Henry Calderwood

The Parables of our Lord

Interpreted in View of Their Relations to Each Other

Henry Calderwood

The Parables of our Lord
Interpreted in View of Their Relations to Each Other

ISBN/EAN: 9783744792561

Printed in Europe, USA, Canada, Australia, Japan

Cover: Foto ©Lupo / pixelio.de

More available books at **www.hansebooks.com**

THE PARABLES OF OUR LORD

INTERPRETED IN VIEW OF THEIR RELATIONS TO EACH OTHER

BY

HENRY CALDERWOOD, LL.D.
PROFESSOR OF MORAL PHILOSOPHY, UNIVERSITY OF EDINBURGH

London
MACMILLAN & CO.
1880

TO

THE REV. JAMES BUCHANAN,

THE ELDERS, MANAGERS, AND MEMBERS OF

GREYFRIARS' UNITED PRESBYTERIAN CHURCH, GLASGOW,

This Work is Dedicated

BY THE AUTHOR,

IN TOKEN OF AFFECTIONATE INTEREST

IN HIS ONLY CHARGE

IN THE MINISTRY OF THE WORD.

PREFACE.

THE aim of the present work is to present an exposition of the Parables of our Lord for popular use, not a critical commentary on the Sacred Text. The special feature in the design is an attempt to ascertain the relations of the Parables to each other. Contemplated as "The Parables of the Kingdom" of Grace, they are regarded as a unity,—a Revelation within the Revelation of God. This conception of the unity of parabolic teaching in the Gospels has determined the grouping of them, and also the interpretation of each parable in its order.

The acknowledged eminent ability of existing works on the Parables of our Lord has led me through many years to shrink from publication of materials long accumulated, and used in a variety of ways. The special plan here adopted has, however, encouraged the belief that many whose delight it is to "search the Scriptures," according to our Lord's counsel, may find some aid in their study of a peculiarly attractive feature in the structure of God's Word. At the same time, in preparation of these pages, I have never been without the consciousness of a measure of unfitness for the self-imposed task, acknowledgment of which should here be made. For adequate treatment of the Parables, the artist's eye and the poet's fancy are both needful, and neither belongs to the writer. The lofty imagination of such writers as Jeremy Taylor and John Howe, Richard C. Trench and James Hamilton, Thomas Guthrie and William Arnot, had much service to render in the work of Bible exposition. No addition to such service is here contemplated. But the Parables present, besides, a most attractive subject for analytic treatment. This attraction has afforded me unabating interest in their study, and has induced me to attempt a single contribution to the great work of Bible exposition.

The necessity for giving the first place to the

duties of a Philosophical Chair has led to long delay in the promised publication of these pages. They appear now as reminiscences not only of Wednesday Evening Meetings in Greyfriars' United Presbyterian Church, Glasgow, but also of Sabbath Evening Meetings in Morningside, Edinburgh; while some part of the expositions was published several years ago in the pages of the *Family Treasury*, from the press of Messrs. T. and W. Nelson, Edinburgh.

H. C.

EDINBURGH, 17*th April* 1880.

CONTENTS.

	PAGE
PREFACE,	vii

CHAPTER I.
THE USES OF THE PARABLES, . . . 1

CHAPTER II.
THE RELATIONS OF THE PARABLES, . . 9

Division I.
MAN'S ENTRANCE INTO THE KINGDOM OF GOD.

CHAPTER III.
SALVATION OF THE LOST.
SEARCH FOR THE WANDERER—THE LOST SHEEP (Luke xv. 1-7), . 18

CHAPTER IV.
THE VALUE OF THE LOST ONE.
THE LOST PIECE OF MONEY (Luke xv. 8-10), . . 32

CHAPTER V.
WELCOME TO THE RETURNING.
THE PRODIGAL SON (Luke xv. 11-32), ... 48

CHAPTER VI.

CONFESSION AND SUPPLICATION OF THE PENITENT ONE.

THE PHARISEE AND PUBLICAN (Luke xviii. 9-14),   PAGE 81

Division II.

THE PRIVILEGES AND DUTIES OF GOD'S KINGDOM.

CHAPTER VII.

STORES OF BLESSING WITHIN THE KINGDOM.

THE GREAT FEAST (Luke xiv. 16-24),   98

CHAPTER VIII.

UNION WITH THE SON IN THE FAVOUR OF THE FATHER.

THE ROYAL MARRIAGE FEAST (Matt. xxii. 1-14),   115

CHAPTER IX.

THE PRIVILEGE OF ASKING FOR OTHERS FROM GOD'S STORES.

THE FRIEND AT MIDNIGHT (Luke xi. 5-8),   135

CHAPTER X.

ENCOURAGEMENT TO PERSEVERANCE IN ASKING.

THE IMPORTUNATE WIDOW (Luke xviii. 1-8),   147

CHAPTER XI.
THE SERVICE OF THE KING.

THE TWO SONS (Matt. xxi. 38-32),	AGE 163

CHAPTER XII.
SERVICE TO GOD IN SERVICE TO OUR NEIGHBOURS.

THE GOOD SAMARITAN (Luke x. 25-37),	175

Division III.
RELATIONS OF GOD'S KINGDOM TO THE PRESENT STATE OF THE WORLD.

CHAPTER XIII.
SOWING OF GOSPEL TRUTH; FOR AWAKENING OF SPIRITUAL LIFE.

THE SOWER (Matt. xiii. 3-9),	187

CHAPTER XIV.
PROPAGATION OF A GODLESS LIFE IN THE WORLD.

THE TARES (Matt. xiii. 24-30),	199

CHAPTER XV.
THE BENEFICENT INFLUENCE OF GOD'S KINGDOM IN THIS WORLD.

THE MUSTARD SEED (Matt. xiii. 31, 32),	214

CHAPTER XVI.
THE ASSIMILATING POWER OF GOSPEL TRUTH.

THE LEAVEN (Matt. xiii. 33), . . . 224

CHAPTER XVII.
THE EXCEEDING VALUE OF SPIRITUAL GOOD FOUND IN GOD'S KINGDOM.

HID TREASURE (Matt. xiii. 44), . . . 234

CHAPTER XVIII.
WISDOM IN SEEKING AND DISTRIBUTING SPIRITUAL GOOD.

THE MERCHANTMAN (Matt. xiii. 45, 46), . 246

CHAPTER XIX.
GATHERING OF GOOD AND BAD WITHIN THE KINGDOM.

THE NET (Matt. xiii. 47-50), ... 256

CHAPTER XX.
WISE USE OF THIS WORLD'S POSSESSIONS.

THE UNFAITHFUL STEWARD (Luke xvi. 1-10), . . . 266

CHAPTER XXI.
WORK AND WAGES IN GOD'S SERVICE.

THE LABOURERS IN THE VINEYARD (Matt. xx. 1-16), . 291

CHAPTER XXII.
UNFAITHFUL OFFICE-BEARERS IN GOD'S KINGDOM.

THE WICKED HUSBANDMEN (Matt. xxi. 33-44; Mark xii. 1-12; Luke xx. 9-18), ... 317

Division IV.

RELATIONS OF GOD'S KINGDOM TO THE FUTURE STATE OF EXISTENCE.

INTRODUCTORY.

THE CONNECTING LINES OF TWO WORLDS,	PAGE 340

CHAPTER XXIII.
CONTRASTS OF EXPERIENCE IN THE PRESENT AND FUTURE STATES.

The Rich Man and Lazarus (Luke xvi. 19-31),   347

CHAPTER XXIV.
CHRIST'S COMING, THE TEST OF CHRISTIAN PROFESSION.

The Ten Virgins (Matt. xxv. 1-13),   383

CHAPTER XXV.
DIFFERENT TALENTS YIELDING EQUAL REWARDS.

The Talents (Matt. xxv. 14-30),   404

CHAPTER XXVI.
EQUALITY OF GIFTS WITH DIVERSITY OF RESULTS.

The Pounds (Luke xix. 12-27),   427

CHAPTER I.

THE USES OF THE PARABLES.

THE first impression made by our Lord's parables was unfavourable. Even His disciples wondered at them, being perplexed as to the reason for employing this mode of address. The wonder and perplexity have not been continued in later times. There is a complete contrast between the view taken in modern times of the value of the parables of our Lord, and that taken by the audiences to which they were first delivered. Even those who are averse to accept Bible teaching have an admiration of these Gospel parables. To the great majority of Bible readers they are amongst the most attractive features of the written revelation; to those who heard them they were the most perplexing parts of Christ's discourses. To us they are as "the green pastures by the still waters;" to them they were as stumbling-blocks and barriers lying across the path to the pasture-ground.

Mere contrast of *position* does not account for this. Difference of position may go far to explain diversity of view as to the words of forewarning bearing on the violent death which Jesus expected. It goes only a little way to account for the contrast of thought and feeling as to the parables. The main part of the explanation lies in the *nature of the parable*. Teaching in parabolic form perplexes at first. The parable has a dark side and a bright, giving it power to confuse and power to instruct. These contrary features belong to the very nature of parabolic teaching. Another thing is to be observed: the dark side is always seen first; and accordingly the confusing power is first experienced. On this account it happened that the disciples were surprised, and almost offended, at the frequent use of parables in the public discourses of their Lord. Coming, as these parables often did, in rapid succession, without the slightest expository remark, and giving strangely different views of "the kingdom of God," there is little wonder that the perplexity of mind was great before a discourse was finished. We have in the completed Bible a key which easily opens the door leading to the inner chamber of truth. It is therefore difficult for us to imagine how great was the puzzle for those who gathered about the door exercising their ingenuity in the attempt to effect an entrance. Those who had an eager desire to understand, were constrained to close around the Great Teacher, when He had finished, exclaiming, "Declare unto us the parable." Make it clear! If, however, the dark side is seen first, it is no less certain that when the brightness is once seen, the darkness permanently disappears. The dark side alone may be turned towards many beholders, but when any are led to the position where the brightness breaks upon the view, there is thenceforth nothing but brightness perceptible. Each parable is a deeply-shaded picture, on which the full sunshine must fall before it can be rightly seen and appreciated. When the disciples were alone with the Lord, He threw fresh light on the scene. Immediately a new wonder displaced the old, as they saw His meaning. From that day till this it has been recognised that the Parable, when laid open to view, affords an illustration at once fresh and suggestive of some selected doctrine of grace. In our Lord's Parables the cross-lights of many analogies play freely over the wide region of revealed truth. Like the stars glistening in the sky, these parables in the firmament of Revelation are hung over our world as it lies in the darkness of sin, guiding the thoughts of men heavenward.

Even in the hands of our Lord Himself, the parable could not lose its double character. It could not fail to exert a twofold influence. As parable, it must be at once dark and bright; in its effects it must be both beclouding and enlightening. The Divine Teacher *meant* that it should be so. He selected the parabolic form of address, *notwithstanding* the risk of perplexing some while instructing others; in part also, *because* it was capable of producing this double effect. His disciples were surprised at the use of a form of discourse fitted in any degree to confound. Hence the inquiry which came hurriedly from their lips when the audience had dispersed—" *Why* speakest Thou unto them in parables?" This question He did not answer by referring to the poverty of ordinary language, or the insufficiency of more simple forms of illustration. He said distinctly that He meant both to puzzle and to instruct. There can be little doubt that this answer occasioned increased perplexity for a time. Their Lord intended to hide the truth so that men should need to search about for it. He meant in a way to bury the truth, so that men should need to dig under the surface for it. He was not making His teaching as clear and simple as He might have done, but was even taking pains to wrap it in a covering fitted so far to conceal it. To the "*why*" of the disciples, this was the Lord's answer—"*Because* it is given unto you to know the mysteries of the kingdom of heaven, but to them it is not given." In this reply there is a double reason, harmonising with the double nature of the parable. There is a "*because*" which applies to the light in a parable, and a "*because*" which refers to the darkness in it. 'Why speak I in parables? (1.) Why speak thus to you? Because unto you it is given in these parables, and by their aid, to understand the mysteries of the kingdom,—the things of grace long hidden from men. Being first puzzled, you will be the better taught. But do ye ask, (2.) Why do I speak *unto them* in parables? Because unto them it is not given to understand the mysteries of the kingdom. These parables, revealing the mysteries to some, really conceal the things of the kingdom from others.' The teaching of the Saviour wears this parabolic form, that it may carry in it *reward* to the inquiring and *penalty* to the uninquiring. And if both reward and penalty are carried in the one utterance, the result in each case agrees with the moral condition of those who hear or read. To those who are seeking light, light is given. To those who do not value and do not seek the light, darkness not only remains, but is deepened. The Parables as set in the Gospels are illustrations of the great principle determining the distribution of spiritual good. "Ask, and ye shall receive; seek, and ye shall find." The true spirit of inquiry is a prayer for light. Ask that, and light will straightway fall softly on the eyes, discovering beauty and grandeur around and above. Ask it not —come to the source of it, and yet account it not worth asking—and thou shalt continue groping in the dark; thou shalt be even more uncertain as to truth than before. "Therefore speak I to them in parables: because they seeing, see not; and hearing, they hear not; neither do they understand" (Matt. xiii. 13). Or still more solemnly, even awfully (Mark iv. 12)— "That seeing they may see, and not perceive; and hearing they may hear, and not understand; lest at any time they should be converted, and their sins should be forgiven them."

There is something testing, we may say even trying, to us in the reception of this explanation. We ourselves may have gladly received the teaching of Christ, enjoying that discovery of light before which darkness flies away. Still, we are left asking, Why should others be taught in such a way as to keep them in darkness? Why should the darkness be deepened, occasioning to them increased perplexity? Why should "the Word"—the Revealer of the Father—the Great Teacher of truth—open His mouth in parables to hide His meaning?

Seeking an answer, we are reminded that there are moral conditions necessary for the understanding and reception of the truth. There is personal responsibility in this matter. A reference to this affords a fuller explanation of the uses of the parables. Amongst our Lord's hearers there were some who craved to be instructed, but there were many more who had no such longing. Some acknowledged their need, and looked to Him for help; others felt no need, and would make no appeal for enlightenment. No hearers were left to appeal in vain to this Teacher. But, as certainly, those who rejected His teaching found in His words a witness against them. Both results flow directly from the frame of mind which hearers cherish. In the parables, then, there is lying hid a reward for inquiry; while, perhaps more conspicuously, because on their surface, there is the punishment of indifference to the message they bear. These parables are ever repeating the Saviour's warning, "Take heed how ye hear."

There is mercy, however, mingled with judgment in the use of this instrument of teaching. The parable is a picture so far telling its own story. Men seeing the story in the picture become attracted. If only they trace the lesson through the story, the truth becomes more clear and impressive. If they look at the picture and do not detect its story, the picture may indeed darken their eyes to the truth, and send them away thinking of nothing higher than the figures on the canvas, the colouring, and the artistic effects. As often happens with Bunyan's *Pilgrim's Progress*, the incidents of the story awaken interest, but the embodied truth escapes observation, and for the time vanishes like the breath of a speaker. And yet a picture will live in the imagination—a story will be brought forth again by the memory, when the simplest, most direct teaching lies unstirred. How effectually, for example, has the parable of the Prodigal Son preached in this way! Thus mercy appears in the use of parables, even though for a while they place truth under a covering. The story, so simple and natural, not understood at first, —possibly misunderstood,—coming again before the mind, a flood of light then falls upon it, discovering a significance unseen before. Then truth enters, hand in hand with the story, to find a welcome and an abiding place within the mind. "The eyes of the understanding being enlightened," God has become the teacher of the soul.

Such use of parabolic forms as a covering for truth is in perfect analogy with the ordinary moral government of God. The lives of men are full of parables. God is ever teaching us by experience. This is what we mean by the lessons of Divine Providence. One sees an incident, and solemnly reads the lesson. One, less inclined to be instructed, observes the incident, but perceives no lesson, and the event is allowed to pass. God does not interpret His providences. The lesson comes under the garb of incident. To some the writing is invisible, to others it is conspicuous as the largest letters. To one there is no voice, to another the still small voice of God is distinctly audible—now sweetly attractive as the Sabbath bell, anon solemn as the bell swaying amid the heaving billows. Death enters a household, and the warning is given, "Be ye also ready." The sufferings of a profligate attract notice, and a voice is heard saying, "The way of transgressors is hard." A good man is suspected, his good name seems lost, but by and by his reputation is vindicated. The assurance is confirmed, "He shall bring forth thy righteousness as the light." "Superstition," says one; "Mere fancy," says another; while many pass heedlessly by, having neither time nor disposition to inquire whether the interpretation is wise or foolish. It fares with the lessons of Providence as with the parables of Scripture. The explanation, in part at least, is that the lessons of Providence are parables. Something of this there must be, indeed, in connection with all teaching, whatever its form or matter. Teaching implies *learning*, and this requires attention and labour. Some *means* of instruction there must be in order to convey truth; and these means must be carefully used, that truth may be received. Those who would know anything must at least open their eyes, and direct their observation. For the secrets of nature, we must search beneath the surface of things. Those who would understand Revelation must "*search* the Scriptures." The parables present no exception to the common demand. They are a touchstone for the inquiring spirit. They become lamps for the path in the hands of those who diligently search for truth.

CHAPTER II.

THE RELATIONS OF THE PARABLES.

OCCASIONAL and cursory perusal of Scripture is apt to induce a reader to regard the parables merely as pictures on the page. It is as if the Divine hand had illuminated the pages of the Holy Bible. These parables are the illustrations relieving and adorning the Book. But such portions of Scripture are not merely ornamental borders accompanying the text. Each one of them infolds a portion of Gospel truth. When the illustration is fully appreciated, the exceeding value of the truth becomes more apparent. By its very nature, and in accordance with the Saviour's design, as we have seen, the parable primarily conceals the truth, but ultimately discovers it more clearly in full relief. The story selected from ordinary scenes of life affords a setting in striking harmony with the truth in the midst of it, and with the requirements of the eye gazing upon it. The observer must, however, linger long over the scene in order to appreciate what has been depicted.

A further subject requiring attention prior to an examination of the parables themselves, is the relations of the parables to each other. These stories did not come from the lips of the Saviour casually according to the suggestions of passing events. There is a method discoverable in them. They were presented in relations deliberately chosen by the Great Teacher. They very commonly appear in groups throughout the Gospels, and are recorded as if uttered consecutively. Simply taking this fact, patent on the surface of the narratives, and without any minute criticism of the text, we may satisfy ourselves of the reality of close and important relations subsisting between the parables. They were presented on a definite plan, thereby making a consistent whole. They appear as a gallery of pictures, giving in successive views the grand outlines of truth which Jesus otherwise presented in more formal discourse. The pictures may be hung on a variety of plans, considerably varying the relative effects, but the general result will be the same. The gallery is complete, and in any case, the general effect is secured.

Take, for example, the parables in the fifteenth chapter of Luke's Gospel. The chapter contains three parables, which are three pictures of the same truth. Each is so different from the other two as to present quite a distinct phase of the truth; while their relation is so close that all three are needed to give a full view. The parables are, the Lost Sheep, the Lost Piece of Money, and the Prodigal Son. When these three are taken together, they present for all times the answer to these questions, Why does God receive sinners? and, How does God receive them? The source of salvation for guilty men is depicted in a wonderful way in these three pictures. The plan of salvation is sketched with sharpness of outline and minuteness of detail not often found concentrated in a single passage. Of a formally didactic kind, the third chapter of John's Gospel comes most closely into comparison with this fifteenth chapter of Luke. To these two the inquiring student of the Christian revelation may well turn. Upon these two the faith of Christian men will rest with increasing satisfaction while the Bible continues their guide in studying the Divine plan of salvation.

Taking first these three parables in the single chapter of Luke's Gospel, it is clear that they are essentially connected with each other. Each one of the three is the complement of the others. Take any one of the three from its place, and an important part of the Divine revelation is withheld. Like a triple picture representing dawn, noon, and night, which artists delight to present in a single frame, these parables must hang together before the eye, else the effect is lessened.

Inquire as to the source of human salvation, Why does God bring salvation to the guilty? Each of these parables supplies an answer. Each answer is distinct from the other two, yet harmonises with them, and manifestly supplements what is given in the others. There is thus a threefold answer. Look on this picture of a shepherd following on the track of a wandering sheep. Look next on the sketch of a woman searching eagerly for a piece of silver lost in her dwelling. Look again on that household full of rejoicing over the return of a prodigal son. These are the three answers; and the three are one. What is the source of human salvation? It is Divine Love. But the answer cannot be reduced to simple unity, for one picture would not suffice to convey an adequate representation. Divine love toward sinners is a love which seeks every wanderer, and the scene in shepherd life will admirably convey this aspect of the truth, while harmonising with what is otherwise recorded in the tenth chapter of John's Gospel—a discourse in which Jesus spoke of Himself as the Shepherd of the flock. Again, Divine love towards sinners is a love which values the lost one, however the worth of the soul be obscured by the corruption into which it has fallen. A woman's search for a lost coin will suitably depict the wonderful truth. And yet again, Divine love towards sinners is a love which welcomes with joy every returning wanderer who comes to seek pardon. The scene which brings out a father's joy in receiving as from the dead a long-lost son, will vividly portray this great reality, so far as pictorial representation can. A Divine love which searches for the lost, and which rejoices in their recovery, is the love which has provided salvation for men. Remove any one of these parables, and the representation of the grand truth is glaringly incomplete.

But these parables not only teach that salvation is altogether of love; they also strikingly present to view the manner in which Divine love brings salvation to the lost. As before, each parable gives a separate answer, and all three answers are required that the reply may be complete. Dogmatically it may be simply affirmed that love is the source of all, but pictorially this cannot be brought out without at the same time showing how love works to the accomplishment of its end. Look first on the scene in pastoral life. The shepherd appears toiling and suffering in his pursuit of the wanderer until he finds it, when he lays it on his shoulders and bears it back to the fold in triumph.

This scene is one part of the answer. As the shepherd searches for lost sheep, so does God seek for sinners. But this is only a partial statement, for pastoral life cannot represent the whole truth. Look, then, on this other picture, which is in character "an interior view." A woman with lighted candle sweeps her house as she searches for a lost piece of money. The indications of suffering in the former view disappear, but new aspects come into view, specially the disturbing process in the search, and the need for having light to play strongly on the scene. God causes a heavenly light to fall on those lost in darkness. Nor is this enough. Something more nearly approaching the great reality is wanted—something which will supply at once what is darker in the lost state, and what is brighter in the saved state—something penetrating more completely to the heart of human relations. And all this is provided in the matchless parable of the Prodigal Son. Matchless beyond doubt it is; and yet, had this been the only representation of the manner in which God brings salvation to men, parabolic teaching on the subject would have been incomplete. Still more incomplete, however, would that teaching be if the other two stood alone without this wonderful accompaniment. God loves a repenting sinner as a father loves and welcomes a returning son.

Having thus found a threefold answer to the question, How does God bring salvation to men? we may compare this answer with what is said on the subject in other portions of Scripture. Take, for example, the third chapter of John's Gospel, to which allusion has already been made. There we find a reference to the Spirit's part, the Son's part, and the Father's part in the plan of salvation. Men are to be saved by being "born of the Spirit,"—"drawn" to the Son, who has been "lifted up" on the cross for them,—and they are blessed in the experience of the forgiving mercy and gracious love of the Father manifested through the Son. Just so is it that the threefold aspect of the plan appears parabolically in the fifteenth chapter of Luke's Gospel. That the Shepherd is the Son, and that the invisible Spirit kindles the light of truth for the discovery of the lost soul in its darkness and pollution, and that the father of the returning prodigal represents the Divine Father, will be admitted as essential to the interpretation of the parables. If these things be plain, the relation of the three parables is not only intimate, but necessary for completeness of representation.

Similar evidences of close relationship between successive parables can be traced in other passages. For example, in the thirteenth chapter of Matthew's Gospel, there is a series of parables representing the spiritual kingdom in its relations to the world as a whole. First in this series stands the parable of the Sower, illustrating the fact that in some cases the truth produces no result, in others only a temporary result, and in some a permanent result. Next comes the parable of the Tares, illustrating the sad reality that evil is also broadcast over the world, taking root and flourishing alongside the good seed of the Word. Thereafter, we have the parable of the Mustard Seed growing up till it becomes a great tree, representing the spiritual kingdom as a whole, and the outward benefits obtained by its presence in the world. And, finally, we have the parable of the Leaven, representing the hidden but constant influence of spiritual truth, silently subduing the world to itself. That a very close relation subsists between these parables is a fact so obvious that it need not be insisted upon.

The examples of relationship now adduced may suffice to show that the parables of Scripture have been constructed and set in position upon a definite plan, such as may fairly warrant us in seeking here a systematic revelation of Gospel truth, even apart from other portions of Scripture. Any scheme of arrangement will leave unaffected the interpretation of separate parables, and yet order may throw additional light upon their value as portions of Revelation.

If, then, a plan of arrangement is to be not merely fanciful, but evidently reasonable, it becomes important that we discover some central point of connection—some key to the system. And such a key we seem to have in the introductory form, explanatory of their reference, so frequently found preceding the parables. In Matthew's Gospel this form is commonly, "The kingdom of heaven is like unto;" in the Gospels of Mark and Luke the designation is, "The kingdom of God," and the introductory form at times assumes the character of a question, thus, "Whereunto shall we liken the kingdom of God; or, with what comparison shall we compare it?" This introductory reference is not by any means invariable; but it is sufficiently common to warrant the conclusion that it may properly guide us in the attempt so to group the parables as to obtain a general view of their unity. There appears little risk of error, if we regard the parables as a consistent and complete representation of "the kingdom of God" in this world. As to the meaning of the phrase, "Kingdom of heaven," or, "Kingdom of God," there is hardly room for dispute. The reference is to the spiritual kingdom which God has established in the world through the atoning work of the Lord Jesus Christ. By the death of the Saviour, the throne of mercy has been set up in the midst of our sinful world —the benefits of the kingdom have been freely offered to men—the gate of faith has been set open that men may enter. This spiritual kingdom is represented in the parables. This, then, being the key to the unity of the parables, it is easy to trace their relations to each other. They depict different aspects of the kingdom. First, there are those which are concerned with entrance into the kingdom; next, those describing the privileges and the duties of the kingdom; thereafter, those setting forth the relations of the kingdom to this present world; and, finally, those which illustrate the relations of the kingdom to the world beyond. All the parables readily come within these four divisions; and when so placed, we obtain a most impressive view of their unity as a revelation of truth. Further, if they can be so distributed, the order in which the subjects have been set down is the natural order for their consideration. It is reasonable that we should first consider entrance to the kingdom; then what is within the kingdom; thereafter, the relations of the kingdom to what exists around; and, in conclusion, its relations to what is to come. By this order, then, I mean to keep.

Here, however, it is needful to introduce a concluding remark as to what is not found in the parables. The kingdom is described as an existing kingdom; but there is no representation of the laying of its foundations. There is nothing in the parables as to the eternal purpose of God—nothing as to the everlasting fountain of love out of which the reign of grace has sprung. Of those deeper, more mysterious, but essential realities, there is no indication in the parables. There could not be parabolic representation of such truths. These things are hid, as are the foundations of a building. The parables trace only what admits of analogy with human experience. For this reason also, we have no parabolic representation of the death of the Saviour, nothing which comes even so near the grand truth as the figurative saying of our Lord: "The good shepherd giveth his life for the sheep." We are not, indeed, without some reference in the parables to the death of the Son of God, as in that of the Vineyard; but it is only in illustration of the rebelliousness of those who cast Him out from the vineyard. Of satisfaction to the holiness of God, there could be no parabolic representation, for there is no analogy of human experience which could be employed for such a purpose. No parable depicts to the eye the anguish of Gethsemane—the lifting up of the Saviour, that men might be drawn to Him—and that unfathomable experience of our Lord, when He made His *soul* an offering for sin, after which He "bowed his head, and gave up the ghost."

Division I.

MAN'S ENTRANCE INTO THE KINGDOM OF GOD.

CHAPTER III.

I.—*SALVATION OF THE LOST.*

SEARCH FOR THE WANDERER—THE LOST SHEEP.

LUKE xv. 1-7.

THE opening verses of this chapter explain the circumstances in which this and the two following parables were uttered. The preaching of Jesus repelled the self-satisfied, but attracted the self-condemned. The Preacher Himself was a mystery and an offence to the more conspicuous religious men of the country. He denounced them for their formalism, and He welcomed penitents who had been notable not only for indifference to religion, but even for open sinfulness. "This man receiveth sinners, and eateth with them." The fact seemed a testimony against Jesus. The parables present the explanation of His conduct as a Teacher and Leader. This parable of the Lost Sheep, standing nearest the utterance of the difficulty, plainly applies to the speaker Himself. He would be regarded as a

Shepherd in a strange land seeking his wandering sheep.

Verse 4.—"*What man of you, having an hundred sheep, if he lose one of them, doth not leave the ninety and nine in the wilderness, and go after that which is lost, until he find it?*" Instead of direct narrative, this part of the parable is thrown into the form of a question. Our Lord thus deals more pointedly with the objection taken against Him by some in His audience. He does not begin with a narrative of a shepherd's wanderings in search of a lost sheep. He was in a pastoral country, where the sight was familiar, and He asks what any one of them would do if, when counting his sheep in the morning, one of the flock were wanting. Is it not natural for the owner to go in search of the lost one? Which man of you would do otherwise in such circumstances? They could not say that the opposite course would be reasonable, and this was our Saviour's vindication of Himself. They asked: Why do ye receive sinners? His answer is: I act as ye would in seeking a lost sheep.

How guardedly our Lord puts the case when He addresses this question to those who marvel at His conduct. Multitudes of sinners were flocking to hear Him, and to all of them He gave a welcome. He might then appropriately have spoken of hundreds of lost sheep; but He narrows attention to *one*. Here, then, is one lost sheep. It was not the only sheep belonging to its owner. He was not like the poor man of Nathan's parable, who "had nothing save one little ewe lamb, which he had bought and nourished up; and it grew up together with him and with his children." This sheep did not reckon even as one in two or three score.

The one lost was but one in a hundred: its wandering from the flock involved no ruinous loss to him who owned so many. Still this one was *lost*. The shepherd makes his flock pass before him, and one of the number is wanting. Once more they pass under his hand, but still the reckoning is ninety-and-nine. There is a lost sheep! Widely the eye ranges, but no trace is found of the wanderer. And how helpless is a lost sheep! Wherever it be, it is the most helpless of creatures. Other animals, taken far away from their accustomed haunts, turn their faces in the right direction, and pursuing their course by day and night, reappear on the familiar ground. It is not so with the sheep. Separated from the flock, it wanders, not knowing whence it has come, not knowing whither it goes. There is not a more affecting example of helplessness. Bleating vainly for help, startled by everything that moves, hurrying as if danger were behind, it hurries on to exhaustion and death. It cannot rest in separation from the flock, and be content to feed where pasture is found; it cannot move deliberately as in familiar walks, but must hurry excitedly on; it cannot save its strength, but wastes it, and hastens the ruin it dreads. Amongst animals, none gives so striking an example of unrest, useless expenditure of strength, and utter helplessness in wandering.

The shepherd's care is the only hope for the lost sheep. He will soon discover the loss, and start in search of the wanderer. When a sheep is missing, the fact at once determines the shepherd's most pressing task. Other things may claim attention; this must come before all. Every hour's delay may render discovery more difficult, and may expose the sheep to danger, or even to destruction. Instantly, therefore, *the shepherd leaves all the rest*, that he may find the one. He has no other to tend the flock while he is absent. Such help is not hinted at in the parable; and the absence of this possible provision for the emergency is to be observed. But even though there be no other to turn an eye on the flock, he leaves them that he may start in pursuit of the one which has gone astray. They are together, and may keep together, however far they wander on as they feed. Some may stray, yet this risk cannot restrain him meanwhile. On his return he may have to go in search of others, but for the present he must seek for the lost one. For this one he leaves the ninety-and-nine. We must note *where* they are left. "Doth he not leave the ninety-and-nine *in the wilderness?*" This reference to the place stands prominent in the statement: we cannot pass it by, as if it were merely accidental and unimportant. He will leave them just where they are—not in the field, not in the fold, but in the wilderness. If he had had any enclosure for them, any limits even which would have hindered them wandering further, it would have been a gain now. If their feeding-place had been a field, out of which the straggler had wandered through some breach in the fence, he could first have restored the fence before going in pursuit of the lost one. If their pasture-ground had been even a hillside, such as is familiar to us in Scotland, every corner and crevice in which is well known to the shepherd, the risk of leaving the flock would have been comparatively slight. But this shepherd has been feeding his flock in a wilderness—such a wilderness as was familiar to Jewish minds as the pasture-ground of the flocks and herds. It was not indeed a place in which there was no grass. In the wilderness both the Forerunner and the Messiah often taught, and we know that Jesus found "much grass" in such a place, on which He made the people sit down. This wilderness, then, is that into which the shepherds were wont to guide their flocks, having in it verdant places where the pasture was plentiful, with wide stretches of barren soil, over which the flock must be led, in order that they may find fresh pasture. On such a grassy place as was to be found in this wilderness, the shepherd leaves his ninety-and-nine sheep, not knowing how far they may have wandered in search of other feeding-ground before he comes to them again, or how many more stragglers there may be.

Leaving his flock, the shepherd will start in search of the lost one. And doth he not "go after that which is lost, *until he find it?*" He will not return without success. Once discovering its track, he will pursue that track until he come in sight of the wanderer. If he see the sheep hurrying still further away, he will follow with increased speed, until he overtake it. If he find it fallen into a pit, he will lift it out. If he find it fast in a thicket, he will clear it from the thorns. If he see it bruised and bleeding at the foot of some rocky place over which it has fallen he will let himself down over the rocks, risking his own life that he may save the life of the sheep which otherwise must speedily die. The shepherd will find the lost sheep.

Verse 5.—"*And when he hath found it, he layeth it on his shoulders, rejoicing.*" The toil of seeking the lost sheep is a small matter to the shepherd, if he has the joy of finding that lost one. From the moment when he reaches it, its safety is secured. However worn out it be by its wandering—however injured by the disasters it has encountered—he will save it from exhaustion and death. He lays it on his shoulders and carries it all the way back again; great as his toil proves, he rejoices within himself, while he retraces his weary way, bearing the heavy burden. "And when he cometh home, he calleth together his friends and neighbours, saying unto them, Rejoice with me; for I have found my sheep which was lost." It must be remarked that he is represented as *coming home* with the sheep. This cannot be identified with the wilderness, where he has left the ninety-and-nine. However true it be that there is pasture in the wilderness, where the sheep may feed for a time before they are led to other places for grazing, there are no homes in the wilderness. The shepherd does not erect his dwelling there. Whatever satisfaction he may find in tending his flock there, and meditating in the solitudes, he cannot call together friends and neighbours to rejoice with him in any joy he has. The home to which he carries the wanderer is different from the wilderness where he leaves the flock. The lost one is so exhausted that it cannot follow the flock. It will need special care, and he carries it home. So soon as he arrives there, he calls together his friends and neighbours, that they may rejoice with him. If this sheep had not wandered, the shepherd had not appeared at his home at this time; the sheep would have been feeding quietly with the others; the shepherd would have counted it among the number of his own, as he does now; yet would there have been no such scene of rejoicing. But returning as he does, carrying the sheep, he tells his neighbours of his long and anxious search; he describes the circumstances in which he found the lost one; and they rejoice with him, that that which was lost is found. In this scene of rejoicing the story ends. There is nothing said as to when the shepherd returned to his flock; not a word more is uttered as to this sheep, whether it was kept thenceforth within the enclosure by the house, or led out to other pasture-ground. So far as our Lord was in need of any story to convey the explanation of His welcome to those who bewail their wanderings in the ways of sin, the parable is sufficient, and here it ends.

The parabolic meaning is clear, very beautiful in itself, and very affecting to us dwelling in a sinful world. When from the perfect moral character of Jesus as depicted in the Gospels, and from the evidence of His glory as "God manifest in the flesh," we turn to consider His mode of dealing with men, marking specially the encouragement He gave to the publicans and sinners when they came to hear Him, and ask, Why does Jesus so encourage even the chief of sinners? the answer He himself would give lies before us in this parable of the Lost Sheep. Each of these sinners in whose return He rejoices is represented by the sheep which went astray; and He by the shepherd. This is made so plain by the manner in which the parable is introduced, that there is no need for argument in support of it. "This man receiveth sinners and eateth with them," say the objectors; and this parable is the explanation of His conduct, and its defence, if such a thing be required.

If we compare the representations of the three parables, the Lost Sheep, the Lost Piece of Money, and the Lost Son, all represent the sinner in his separation from God. The three descriptions do not apply to three different *classes* of sinners, but are three distinct views of the condition of every sinner in his wandering from God. Bengel, in his own terse style, made a threefold classification of sinners to suit the three parables; and his view has been very generally adopted. With his usual brevity, nothing is said in support of it. The classification is sharp in outline, and happy in its appearance of harmony with the main features of the parables; but I think it cannot stand the test of rigid scrutiny. He says there are some sinners who are stupid in their wanderings, as the lost sheep; some ignorant of their state, as the lost piece of money; and some wilful in their transgression, as the prodigal son. There is much that is striking in this way of grouping sinners; specially, an apparent roundness of figure which is apt to prove attractive to an interpreter. There is, besides, a measure of truth in the classification, although there must be considerable strain in order to reach the analogy in the case of the money, if it also must be applied to a distinct class of sinners. There are some who are conspicuous for their stupidity, others for their ignorance, and some for their wilfulness; but there is no sinner of whom all these things may not be said; nay, more, these are things which must be said of every sinner, if his condition is to be accurately described. There is no one who is not unreasoning, ignorant, and wilful in his wandering from God. The three things are so connected that they cannot be separated. To sin is wilfulness, and that is acting from blind, unreasoning impulse; to continue in this is to continue wilfully indifferent and ignorant as to what is really involved in such a state. These go inevitably in company.

Man wandering in the ways of sin is a sheep straying from the flock. This view of his condition awakens the compassion of our Divine Saviour. Man is a wanderer from God's care and keeping! Thinking it better to be free from God's control, and to act as he inclines, he wanders on, not knowing whither he goes. With all this uncertainty, he keeps on the course which he has begun; he even hastens onward, and in doing so hurries towards destruction. If escape be sought, safety proves difficult to reach. The sinner is helpless; his case is hopeless, even with all his strivings, though thereby he exhaust himself. He has wandered, and cannot return. He cannot undo the past. He cannot retrace his steps, and stand again safe under the gracious keeping of his God. Helpless and hopeless, he continues wandering as a lost sheep. In all this the *sinfulness* of the wandering is not indicated; only the helplessness and the sure ruin of such wandering, are conspicuous. So accurate is this view of our case, that if we would describe it aright, we must be willing to take up the words of the prophet and make them our own: "All we like sheep have gone astray, we have turned every one to his own way."

But, for the helpless wanderer help is found in One who is mighty. This helper is the Divine Saviour. He it is who calls Himself "the Son of man," and whom the Father calls His "beloved Son, in whom He is well pleased." He toils to save the lost. They are away from the fold of God, outside His kingdom, and exposed to the greatest hazards. He goes forth to seek the sinful, even while they continue to wander. Here we view the Saviour's work, not as that of suffering in the room of men, of which there is no parabolic representation, but as that of seeking the wanderers, that He may rescue them from destruction.

The first part of the parable may seem more obscure. It implies leaving some, in order to seek others. "Doth he not leave the ninety-and-nine in the wilderness?" What is the significance of this forsaking of some, in order to rescue others? What is plain in the case of the shepherd, is not by any means so clear in the case of the Saviour. While the shepherd must leave the flock in order to seek the straying sheep, this necessity is not so obvious when the Saviour would seek some wayward soul. Does Jesus in reality leave some men to themselves while He seeks others? So it is made to appear. But it is the whole flock which is left in this case. Does, then, the Lord forsake His own people in seeking for those who wander in the ways of sin? Did He ever speak as if this were the case, or did His disciples ever feel as if it were? Assuredly not. Whosoever is delivered by Him is thenceforth cared for and kept by Him. They are defended, and fed, and folded by Him. For His relation to His disciples, as represented under the image of a shepherd, we must turn to the tenth chapter of John's Gospel. There we find the Good Shepherd and the sheep which know His voice, and the fold in which they are kept, and the practice of the Shepherd in leading them out to the pasture. In such a picture, there is no indication of the sheep of the fold being left unprotected, as in the case before us. There is, then, nothing in Christ's dealing with the saved ones, which can be represented as leaving them in the wilderness, while He goes in search of the wandering. The analogy of parabolic teaching is against this view; the more direct teaching of the whole Bible is against it; the experience of the early disciples gives no clew to such a thing; and even the structure of this parable is adverse to the supposition. Look at the connection in which it is recorded. The disciples are not said to have wondered at Christ leaving them in order to welcome the publicans and sinners. But the Pharisees and scribes murmured. They felt that Jesus had withdrawn Himself from them; that His words of encouragement and warning and instruction were not for them, but for other classes of the people. This was indeed the case; Jesus intended that it should be so; and the parable at this point carries an admission of the fact. Seeking the deliverance of the lost, He *must* separate Himself from those who think they have no need to be delivered. In so far as the Teacher interprets His teaching, this is confirmed; for in the seventh verse the flock which is left is described as "ninety-and-nine just persons *who need no repentance*." Does the Saviour ever describe His people thus? Quite otherwise. This is His description for the self-satisfied, who do not mourn their sins, and do not feel their need of a Saviour. Such are indeed left by Him in His seeking after the lost. They are left, not in the fold, but in the wilderness; yet not without pasture, but rather in the very midst of it; nevertheless unprotected by the Saviour's power, and completely exposed to danger. Often He is with them. But, in seeking the wandering and the troubled, He is ever leaving them in the state which they account sufficient; for they think not that they need repentance, and pardon, and Divine help, to save them from impending ruin.

Passing this view of separation from some, we see the Saviour going forth in search of the lost sheep, to engage in the work on which His soul is set, delivering those who are ready to perish. He seeks the wandering, who feel the misery of their condition. However far sinners wander, there is no extremity to which the Saviour will not follow. The Most Holy will seek after the most guilty. Unwearied by the effort, unchanged by their folly, full of compassion and love for them in their perplexity and suffering, He will still pursue His work of mercy, and be ready to save them in the hour of their extremity, when they feel as though they were ready to die. This was the Saviour's great work when He sojourned on the earth. A God-like work! Of this He was wont to speak with zest as His work. "The Son of man is come to seek and to save that which was lost." And now that He has gone to the heavens, He still carries forward the same work by the Spirit of truth, who shall glorify Him in the salvation of men, according to the promise of the Saviour, "He shall receive of mine, and shall show it unto you."

The Saviour's work, however, is not merely seeking, but delivering by the exercise of His own strength. As the sheep in its exhaustion is powerless to return, so the sinner is helpless. The deeper the sense of sin, the more distressing will be the sense of the utter hopelessness of any attempt to escape the crushing weight of condemnation. Burdened with sin, how can the soul venture on return to God? Troubled with the fear which self-condemnation awakens, and weakened by reckless, foolish wandering, there is not strength to return. To such an one the Saviour comes as the shepherd to the lost sheep. His voice is gentle and familiar as a shepherd's voice to one of his own flock. And when He finds the sinner, mourning over his lost condition, He does not merely, by His higher knowledge and by His grace, show him the way to safety, as any disciple of the Master might; He does not merely lead him along the way, as one of like experience might; but in the exercise of Divine strength He bears the troubled one to the Father's presence, and there sets him down in peace. Such description as this is unspeakably precious. No reflection however anxious, no philosophy however profound, can bring anything so valuable to the sin-burdened family of men. Thought only exasperates and exhausts; the power of the Saviour brings help all-sufficient. In such an assurance there is balsam for the sorest wounds—there is healing for all the nations. If anything in the form of the assurance could enhance its value, it is provided when the Saviour represents Himself as bringing help to one sinner, as though there were no other straying at the time. Love concentrates on the individual wanderer.

One thing more there is in this description to crown what has already been said. "And when he cometh home, he calleth together his friends and neighbours, saying unto them, Rejoice with me; for I have found my sheep which was lost. I say unto you, That likewise joy shall be in heaven over one sinner that repenteth, more than over ninety-and-nine just persons, which need no repentance." Even the sinner's deliverance is placed beneath the fulness and freshness of the Saviour's joy. When He has brought the sinner back, He rejoices. Into His own home in the heavens

The Lost Sheep.

He brings him; and calling together those who dwell there, He says, "Rejoice with me, for I have found my sheep which was lost." As it was with the shepherd in his humbler way, so shall it be with the Divine Saviour in His heavenly home. We have the assurance in His own words: "I say unto you, that likewise joy shall be in heaven over one sinner that repenteth, more than over ninety-and-nine just persons, which need no repentance." Joy over *one sinner!* More joy over one than over *ninety-and-nine who need no repentance!* We are in close contact with the greatest realities of life in considering such words. It will be well for those who think they have no need of a Saviour if they ponder this profound measure of divine love and justice. And for those who are "fellow-workers with God," seeking the deliverance of them who are ready to die, it shall be well if they draw encouragement from the teaching of the Saviour in this place, and strive with growing zeal, in face of extended toil, to "enter into His joy."

CHAPTER IV.

II.—*THE VALUE OF THE LOST ONE.*

THE LOST PIECE OF MONEY.

LUKE xv. 8-10.

THIS parable has a similar application; and, at the same time, is sufficiently unlike the former in structure to give a representation of the case quite different. The contrast between the two is strongly marked, suggesting that the Teacher felt the need for a distinct addition to the instruction already communicated.

Verse 8.—"*Either what woman, having ten pieces of silver, if she lose one piece, doth not light a candle, and sweep the house, and seek diligently till she find it?*" A woman possessed of ten pieces of silver, loses one of them in the house. Concerned at her loss, she lights a candle, and sweeps the whole house, searching for it until she finds it. When she has found it, she is so full of joy that she calls together her neighbours, who had already heard of her concern under the loss, and tells them that she has found the lost piece. So it is, says our Lord, as to the loss of the sinner, and the joy over his recovery from the sinful state. Such a parable puts man's sin and salvation in a new light, presenting for consideration a distinct order of facts. Man may be likened to a silver coin. In his sinful state, it is with him as with the coin which has rolled off to some obscure corner. When recovered, his value is exactly as it was when lost.

A lost piece of money!—This is the chief feature of the parable, around which the whole interpretation gathers. Our Lord selects a piece of money to represent a man; and it is a silver piece.[1] In taking this silver coin to represent the lost soul, our Lord chooses the money of highest value in common use. Gold coin there was, no doubt; and in our times this form of currency would probably have been preferred, for gold is elsewhere used in Scripture when the currency is not in question, as when reference is made to the trying of men in the furnace. But silver coin was the highest in regular use in the days of our Lord. Anything higher certainly could not be in the possession of the woman who reckons up her little stock at ten drachmas. It cannot appear, then, to an interpreter as if our Lord were selecting a secondary value. This silver piece must be taken as the highest form of coin in general circulation. Man, then, is like the silver, which is precious by its very nature. Inherently valuable he appears even in the eyes of the Great Proprietor, who made him the chief of all His works on earth. Further, it is not silver ore, but silver coin, which has been taken for illustration. And in this has been uniformly recognised an allusion to the image of God in

---

[1] The Greek *drachma*, the same in value as the Roman *denarius*, was the silver coin in ordinary use in our Lord's time,—rendered in our English version "a penny." Its value is about sevenpence three-farthings of our money. The whole money, therefore, in the possession of the woman at the time of her loss is about six shillings and sixpence of our currency.

the soul of man, the distinctive feature of His excellence, as the image of the sovereign is the common mark of the coin of the realm. The accuracy of this allusion is not affected by the fact that the Greek drachma had often upon it the image of some animal, and sometimes of one of the national deities, instead of the effigy of a ruler, as on the Roman denarius. In any case, the imprint marked the piece as belonging to the coin of the country, having its character and value determined by the ruling power; and this sufficiently represents the image of God imprinted on the soul of man. Even the likeness of a heathen deity neither destroys nor mars the analogy. If any idolatrous nation marked their coin with the fancied likeness of one of their gods, our Lord may well compare with such coin bearing the stamp of the national mint the spirits of men having the traces of His Father's image upon them. In such comparison there is testimony to the superiority of the true God over idols, and of that which is valuable to Him over the treasure of the kingdoms of this world. Here, then, are the two points of analogy given us; man is inherently precious in God's sight, as is silver among the things of the earth; and man is distinguished by the imprint of the Divine image, as is every piece of silver sent forth from the national mint. Take any one of these publicans, however grasping, unfeeling, and harsh in his treatment of those from whom he seeks to obtain the sums levied upon them. Or take any one of these dissolute women, however irreligious, profligate, and profane she may have been. The Saviour seeks to rescue every one of them. Why should He welcome such as they, even though they come with penitential confessions? His own answer is this, Each one is precious in my sight as the silver coin in yours, which you gather and seek to save; precious in my Father's sight as is the currency of the kingdom in the eyes of the king.

This parable is entirely different from the other two in this respect, that it alone introduces likeness to an inanimate object. This it is which presents the specialties of the parable. Valuable as the silver is, there is manifest difficulty in selecting a lifeless object as the basis of comparison, when the intention is to illustrate not only the value, but also the sinfulness of man. In this view the use of such a comparison may at first seem unpromising. Assuredly the lifeless cannot represent the living, least of all responsible life. Here all analogy with action is surrendered; the view of human responsibility disappears for the time. But what is in this way laid aside, is very fully and carefully indicated in another of the companion representations. If in one of His parables our Lord thus turns away from the essential facts of personal responsibility, it is to add important features which the other two parables were insufficient to indicate. And here certainly is obtained the most startling representation of utter *helplessness* in a lost state that any such form of teaching could provide. The moral helplessness characteristic of the sinful state is certainly one of the most difficult to set forth in parabolic form. In this appears the need for resorting to more than one parable. That of the Prodigal Son most impressively brings out individual responsibility; but, at the same time, it discovers, with least exactness, the utter inability of the sinner to undo the past, or escape from its consequences. Helplessness of a kind is illustrated by the sheep, so destitute of knowledge to guide, while it has the power to hurry along, thereby wandering still more hopelessly. But the inability to do what needs to be done in order that the soul may be rescued from its sinful state, one of the most sad features of the sinner's case, is most vividly set forth here. In the parable of the Sheep, this appears in the act of the shepherd carrying back the sheep, rather than leading or driving it back. But it might be supposed that this carrying was, in such a case, more compassionate than needful. Here, however, the reality is brought out most vividly. Where a piece of silver falls, there it must lie, unless some hand be stretched forth to lift it. Power in itself to affect its own position there is none. So is it in a most important sense with the sinner. To undo the past is hopeless. To go back to that state from which man has fallen is impossible. To change his position in relation to God from that of a sinner to that of a holy one accepted of God and doing service according to His will, is an impossibility with one condemned of his own heart, and still more condemned of God. As well might we represent a piece of money as rolling back from the corner into which it has fallen, and leaping again into the hand of her who is most anxious to obtain it. A special part of the explanation of the Saviour's selection of this inanimate object for representation of a responsible being is to be found in this suitableness for the illustration of spiritual helplessness. If man by nature is valuable as the silver, in his sinful state he is as a lost piece of silver. In this way due prominence is given to the fact, that in the parable it is not only the inanimate though precious silver which represents man; but *a lost silver piece* illustrates the state of a lost man. And very fitly in other ways does the analogy prove serviceable. A piece of money *does not lose its value*, though it be for the time lost to its owner. So the intelligent immortal spirit continues to be precious in the sight of God, even when separated from Him by all the distance which sin implies. Yet lost silver is soon *tarnished*, and is the more obscured the longer it continues in neglect. In this respect silver represents, even more accurately than gold, that sensitiveness to corrupting influences which is characteristic of the soul of man. The soul separated from God quickly loses the beauty of holiness, and is easily tarnished by contact with evil around. In this the silver coin is the true type of the human heart. But *lost money is useless while lost*. It continues of the same value; but while lost, present usefulness is gone. It is all the same as if it were of no worth; it is not capital in any proper sense. It is not only itself lost, but what it is capable of producing is lost also. The increase it might have brought to its owner is sacrificed. So does God lose the service which man was created to render, and which he would have rendered but for this separation from righteousness. Something worse than this there is, as we know, in this sinful state, which the piece of money cannot represent. If the money is lost, the loss is summed up in the amount of its own value, with such increase as it might have brought. But the soul which sins, not only yields no return to God, robbing Him of his own, but goes on to do evil, in defiance of the will of God. In this again appears the insufficiency of a single parable to illustrate the many-sided aspects of man's state. To the parable of the Prodigal Son we must turn for evidence of progress in sin.

Continuing, however, the attempt to interpret the parable before us, we concentrate attention upon what is characteristic of the inanimate object here selected. *A piece of money cannot lose itself.* It is lost either by the misfortune or by the carelessness of one to whom it belongs, or who has it in charge. Whether in consequence of the one or the other in the case before us is not stated. That is left indefinite, and intentionally so, in order that the story may apply to either mode of losing. But if a piece of money be lost, there is responsibility somewhere. Not being in the thing lost, it is in the loser; and hence it is that the person seeking the lost in this case has the responsibility of losing, and is therefore not a representative of God, as the shepherd is, and as the father is in the succeeding parable.

A woman with lighted candle.—She bears the evidence of imperfection as a seeker, while representing one somehow related to God in the search for the lost. The shepherd seeking the sheep may represent the God of salvation, so also may the father receiving the penitent son, but not this woman sweeping the house, and searching by the aid of candle light. What seemed quite simple in the other two parables is complicated here. And yet the complication, which may have been puzzling to the first hearers of the parable, must appear very attractive to those who contemplate the search for lost souls by the believing people of God in this world. Why does our Lord in this parable represent a woman as the seeker for the lost piece of money? We cannot find the explanation in anything so superficial as the fancy that women in His audience were assenting to the objection taken against the Saviour's conduct in receiving penitent reprobates. There is no value in the supposition. The explanation will appear if we attend to the structure of the parable itself. There is some truth as to the seeking of sinners to be illustrated in this way, and which is not brought out in either of the other parables. To His audience the first parable must have appeared a very direct and full explanation of His conduct in receiving sinners. When He passed on to another mode of illustration, it may have appeared to His hearers that He was only varying the form. They could see at once, for these things lie on the surface of the stories, that He somehow accounted even the worst of sinners as His own lost ones; that He strove to save them; and that He had joy when successful in doing so. But when we consider the details of the parables, there are specialties which need some distinct interpretation. In this way we have been led to give prominence to the fact that the loss of the coin is to be accounted for by responsibility of its possessor, showing that in this parable the woman cannot represent the Saviour Himself. And, without anticipating the interpretation of what is to follow, it is evident that the need for light in order to seek for sinners, points to some need which the Saviour Himself did not feel. The woman, therefore, does not directly represent Himself. Yet the seeking here strikingly described must be so closely analogous with His own, and so truly connected with Himself, that it must somehow be possible to account of it as if it were His own. With these considerations before us, we find that His subsequent teaching throws clear light on this parable. He invariably urged it as the common and constant task of His believing people, that they should seek to save others who were lost. The prominence of this to the Saviour's mind is peculiarly obvious in the sublime intercessory prayer recorded in the seventeenth chapter of John's Gospel, in which He speaks of the mission given to Him as exactly that which He has given to His people: "As thou hast sent me into the world, so have I also sent them into the world." Thus it is that when He is to take His departure from the world, and is no more in person to do the work of the shepherd seeking the lost sheep, He regards His people unitedly as taking His place and doing His work in this respect. Therefore He says: "I pray not that thou shouldest take them out of the world, but that thou shouldest keep them from the evil." When He goes, they are to be left behind; when He is wanting, they are to take His place, in so far as the seeking of sinners is concerned. Their seeking thus becomes as it were His own. With this the parable before us agrees. It is not He himself who is the seeker, and yet it is as if this were His own seeking. The parable is the answer for after-times to the question, Why does the Church of Christ willingly receive publicans and sinners? just as the parable of the shepherd is the answer to the question why He personally was found doing so on that day when these three parables were uttered. The Church seeks sinners just as her Lord and Master did; and she it is who is represented in this woman seeking for the lost piece of money. Most naturally this parable comes after the former—after, and not before, as the Church's work follows Christ's;—and comes necessarily, as Christ's work is not complete without the Church's work, hers being in reality His work continued down through all time. These hearers of our Lord, being Old Testament readers, could not have much difficulty in perceiving the fitness of the parable, familiar as they were with the representation of the Jewish Church as "the daughter of Zion." Readers in later times, being New Testament readers, may see it more clearly still, familiar as they are with the representations of the Church as "the bride," lifting up her voice and saying, "Come!"

If, then, the woman in this parable be a type of Christ's Church, how fitly the little Church of these early days seems represented by this poor woman with her ten pieces of silver; and how precious also is a soul thus made to appear, when it is as one piece out of ten. She dwells in a small house, and these ten pieces of silver now in her possession are required that she may hold that house as her own. By and by her house may be enlarged—it may even become one of stately proportions—and if it do, the seeking for the lost piece of money will be a search more widely extended. Here, however, we are coming upon another complication. Have we not made the lost piece of money represent the lost soul, and if the woman be the Church, is not every saved one absorbed into that Church, thus being at one time the sought, and at another the seeker? No doubt this is the case, and when we think of it, there may appear some entanglement. Yet this complication exists in reality. Men who were first in the position of the lost are afterwards in the position of the seekers. We may therefore expect that this double relationship to Christ's work will involve some complication in a parable which puts both things into one story. But the parable may be regarded as giving the Church's position at a definite point in her history. At each successive period to which the narrative applies, the unsaved soul is the lost piece of money, and the Church is the seeker. The representative story will thus be constantly applicable. And if we shift our view from the position of the sought to that of the seeker, it will be found that the form of this parable wonderfully suits the reality. As possession of money is to the support of the household, so is the ingathering of the lost to the maintenance of the Church. There is no analogy which can better indicate this than that afforded by money. The Church's wealth is increased by conversions, the house is enlarged, and the resources at command are sufficient to support all the demands of the extended establishment. No doubt the imagery is becoming complicated when we think of such things, but it is also enriched by the complication, as the Church is by the increased number of those lost ones who are found. The wealth of imagery which is here was recognised by the Teacher who shaped the parable. And in confirmation, it is to be noted that the Lord does not compare the nine pieces which remain to those who need no repentance, as He did compare the ninety-nine sheep left in the wilderness. The Church is spiritually richer by every piece which she finds. The silver of the Lord's house is multiplied; its treasury is replenished; and the Lord is "seeing of the travail of his soul, and is satisfied." The Church herself may or may not have had the responsibility connected with the position of those who are lost; but she shall at least have fresh gladness in every lost piece of silver which she replaces in the treasury. She shall then dwell joyfully and gratefully in the house provided for her, and her home become a centre of activity and cheerfulness in the land.

Search for the lost piece.—The picture, so sharp in outline and definite in figure, is such as may engage the fancy of an artist, and supply an attractive subject for the pencil. The lighted candle, the thorough sweeping, the diligent searching, are highly artistic. And they are spiritually full of significance.

1. *The lighted candle* is the first requisite for the search, and is altogether peculiar to this parable. Need for it presents evidence of imperfect ability for the search. The candle is instrumentality which supplies want. Without light we cannot see to search, and the candle provides the requisite. The candle is a *prepared medium of light*, ready to the hand of the woman when she would use it; and *a moveable light*, which can be carried in the hand or shifted from place to place as the searching proceeds. The light with which the Church searches is the truth. The candle is the Word. The familiar analogy of Scripture is drawn out in harmony with this, as under the imagery of the golden candlestick in tabernacle and temple, and again in the candles and candlestick of the Apocalypse. The Word of truth is the candle prepared by the Spirit of truth to the hand of the Church, that she may be equipped for her searching. This parable is, therefore, that in which the Spirit's part in the salvation of men is brought into view. Invisible He himself continues, in accordance with all that is otherwise taught in Scripture, as to His working; but the light of the truth, wherever it appears, is the evidence of His preparation for the work of the

Church in the salvation of the lost. And in this connection we are elsewhere taught to believe in His presence with the Church in working, and His power accompanying the work, so that while the Church searches, He, too, is the invisible Searcher who needs no light. This, however, cannot be introduced in parabolic representation. There is, then, light provided for the salvation of lost men, as to which the Bible is full of allusions. Christ is the light of the world, His Word is light, His Church herself is light. The harmony is clear. The Word lightens, but it is the work of Christ, as set forth by the Holy Spirit, which gives the illuminating power, and it is the Church which holds up this divinely-provided light. The candle is a *moveable light*, carried by the woman from place to place. Wherever a lost piece of money is to be sought, there the candle must be carried that the searching may be thorough. This carrying of the candle, first into one place and then into another, is the Church's part in seeking for lost souls. While the whole truth for man's salvation is presented in Holy Scripture, and any man who would inquire as to the way of life may there find the light he needs to guide him aright, men do not readily search the Scriptures for themselves, that their own souls may be saved. In recognition of this neglect, illustrated in one way under the image of the wandering sheep, in another under the image of the lost piece of money, the necessity for the active work of seeking is acknowledged by the Church, as it is here taught by the Saviour. The Bible is thus to the Church as the store of candles which the householder keeps ready for immediate use. The truth stored in the Bible is taken up, carried in the hand, and applied to the souls of men, that its light may fall upon them, discovering their condition and the way of escape. Where earnest desire to save the lost exists in the Church, such as was exemplified by the Saviour, and is illustrated in the case of this woman, there will be constant use of Gospel truth in order to secure the deliverance of men. And this is not gained by simple preaching of comfort, which may be disregarded in the hearing of it, as it often is in the reading of it; but by such preaching as shall make God's truth fall upon the soul to the discovery of its own lost condition. The candle burns as clearly when the search is unsuccessful as it does when its light is reflected on the surface of the lost piece of silver. The difference is, that in the latter case, by continued faithful searching and the Spirit's influence, it is brought to bear upon the lost. There must be much unsuccessful carrying about of the truth, attended with much labour; but wherever there is success in searching, it is the result of close application of Gospel truth.

2. *The sweeping of the house.*—The woman determines to leave no corner unexamined, no article in the house unmoved. As the soul is amongst the corrupting influences of earth, so is this piece of silver fallen among the dust, where it may be tarnished, and its real nature may be in consequence hard to recognise. Difficulty was felt by the Pharisees and scribes as they looked upon these publicans and sinners. In such characters the glance of the silver was not apparent. The naturalness of their perplexity the parable at this point allows. Tarnished silver has its value obscured. But, knowing the sinful condition into which men have fallen, and how in that state their real value may be con-

cealed, the Church will diligently continue the search, even in most unlikely quarters, determined at least not to be misled by unfavourable appearances, or by captious objections from onlookers. As in the case of the woman, the Church can carry out the search only at the cost of considerable disturbance all around, and discomfort to herself. As Bengel has said, the work is not done without raising much dust. The woman, however, is not deterred, she is hardly influenced, by the confusion occasioned and the dust raised. So eager is she in the search, that she hardly takes heed to these things. So much anxiety of heart does she feel in reference to the piece of silver which she has lost, that she cares nothing for discomfort. This is the ideal of the Christian Church as sketched by the Saviour's hand; a woman who grudges no trouble, and is undeterred by the disturbance her work occasions. The one object kept in view is the discovery of that which has been lost; and when success at last crowns the effort, her reward is sufficient, her joy is great.

Joy over the finding of the lost piece.—In her gladness of heart the woman calls together her friends and neighbours to rejoice with her. It is interesting to observe that the Saviour does not in this case say that there shall be joy *in heaven*, as He did when speaking of the shepherd taking home the lost sheep. Here he says simply (verse 10), "There is joy in the presence of the angels of God." It is still joy to the angels in the salvation of lost men which is here represented, as in the former case; but here it is the joy of those angels when they are sent forth to the earth, beholding the efforts of the Church, and ministering to them who are heirs of salvation. There is joy in heaven to the angels, and there is joy to them also, as they are visitors to the earthly house, beholding the Church's work. Within the house of privilege, where the Church has her home, and where provision for her need has been made from the fulness of Divine favour, there is great rejoicing when a lost one is found, and that joy is shared by invisible witnesses who are interested in all that concerns the working of Divine grace in the midst of the sinful race of men. As Bernard has well put it, though out of harmony with the analogy in the parable, "The tears of the penitent are angels' wine." Keeping to the figure, we may say that the Church's joy wakens a sympathetic gladness in the midst of a group of witnesses, invisible to human eyes, belonging to a higher race, attracted to the sight by the importance of this great work to which the Church on earth gives herself, in the name and with the blessing of her Lord.

CHAPTER V.

III.—*WELCOME TO THE RETURNING.*

THE PRODIGAL SON.

Luke xv. 11-32.

As a picture, the parable of the Prodigal Son needs a large canvas, bringing out in due perspective a father's house in the foreground, and a far country in the background. Perhaps it might rather be said that the story affords material for a portfolio of views, all the pictures having the same subject. The father's house is first presented to view; thereafter different points in the landscape are successively brought into prominence, under varying light and shade; until, in the last view, the house is again seen in the foreground, in the full brightness of an unclouded day, the scene of special rejoicing. A single sketch, however, will best serve the purposes of exposition. A spacious dwelling situated in a wide territory is conspicuous in the picture; a father and two sons compose the family; a large number of servants are in the dwelling. This father is ruler over the whole territory. In a far part of his dominions the inhabitants have established themselves in opposition to his authority. The younger son, after receiving a large share of his father's wealth,

The Prodigal Son. 49

leaves his father's house, and wanders into the region of rebellion, where he joins the rebels and wastes his substance in riotous living. Coming to wretchedness, he after a great while repents, and sets out for the long deserted home. He is welcomed with great joy by his father; in that joy the servants of the household largely share; but the elder son, who had continued at home, stands outside in sore displeasure. Sketched only in outline, this is the representation of the kingdom of God in its relation to a sinful world. God is as a Father amongst men, who takes delight in receiving to His favour and home all who return in penitence from wandering and transgression. Self-righteous and supercilious men may wonder at it, but this is the very truth, a Divine Father "receiveth sinners and eateth with them."

Verse 11.—"*A certain man had two sons.*" At first our attention is fixed on the family circle within the dwelling. There is a father, and there are two sons. These make up the family. The mother does not appear in the story. Her absence is quite marked, and yet is never painfully felt, because there is nothing in the story which involves even an allusion to the fact. This is a studied silence, for the simple reason that human relations never can be made fully to harmonise with the higher relations subsisting between God and men. Hence it happens that the gentle, penetrating, and most powerful influence of a mother —the finest moral and spiritual influence working in the midst of family ties—is necessarily absent from a story introduced for parabolic service. At the same time, it is to be observed that the subtle power of tenderest, purest affection is not absent. The sons are not represented as if suffering from the want of this. On the contrary, there is an unusual tenderness of feeling, and very striking expression of it, when the father meets his returning son. To every one who considers how a father would act in such circumstances, and how a mother would, it must be clear that the motherly influence is not wanting, but rather conspicuously present. It is the strongest and tenderest love of the family circle which is discovered at that point in the narrative, though even in such love there is, no doubt, only a dim shadowing of the love which "passeth knowledge."

There are only *two sons*. In the three parables here set together, there is a striking difference in the numbers spoken of in the illustrative cases. There is indeed in each case a single object conspicuous. It is a solitary wandering sheep, which is alone on the mountain; a single piece of money, which has rolled off into some darkened corner; and one prodigal son. But the single object is put in different relations in the successive stories, and with some regard to what is natural in the form of illustration. There is one sheep from a flock of a hundred belonging to the shepherd; one piece of money out of a little store of ten pieces which a woman has in her possession; one son from a family only two in number. The flock of sheep affords in some ways an appropriate line of illustration, but it is furthest removed from the reality. The piece of money comes nearer the case in the illustration of enduring value, yet the relative importance of it to the holder is heightened to one in ten. The family circle comes unspeakably nearer the truth, yet still the effect is heightened, and the lost one takes rank as one of two. This is the impressive mode of disclosing the fact that God cares for each sinner apart, as if he were the only wanderer;—as if the world were but a small domain, and in it only a single sinner, so watchfully does God care for each lost soul. This is the parabolic form for "*whosoever* will, let him come;" and for the distinctly personal assurance for "every creature,"—"*him* that cometh unto me, I will in no wise cast out."

And here let us mark quite decidedly that it is a father's love which yearns over the lost one. So our Lord describes it; and so every sin-burdened heart may regard it. A father's love is the key to the glad tidings of peace. "A certain man *had two sons.*" This is quite a different "having" from having sheep, or having silver pieces. A father's relationship is concerned, and he has not even a large family circle. The whole strength of his affection is concentrated on two sons, and of these two, one is a prodigal.

Verse 12.—Our attention is to be given chiefly to this younger son, who becomes a wanderer in the ways of folly and vice. We see the separation of this son from his father, to the father's deep displeasure, and to his own speedy ruin. What leads to this separation of father and son? Nothing in the father's character or treatment of the son; nothing in the circumstances of the family; but something in the moral condition of the young man himself. He is restless, longing after what he has not. He craves more than is given him in his father's love and the fulness of his father's house. What is worse, he desires what it is impossible to have in the sunshine of his father's favour. He is prepared to sacrifice a father's love in order to gratify his own desires. Two things he specially longs after,—goods completely his own, and separation from his father in order to unrestricted use of them. These two give form to a plan which he sketches for his life, or at least for as much of it as he cares to forecast. There may be a Beyond,—he does not inquire into that, and is content to leave it a blank. While, however, the two things are present to his mind, only the first is uttered. There is a half-truthfulness attendant on an evil purpose, which is falseness, and prepares the way for evil-doing. Such half-truthfulness is the device of this young man now. "*Father, give me the portion of goods that falleth to me.*" Property which I can call my own is my want. He speaks as if he only wished to make a beginning for himself, as every young man may properly desire, and as it is well for him that he should be induced to do, whether he have a large capital to start with, or no capital but willingness to work, character to guide him, and determination to learn. But this young man does not contemplate work. He does not think of entering upon his possessions with a sense of responsibility, meaning to do a manly part in making a wise and benevolent use of his property. He is quite willing, indeed, that his father should regard his request in this light, but quite unwilling to have his actual design explained. The desire for property is occasioned by what is meanwhile unacknowledged—the desire of self-indulgence away from a father's control. The father gives his son what he asks. So God gives to man, with freedom to use, according to personal choice. Deceived neither by half-truthfulness in utterance, nor by the nature of the purpose but half acknowledged in the heart, God freely distributes property, even though men make a god of it and utterly forget the Giver. Too often men desire the gifts while caring little for the favour of the Giver, and unrestricted use of His gifts rather than their use according to His will. The explanation of man's separation from God is twofold: Inwardly, self-indulgence is more valued than experience of Divine favour under the restraints of obedience; Outwardly, God's gifts are esteemed more than God Himself. These elements mingle in all sin.

Verse 13.—Half-truthfulness, which has a covert end to serve, discovers its real falseness as soon as that end seems sure. The young man could not long keep up appearances. But a few days could he brook delay, when he makes a complete break-off from home restraint. "*Not many days after, the younger son gathered all together, and took his journey into a far country.*" Such beginning is the start on a course of sin. In such exploring a man may travel long, and penetrate far into the dread mysteries of unrestrained wickedness. As we look upon the young man hasting away, we do not see the worst. With stores of money in his possession, he is hurrying from his father's house, glad to widen the distance between him and a father's commands. His mind is full of purposes and high expectations. Property and prospects together are here a preparation for iniquity. This young man is mighty to do evil, and eager to make a beginning. Sad it is for the man himself, and very sad for those to whom he comes, when youth and wealth go open-handed into the dwelling-places of vice. Sad for him, for he may perish, though a possibility of escape remains, through which he may come out, though scathed as by fire.

Sad for them who are dwellers in the abodes of sin, increasing the power of those influences which ensnare them, establishing the strongholds of evil. By such events, those who have sold themselves to sin become still more entangled in their captivity.

How, then, does it fare with this youth? He reached the desired country, and "*there wasted his substance in riotous living.*" It is quickly told. The Bible condenses the description of such scenes. These few words give the Bible representation of folly and vice. The picture is only in outline. It does not aim at telling much, for there is an ignorance which is precious above thousands of gold and silver. It is ignorance of such scenes as those with which this young man was now daily familiar. Happy is that man whose memory carries no imprint of them. This youth has now a knowledge which is a living curse. Enough is sketched in this picture to show in dim perspective the hatefulness of the life. "Wasted his substance in riotous living." Reckless folly. The reins which reason holds are snapped and dangling in the breeze; passion has sway; the sight of ruinous waste fails to deter. Some sin is wily in its working, and does not part company with prudence; but not such as this. Vice can cut short its own course by ruining its devotee. Earthly substance cannot endure under riotous living. Like snow before the sun, it melts away. The profligate awakes; his eyes are cooler and clearer; his wealth is gone. In wreck of substance is the reign of debasing vice. Terrible is the close for the man who delights to dwell among its devotees. The law which conscience gives is first shunned; afterwards it is brought forth to provide materials for jest; lofty aspirations are cast away as cumbersome treasure on the line of a retreating army; and the novice in vice goes headlong into pollution, soon fitting him for companionship with the worst. This "far country," where substance is wasted in riotous living, is the kingdom of wickedness in this world. It is the kingdom of Satan.

Between the kingdom of vice and the father's house there is a wide territory. In view of the significance of the story, the dwelling of vice could not be near the house. It is in a "far country." The separation is complete. As you look along that wide stretch of moorland between the father's house and the corrupt retreat to which the younger son has gone, you discover no messenger sent to make inquiries after the youth, or to carry words of earnest entreaty for his return. At first sight this is perplexing. It seems so different from the reality represented in other parables, such as the two which precede this. There is significance in the absence of a feature which would have been natural to such a story. Is not this testimony to the deep displeasure of the father with the conduct of his son? The father voluntarily continues as far from his son as the son has voluntarily gone from him. In this completeness of the son's isolation from home—in this absence of the going and coming of messengers—we trace strong marks of a father's moral indignation. It is plainly the more needful to notice this, considering the absence of any manifestation of displeasure, when at length the father meets his son returning from his career of wickedness. The past is then so completely buried, that it is of the highest consequence to note the unbending condemnation so strongly maintained till that moment.

Verse 14.—The narrative, which faintly traces the riotous living, indicates more minutely the bitter experience which comes in its train. "*When he had spent all, there arose a mighty famine in that land; and he began to be in want.*" Such is the dark shading in which the consequences of riotous living are painted. Ruin keeps company with riot. The youth goes unbidden to be the guest of the riotous, and soon ruin comes unbidden to be guest with him. This happens partly as the result of his own action, partly because of events over which he had no control. First, he spends all his substance in self-indulgence, and thus walks deliberately into the inheritance of penury. By his own choice, he brings himself to want. To aggravate his experience, there comes "a mighty famine" upon the whole country. His trouble is deepened by events which involve all around him in a share of distress. The famine in Canaan, when stores were in the garners of the king of Egypt, may represent what is here depicted. The parabolic meaning of the famine is the thing of chief interest. In seeking this, the main points to be noticed are, that its coming is here connected with his spending of his substance, and it involves *him* in additional distress only as it involves all the dwellers in the land. It came when his purse was empty, but it came to all who dwelt there, whatsoever the state of their resources at the time. Not merely has this young man's wealth gone from his hands, but the land into which wealth is carried by headstrong foolish youth, who freely pour it forth till nothing remains for themselves, is a land subject to mighty famines. When such famine comes, the possession of flocks and herds avails little; in some ways it increases the evil. How to provide for them at such a time; how to escape the necessity of driving them to an unfavourable market; how to keep off the hour when there shall be stores of money in possession, but no food to buy,—these are the perplexities of the rich in such times. Money keeps famine at bay only by a few paces. In this way the parable illustrates a spiritual truth. Famine afflicts the life of those who are far off from God, whether in the midst of poverty or of plenty. There is a want which riot cannot satisfy. Licentious indulgence will only excite for a brief season, blinding the eyes for the time to all that is beyond the whirl; but when the excitement is over a great void is left behind. The whirl stops, objects beyond become visible, and the man finds himself unprepared for meeting them. Property cannot satisfy. There is in the land a great famine of all that the higher nature wants for its support and satisfaction. Those who have least property, having least to lean upon, and fewest expedients open to them, are on these accounts likely to feel the pinching most. But all feel it, even to the richest. The greatest possessions cannot buy what the higher nature needs. Afar off from God, the supply is not to be had at any price. There comes a mighty famine.

Verses 15, 16.—"*And he went and joined himself to a citizen of that country; and he sent him into his fields to feed swine. And he would fain have filled his belly with the husks that the swine did eat: and no man gave unto him.*" In the straits which famine brings, and without any resources of his own, he looks around him for help. He makes his appeal to "a citizen of that country." This person, as a permanent dweller there, is identified with the place where the youth has but recently arrived. The citizen has acquired property, has vested interests in the country, and among the citizens is one of those least likely to think of removing. It was plainly of such an one as this that our Lord spoke, when He startled His disciples by saying, "How hardly shall a rich man enter into the kingdom of heaven!" Rendered into the language of this parable, that saying will run thus: "How hardly will a prosperous citizen of the far country depart from it, that he may dwell near to God." To such a settled dweller in the place, the profligate son betakes himself now. The youth would settle if he could, and find a place among the citizens. Companionship in a godless life gives some support. When this cannot be found to any extent worth reckoning upon, even patronage from those who have prospered in ungodliness is accepted as a gain. A very small gain in this case such patronage brought. This wealthy citizen "sent him into his fields to feed swine." And he went! He whose excited imagination had drawn vivid pictures of unmingled delight, accepts to-day the post of a swine-herd. He drives out the swine into the fields, that they may feed under the trees on pods which have fallen from the branches. Heart-sick with disappointment, he is meeting the realities of life in their plainest, roughest form. Separated from his home, forsaken by the companions of his revelry, he is lonely and sad in these silent fields. In his self-produced poverty, hunger is his companion, yet no man gives unto him. In his extremity he sits down among the swine and feeds with them upon the husks. Sad is this picture of humbling, bitter extremity. As we look upon it, let us remember that poverty is in itself no disgrace, though there be many disgraceful paths which lead down to it. Unspeakably better it is, in every way more worthy of man's moral nature, to be an honest swine-herd, feeding on the pods which have fallen from the kharub trees, than a riotous profligate, faring sumptuously every day.

Verses 17-19.—"*And when he came to himself, he said, How many hired servants of my father's have bread enough, and to spare, and I perish with hunger! I will arise, and go to my father, and will say unto him, Father, I have sinned against Heaven, and before thee, and am no more worthy to be called thy son: make me as one of thy hired servants.*" Suffering proved a valuable teacher to this young man. He was in misery now; no help was to be found around him, and he knew of help nowhere save in the midst of that home which he had so wickedly left, and which for a time he had been so anxious to forget. Such thoughts as these came in upon his mind on this day of calamity. In giving a welcome to them, "he came to himself." This brief expression carries in it a vivid reflection of what his previous course had been, as well as a strong testimony to complete change now. The Saviour accounts every one who hastes away from God, hurries into transgression, and seeks to abide in the midst of evil, a man who is "away from himself," as well as away from God, and away from home. This description applies not merely to one course of conduct, such as that described in the parable, but to all courses of action involving wilful separation from Him who is the source of all good. A man is away from himself when he refuses direction of those powers given him for the guidance of his conduct. Ruling impulses may differ greatly in the history of different wanderers, but in all cases they are impulses not suited for the rule which is given to them, and not capable of exercising such rule, except to the man's hurt. Prejudices, opinions, and delusive imaginations are not the man, though cherished by him; evil passions are not the man, though indulged and strengthened within him; wicked actions are not the man, though they are done by him. Under the dominion of false views and evil desires, which lead on to sinful actions, the man is not himself. The wandering from God, which is wickedness, is also the utmost foolishness. The man who goes against God, at the same time goes against himself. The history of this prodigal is the illustration. At length, however, in the midst of self-caused wretchedness, "he came to himself." This return is coincident with the resuming of sober thought. Once brought to this frame of mind, thoughts start up as memories of the pleasant past; in the stillness and sadness of that hour he seems to hear a voice say, "Thou fool!" Then, overleaping the immediate past, which he has filled with spectres of folly, sin, and shame, he sees in a more remote past the exceeding blessedness which he has surrendered, and in the fulness of which his father's servants are now luxuriating. Having abated bodily hunger by sharing husks with the swine he tended, a greater hunger now takes possession of his soul. Lost to all around, he gazes with lustrous eyes on an excellence unseen by those who are near him. He longs for peace, for purity, for such a love as his father's love, even if he cannot have it in all the fulness which he had known when he held the favoured place of a son. He says in his heart—says it aloud, perchance, as he wanders through those fields, with none but the swine for companions—" How many hired servants of my father's have bread enough, and to spare, and I perish with hunger!" Subjection to his father he had disliked and sought to escape. But now, from a sadly changed point of view, and with a greatly widened experience, which had made him weary of knowing what the world contained, he looked on the service of his father as the finest thing the world possessed. How glad would he be now, even if he took the lowest place among the servants! As he thinks of it, he feels as if new life were coming to his heart, as if the treasures of wisdom, so recklessly thrown away, were being mysteriously restored. He says, " I will arise, and go to my father." This is the turning-point. To secure this among men, Jesus lifted His voice and cried, "Repent: for the kingdom of heaven is at hand." Repent and come. Blessed is the least in the kingdom of heaven. That blessedness men may not only see from afar, but enter into, and share freely from henceforth. There is warrant even for such a wanderer as this prodigal to repent of the past, and say, " I will arise, and go to my father." He is right in the instinct which makes him regard this as his last resort. Pity that it had not been his first! There he hopes to find an open and safe retreat for his weary, sin-burdened spirit. Well it is for him that such a resolution should be taken and at once carried out. In this is the beginning of wisdom; the end is everlasting life.

But all who wander do not thus escape from that "far country." The figures of many are dimly traced on the picture, whose movements we cannot descry. They do not appear in the foreground, because none of them are seen to come out from that country and approach the father's house. They dwelt there when that son came to their abodes of evil, and they continue there when he departs. Thus it is faintly indicated that there are many who remain there, and find their graves in the "far country." There are some who prosper, and who settle there, rejoicing in their prosperity. There are some uncomfortable there, who seek to make the best of things they see no way of mending, and who do not brace themselves for an effort to break away from the influence with which they have grown familiar. Others there are, sick at heart, who yield to depression, and, like weary travellers toiling in winter through dangerous Alpine passes, sink into the midst of snow, knowing as they yield to overpowering drowsiness that they will sleep the sleep of death in that cold winding-sheet. From other parables we learn that in the kingdom there is provision for merciful attempts to deliver men from this great danger. To those who will not say, "I will arise and go," there are those who are sent forth, to lift their voices with the friendly cry, "Arise, and come." Yet are there many who remain behind.

When the prodigal son nerves himself for the resolution of returning to his father, thereby discovering his shame and wretchedness, his thoughts grapple with the great perplexity,—How can he meet his father, and what account will he give of his sin? He went out full, he will return empty; he went from the door with great pomp, he will come again to that same door as a beggar; he carried with him all his goods, but they have been swept from his grasp, while he himself with difficulty forded the torrent of vice, barely escaping with his life; he will return with an empty wallet, every eye in the house beholding his shame. But these are not the things which distress him now. How shall he meet his father? is the one question; as the sinner's inquiry must be, How shall I meet God? The one thought which expels other thoughts from his mind, and lies as a great burden upon him, is this, " I have sinned." True it is—and the one truth affecting his position. All other facts in his career lead directly to this as the central fact. However often he may turn aside from it, to this one thought he must always return : "I have sinned." "I am no more worthy to be called a son." In saying this, he sees his only method of approach to his father. In his father he sees his only refuge from perdition. He forms his resolution. "I will say it." This is what the Bible means by confession. It is simple truth-speaking when we approach God ; nothing more, and nothing less. "If we confess our sins, He is faithful and just to forgive us our sins, and to cleanse us from all unrighteousness." By the Saviour's work the way for all this has been set open. We are assured of that which the prodigal son only hoped for with a trembling uncertainty and fear, when, having repented of his folly and sin, he resolved to retrace the long way over which he had hurried in pursuit of phantom forms of liberty and joy. For every sinner it is fit to speak to God as he now determined to speak: " Father, I have sinned, and am no more worthy to be called thy son." To this he adds a request which is proof of the sincerity and depth of his humiliation now : "Make me as one of thy hired servants." In the abjectness of his distress he sees no other thing he can ask. Restoration to a son's place! That seems too much to think of asking He cannot even venture to frame such a wish in words. The hope flits like a condemning spectre about his mind, and frightens him when he dares for a moment to glance at it. No; it cannot be. Fallen for ever from a son's place, I can ask only to be set among those who serve in the house, out of my father's sight, whose hire is recompense. Thus the self-condemned prodigal thinks and feels now. It lies with the father, and not with him, to see how impossible is all this, and how certain it is that the welcome given on his return must be the welcome for a son.

When the prodigal's trouble was at its height, he still confided in his father, believing that he would receive him if he returned. Upon this return he resolved, with the determination to acknowledge in his father's presence the greatness of his sin. From this point all is changed.

Verses 20-24.—"*He arose, and came to his father.*" Travelling back over the ground which he had before crossed so light-heartedly—travelling now in the garb of a beggar, and, what was far worse on that day, agitated with bitter thoughts of self-condemnation— he at length came in sight of that house which had so lingered in his memory as the happy home of his boyhood, and which had seemed to him in his extremity the only remaining retreat which the wide world contained. In sight of the place, his heart beat fast; his anxiety rose to intensity, as he wondered whether that day should make his life one of despair by throwing him back again on his misery, or of hope and returning joy by affording escape from the polluted, hateful past. He trembled under a sense of the greatness of the crisis.

"*But when he was yet a great way off, his father saw him.*" The father who would not go to seek his son, who would not even send to entreat his return, did not cease to watch day by day in the hope of his reappearance. With the quickness which love gives to the observing eye, the father recognised his son when he was just in sight, far in the distance. The servants in the house might have taken no notice of him, or, if they had cast a glance in the direction, they might have failed to recognise, in the weary, poor-looking wayfarer, the figure of that long-lost son, who had departed wearing all the signs of high rank. But "his father saw him;" not only saw, as any of the servants might have seen him, but recognised him as his son. And "he had compassion on him, and ran, and fell on his neck, and kissed him." The intensity of feeling long pent up in that father's heart became apparent. Others might have misunderstood the restraint which he had put upon himself during his son's wilful wandering; but there could be no misunderstanding now. The compassion silently nourished, now rose like a tide; and in the strength of his ardour, he hasted to meet his son. While others may have doubted how that son would be received if he ventured to return—and no one could feel greater misgiving than the son himself, now that he was about to put it to proof—the matter was already settled in the heart of the father; and the decision is quickly discovered to all. The father did not wait the arrival of his son; he did not send out a messenger to receive first the submission of the transgressor; he went forth to meet him, and, as if to lessen, though only by a few moments, the period of their separation, he ran towards him; and when they met, the father fell upon the son's neck, and kissed him. Before a word had been spoken, a welcome was made sure. The combined strength of a father's regard and of a mother's tender love are seen in such a welcome. As in an instant, the light of morning breaks through the darkness of night; so the warmth of home affection revived the man ready to die in neglect.

When our Saviour has sketched this scene, He tells us that in such a father we have a representation of the Father in heaven. He who saith, "No man knoweth the Father, save the Son, and he to whomsoever the Son will reveal him," looks upon this picture taken from earthly life, and says, This is my Father, and thus my Father acts towards a returning penitent. His is a father's love towards a lost son—a father's welcome to a repenting prodigal. A grand truth lies here for all mankind. The value of the representation is enhanced by the fact that the son thus welcomed is one of two. God welcomes each sinner with a strength of love and joy such as a man might feel if the son who comes back to subjection were the only one whose return was expected. God's forgiveness must, indeed, be such as condemns sin and upholds righteousness. The Divine displeasure against sin has been already set forth in the parable, but its uncompromising sternness is followed by the most marvellous sight of overflowing love. With ever-watchful eye, God discovers the first movements of penitence within the heart; before the penitent can be assured of a welcome, the Divine favour is turned towards him; when the sinner comes to plead, the answer is ready before the petition has found utterance. God keeps no man waiting who seeks His blessing thus. "He delighteth in mercy."

Welcomed as the son is in this way, he cannot leave the past unmentioned. He must make confession of his own exceeding sinfulness and unworthiness. And thus it is he speaks: "*Father, I have sinned against Heaven, and in thy sight, and am no more worthy to be called thy son.*" Most comprehensive confession, fit equally for the ear of his father and for the hearing of God, who judges of all such confessions when they are made. "I have sinned;" this brief description applies to all my course since I passed wilfully from under thy control in search of a satisfaction never found. "I have sinned against Heaven;" for this is the first and most dreadful view of my evil course, that I have in all sinned grievously against God, while the sin has been in thy sight, my father, and thou hast had cause to condemn me. It is in the very spirit of David he speaks (Ps. li. 4), "Against thee, thee only, have I sinned, and done this evil in thy sight." And when now he sees and owns what he is before God, he keenly feels how unworthy he is to be owned by his father. "I am no more worthy to be called thy son." 'Father' I must call thee; and yet I am unworthy that thou shouldest call me 'Son.' Such is genuine confession. Yet must we observe what is left unsaid. There is no trace of false-hearted excusing of his conduct, such as we all find so easy. There is no apology for himself, and no making of charges against others. As Grotius has said, "He does not cast the blame upon his youth, or upon his ill advisers, but, without excuse of any sort, he makes naked confession of his guilt." And, on the other hand, it is to be observed that something of what he purposed to say is left unspoken. Before he departed from the far country, we heard his resolution to pass from his confession to the petition: "Make me as one of thy hired servants;" but that prayer is unspoken. The father's welcome has made it impossible, and when he has said in humility, "I am no more worthy to be called thy son," he cannot go further, even though he intended it,—for he must still say, *Father!* These then are the prominent features of this son's state of mind now; he mourns over his sin and loathes it; he feels himself unworthy to be named a son; and yet he desires nothing so much as to be completely under his father's authority again. This is the Saviour's sketch of a true penitent before God. If any are anxious to know who will have the welcome of a Divine Father, they have here the unmistakable reply. As he says, I have sinned, so must we; as he views all his sin chiefly as sin against God, so must we; as he cried unworthy, so must we own complete unworthiness of Divine favour. Then shall we receive that which is given in the exercise of Divine mercy and grace; for "by grace are we saved through faith; and that not of ourselves: it is the gift of God." But it will be said that in selecting such a prodigal to represent the man who appears before God to confess himself a sinner, a very extreme case has been chosen. And no doubt this must be carefully considered. We hope it may be said that the great majority of men shrink from going such a dreadful length in sin as this youth went. But there is obvious reason for the selection, when Jesus would by this story set forth the grand truth that every sinner may come to God and live. The line runs out widely to embrace such a profligate, that it may encourage all. Not, indeed, that this case may be taken as a type of the very worst on earth, for as the dividing line sweeps through the far country, it passes between the abodes of those content to dwell there. But through the midst of these abodes it runs, that it may be clearly shown that any dweller there may yet escape condemnation, if he will only arise and come. On the other hand, it is evident that this description embraces all courses of sin less gross and glaring, in which a man runs a less distance, and returns by a more direct course. While thus the extreme type of illustration is such as to make it all-inclusive, it must be observed that as all sin is self-seeking in disregard of the will of God, so must all the avenues of return converge on the same point of union,—repentance of the wandering, and faith in the God to whom all must return in seeking for peace. And now we complete the view, when, passing from different courses of sin, we consider how each man's sin appears in his own sight when he comes to meet God with confession. Seeing how much men's lives differ in the amount of evil they contain, we may appropriately speak of some forms of life being more wicked in comparison with others. But when each man considers his own sin, as it looks under the eye of the holy God, it appears most dreadful, and there is no true expression of the reality save this: "I am unworthy to be called thy son." The prodigal's confession is accepted as suitable for each; the publican's prayer is the fit petition for all: "God be merciful to me a sinner." There is thus no extreme of self-depreciation, but the natural expression of what is obviously true, when Peter says, "Depart from me, for I am a sinful man, O Lord;" and when Paul, the apostle, who in early life had been a scrupulous observer of all the demands of the law, tells us that in his own eyes he seems the chief of sinners.

From the confession of the prodigal, the narrative passes at once to the orders which the father issues to provide for his son's wants. The son said, "Father, I am no more worthy to be called thy son;" but the father said, "*Bring forth the best robe, and put it on him.*" This transition conveys a deep impression of the all-absorbing determination of the father to prove that the welcome was unhesitating and joyous. While, however, we mark this, we must not fail to observe *the father's silence* in reference to the confession. There is meaning in this. When a son is received in such circumstances, expressing his grief for the past, what he says is apt to give occasion for reproach, or, if a different spirit rule, the father is apt to go to the opposite extreme, and frame words of excuse. It is otherwise here. The father is silent, and that silence is God-like. He receives the confession, for it is true, it is necessary; nothing can excuse the deeds, nothing can change the character of that awful past; but he does not dwell upon the painful subject, he does not open up the wound afresh. As he cannot say a word in excuse, he will not speak at all. His silence is condemnation. Thus God deals with man, maintaining a silence which is merciful. He casts the sins behind his back. "He giveth to all liberally, and upbraideth not."

Having thus received the humble confession, the father orders a robe for his son, a ring for his hand, shoes for his feet, and the killing of the fatted calf that a feast may be prepared. The best in the house is at his command, and a festival is a fit expression of the household's joy over the wanderer's return. In each one of these particular orders some readers see a distinct meaning. The robe is righteousness, the ring is freedom, the shoes represent preparation for service, and the feast is experience of the blessings of grace. No doubt the imagery has a fitness, but we doubt if there be warrant for such use of single phrases; most of all would we object to the attempt to find in the killing of the fatted calf some representation of the death of the Saviour, to which event it bears no analogy. The simple tale is this. The father is full of gladness, and all his resources are called into requisition to give token of it, and mark the rank of the son. All trace of his wretchedness is instantly cast away; he is clothed as a member of the family, and the household is summoned to a day of rejoicing. The key to all is in these words of the father to his servants: "*For this my son was dead, and is alive again; he was lost, and is found,*"— words which carry softly the condemnation of the past, while they celebrate the present gladness. This my son was dead—dead to home, dead to a father's claims, dead to duty; this my son was lost—lost to me, leaving me in gloom to weary for his return, lost to the life of holiness which otherwise had been his honour and my joy; but my son it was who went astray, and my son he still is now that he has returned, let us rejoice together: he was dead, and is alive again; he was lost, and is found.

"*And they began to be merry.*" In the circumstances, this statement is striking. It is not of the prodigal's experience that we are told. We naturally expect to hear how he was soothed, how the great weight of sadness began to pass away from his soul, how he drank in a new joy from the light of his father's countenance, and coveted eagerly the satisfaction of ministering humbly to his father. But we hear nothing of all this. The son's experience is lost in the joy of the father and the household. By the Saviour's teaching we are made to see that this is God's way. Wonderful teaching as to the ways of God! It is even made to appear as if the return of the sinner were the source of satisfaction chiefly to Him. He rejoices over a solitary sinner's return, when He blesses that soul with everlasting life. And it is not upon His gladness alone that our attention is turned. "*They* began to be merry!" Who are these servants? They abide in the house, they are even more in harmony with the father than the sons are, and they find their joy in ministering to these sons at the father's bidding. There can be no doubt as to the meaning of all this. These servants of the household represent the angels in the Father's house on high; there is here the echo of what has been already said in the seventh and tenth verses of this chapter. Look upon that household in the day of their feasting, when the master rejoices over the return of a long-lost son. And now, hear the Saviour translate the scene according to its spiritual significance: "Likewise, I say unto you, There is joy in the presence of the angels of God over one sinner that repenteth." The words were uttered in reference to the recovery of the lost piece of money; but the truth is the same, and the parabolic representation of it is much nearer the reality, when we witness the rejoicing over the return of the long-lost son.

Verse 25.—"*Now his elder son was in the field: and as he came and drew nigh to the house, he heard music and dancing.*" We now enter on a second part

of the story, which is in some respects a return upon
the first part of it, though quite distinct in detail. At
the outset the story spoke of two sons, between whom
this father divided his living; but hitherto the younger
son exclusively has occupied attention. Now the elder
son reappears—the wonder being that he has not
appeared sooner. The explanation of his absence from
the scene of rejoicing comes out in what follows. This
father, with only two sons, had trouble with both;
neither obeyed him with a willing mind, or showed
anything like that measure of sympathy with him
which he had from the servants of his house. What
here breaks upon us as a discovery of the evil disposition of the elder son is evidently nothing new or unexpected to the father. Such an outbreak of feeling has
plainly been a common occurrence. This father had no
such close and happy relationship with his first-born son
as he must have longed for, especially during that weary
season of the absence of the younger. The elder son
had not, indeed, forsaken his father's house; he had
not hurried into profligacy, as the other had done; he
had throughout kept an eye to all that concerned the
property on which they lived. But mutual confidence
was wanting, and free intercourse between them there
had not been. Outwardly the elder son was the better
of the two; but in the end the younger came most
quickly to give himself to his father with a full-hearted
affection. This father was like that other, reported of
elsewhere in the Gospels (Matt. xxi. 28), who had two
sons, to both of whom he issued his commands: and
the one said, "I will not," but afterwards he repented
and went; while the second said, "I go, sir," and went
not. That this is the real state of things in this case is

made very evident. When the younger son returned, the father, full of joy, called his servants; but he sent no messenger to call his brother from the field. The absence of this is a conspicuous feature in the story. It can be accounted for only on the supposition that the father, while lavishing his affection on the younger, and finding in this all sympathy from his servants, expected nothing but discontent if the elder son entered the house. The want of any message to him is the mark of the father's displeasure with the reigning disposition of the only other son he had. The conduct of the father in this respect is the exact counterpart of that on which we remarked at an earlier stage, as he sent no message to the prodigal while he remained absent. In both cases we have evidence of his dissatisfaction by withholding communication. The elder son was absent from the scene because he did not know of the rejoicing; in the midst of it his father sent no message to him, obviously because he expected no joyfulness on his part. Thus it appears he was excluded by his own cherished disposition, which had separated him from his father; and it is only the natural and inevitable consequence which we witness at this crisis in domestic history. The elder son does not appear in the midst of the festivities which celebrate the return, in profound penitence, of the long-absent wanderer.

"*And as he came and drew near to the house, he heard music and dancing.*" When all within the house are partaking of the feast, and the sound of music is high, the elder son is coming slowly back from the fields, where he has been superintending the operations in progress there. He is confounded by the evidence of high rejoicing within the house. But he will not enter to ascertain what has occasioned this unexpected state of matters. He summons a servant, and when he hears the explanation, so far from feeling any impulse to hurry into the presence of his brother, he is full of wrath, and turns away from the door. The father is informed of this, and hastens out now to meet this son, as a little earlier in the day he had gone forth to meet the other. In the former case, the son was the suppliant; in this case, it is the father. The father entreats his own son to rejoice with him in the return of the erring one; but the entreaty is scorned with the utmost bitterness of feeling, and the father is taunted for want of generosity towards a faithful son, and for wonderful sympathy with ill-doing. The words of this son are hateful, coming from a heart full of bitterness; they are words poisoned with malice. No man with a lingering trace of respect for his father could have spoken as he did. He tells his father that there is no generosity, not to say fairness, in the treatment he has experienced as a son. For many years he has served him without transgressing, and he has never received even a kid, far less the fatted calf, to make merry with his friends. He has served as a drudge, kept under continual restraint, without even a day of festivity throughout all these years. "But as soon as this thy son (he will not say 'my brother') is come, who has devoured thy living with harlots, thou hast killed for him the fatted calf." Thou hast no reward for faithful service, and thou hast no condemnation for the wasting of substance in immorality; thou hast nothing but feasting for a reckless spendthrift, who comes home only after he has wasted all that he had. The father's reply is clear, calm, and conclusive; but clear reasoning has no value to a man in such humour. The father says nothing of the bitter, malevolent spirit against himself and against the younger son which breathes through all these hateful words. He can do nothing but condemn them; and he keeps silence, as he did before in receiving the confession of the younger son because of his course of evil. That confession, however, he could receive. This statement which the elder son makes of his past he cannot accept; it is exactly the reverse of the confession of the other, and in every respect it is false. The younger said, I have sinned; the elder says, I have never transgressed: the younger said, I have sinned against Heaven; the elder makes no account of heavenly authority: the younger said, I am no longer worthy to be called thy son; the elder says, I only am worthy. The confession of the younger son the father could receive, for even his terrible sin had not shut him out from return; the self-assertion of the other he could not approve. But a man who stubbornly affirms that he has never transgressed is not to be reasoned with; it is hopeless to convince him that he is guilty of serious transgression in the utterance of the moment. Yielding to sad necessity, the father is silent. Of the charge against himself the father easily disposes. Had he never given this elder son anything? He had divided between the two all his living; and all that now remained of the property belonged to the one who declared he had received nothing. The younger son had indeed wasted his substance in riotous living, but in this he had robbed himself, not his brother, and made himself dependent on the tender mercy of others. And who should show mercy if not his father and his brother? *"It was meet that we should make merry, and be glad: for this thy brother was dead, and is alive again; and was lost, and is found."* In speaking to his servants, that father had given this reason for rejoicing in exactly the same terms, except that then he said, "This, *my son*, was lost;" whereas now he says, "This, *thy brother*, was lost:" for now he would not merely explain his own feeling, but remind a selfish brother what his feelings should be. Having given this explanation, and made this appeal, his father leaves him there.

The dealing of the father with his elder son represents the dealing of the Father in heaven with another type of transgressor. And who is this elder brother? The question has occasioned great perplexity to Bible interpreters. Some have supposed that Christians are aimed at, who are dissatisfied with the welcome of profligates into the kingdom of their Lord. And if we consider only the discontent with the welcome of the prodigal, there is enough to give a colour of sanction to this view. But if we have regard to the entire character described, such an interpretation is hopeless. There is no Christian who could think and speak of God, not to say to God, in such a manner as that adopted by the elder brother in speaking to his father. It may be asked, Of whom, if not of a Christian, can it be said by God, "*All that I have is thine*"? But of which Christian can this be said? And if the words could be thus applied in any sense to a Christian, would he be fierce in his denial of having received anything? Let us be consistent in our interpretation, and carry the meaning uniformly through the whole. The father divided between these two his living—a half he gave to the younger, and the elder became rightful owner of all that remained. In both cases temporal substance is spoken of, which is of unspeakably less value than the father's love; if that which was wasted in riotous living was temporal, so also was this which remained by right to the elder; and in that case, "All that I have is thine," must be held to apply to what is only temporal. To begin to apply this in a spiritual sense is to contradict the principle of interpretation uniformly followed in dealing with the other half of the parable, and is to mix up in hopeless confusion the domestic history and the parabolic teaching conveyed by it. Others have supposed that the elder son is intended to represent the hypocrite; and though this is certainly nearer the truth, the character described is not prominently hypocritical, but rather offensively open in the assertion of his hatred. We discover the application simply by gathering together the leading features of character implied in his own words. These are mainly three—*first*, he has never transgressed; *secondly*, he has had no pleasure in his service; and *thirdly*, he feels as if God did injustice to him by pardoning the profligate. These are the outstanding features of the character. The life of such a man wanders less into open sin than the life of the profligate; but it no less involves separation from God, and even for him there can be no true union to God except by returning to Him in the same spirit as that which the prodigal cherished and expressed. Outwardly decent, worldly, self-satisfied a man may be, wondering how open transgressors can hope to be accepted of God; but he himself must change his thoughts, feel his sinfulness, and take as his own the confession of the prodigal. Instead of saying, "I never transgressed at any time thy commandment," let him say as the prodigal did: "Father, I have sinned, and am no more worthy to be called thy son," and his confession will be received as true, his welcome shall be sure, and he will straightway have a full share in the rejoicing which they have who trust the Divine mercy, and serve God in gratitude for the great deliverance. But as long as the confession of sin is refused, the heart wilfully separates itself from God. The God who forgives the sin which is confessed, cannot approve when the confession is withheld and the need for it is denied. In this case the man is untruthful, and his life is one of rebellion. Such an one is not even called to a share of the joy which is felt in the return of the prodigal, but is left standing without. Thus the parable ends with solemn warning. The high encouragement of the early part is followed by the stern fidelity of the close.

In the three parables which have now been considered there is set forth in figurate representation the grand truth concerning the Divine plan for human salvation. On the lower side we see man's sinfulness, folly, and hopelessly ruined state, followed by a view of man's penitence and repose in Divine compassion and love. On the higher side we see God's condemnation of the sin, and His deliverance of the sinner. Having our attention specially concentrated upon the manner in which salvation is provided, we see the Son, as the Shepherd, going forth to seek the lost, and bearing their weight upon His own shoulders; we see the Church, with aid of the truth, under the Spirit's guidance, used as the instrument to seek the lost ones of the race; and we see the Father, by whom both Son and Spirit are sent, giving a royal welcome to the sinful in the midst of His own glorious home. Here is God's work for the good of man, while man's lowest state before God is exposed to view. Here is Divine truth of the highest order, reflected with prismatic beauty and harmony in these three parables. And most glorious it is to mark that this truth is ever being realised anew in the history of successive generations of men, for God's seeking is a constant seeking, and the Divine joy a continual rejoicing over the everlasting gain which rewards the search.

CHAPTER VI.

IV.—CONFESSION AND SUPPLICATION OF THE PENITENT ONE.

THE PHARISEE AND PUBLICAN.

LUKE XVIII. 9-14.

FOLLOWING the illustrations of restoration to the kingdom of God presented in the foregoing parables, we have seen that God desires men to come to Him, that they may share the blessings of His grace. We have now another view of the arrangements connected with entrance into the kingdom, giving greater prominence to personal responsibility in the manner of appearing before God. Men must plead with God in order to become partakers of His grace. We have heard God calling unto men; we must hear men calling unto God. In accordance with a conspicuous part of the parable of the Prodigal Son, supplication on man's part must be regarded as essential for entrance into the kingdom, and opportunity for such pleading with God is one of the privileges of the kingdom. Men cannot serve themselves heirs to this kingdom by any long course of strivings after great deeds of holiness, but they may have their names placed on the roll of its subjects by lowly acknowledgment of their failures. It is not chivalry, bearing down the selected course through heats of passion, and wearing with pride the signs of its triumphs, which wins the favour of this King; but humility, bending in lowly mien at the gate, owning the imperfection of the past, yet seeking, by God's help, an elevation hitherto unattainable. If the plans of the Lord of the kingdom are to be carried out, they who trust in themselves that they are righteous must be undeceived.

Prayer is, on one side, sense of need; on the other, entreaty for supply. It is need finding expression in the hearing of God. This exercise is the duty of men in coming to God, and thereafter the established privilege of those who have come in faith. The analogy between the two sons in the parable of the Prodigal Son, and the two suppliants here, is very close. An expositor cannot be far astray when detecting in the Pharisee the reappearance of the likeness of the elder brother, who says, "Neither transgressed I at any time thy commandment;" and in the publican the likeness of him who said, "I have sinned, and am no more worthy to be called thy son." The characters are the same, only the development of truth is more advanced. In observing such points of analogy the real unity of the parables becomes apparent.

The peculiarity of the parable of the Pharisee and Publican is, that the true nature of the prayer by which men enter the kingdom is illustrated by two examples entirely opposed in spirit. In other cases the parabolic narrative is drawn from pastoral, domestic, or social life. But the prayer to be offered by men, in seeking admission to the kingdom, is so thoroughly distinct from anything to be found in the relations of men, that such relations are searched in vain for anything sufficiently analogous to serve the end of illustration. This fact our Saviour proclaims, when now, contrary to His custom in other cases, He constructs His parable by selecting illustrative examples of the exercise of prayer itself. Man is, indeed, often a suppliant before his fellow-man, and our Lord will find aid for illustration in this, before He has finished His teaching as to prayer; but no example of this kind will suffice to bring out the true nature of that exercise which is required of those who draw near to God. To serve His end, our Great Teacher must select examples of the homage which is preferred in presence of the Deity. He who knew the heart of man, and needed not that any should testify what was in man, must go into the secrets of the soul, and select illustrative examples of prayer which shall be truly representative. This He has done in constructing the parable before us, setting forth how extremely different are the views of men as to prayer, and how different is the estimate which God sets on a variety of exercises bearing the same name.

Verse 10.—"*Two men went up into the temple to pray; the one a Pharisee, and the other a publican.*" "Two men." This is another example of the selection of two to represent the whole. All suppliants may be included within this comprehensive grouping. But all men are not suppliants. There is another class of men which cannot be here represented. They are strangers to prayer. Their absence is allowed for in the fact that the reference of the parable is exclusively to those who do appear before God in some way, while their case has been dimly indicated in the parable of the Prodigal, where they are mentioned as citizens of a far country; they are by their own choice "far off," while these two at least seek to draw nigh to God. For the present our attention is concentrated upon praying men—upon as many of our race as own that it is rational to pray, and that it is dutiful. Thus persuaded, and in a sense urged, they agree in appearing before God in the attitude of suppliants.

That the representation may be the more striking to the observer, these two men are brought together at their devotions, their meeting-place being the temple of God. Whatever their private life, they have come together for the same exercise, and they meet in the place dedicated to Divine service, where the tokens of the Divine presence have often been given. As they enter the outer court, everything before them conveys instruction as to the true manner of approaching God. Here, in the very centre, is the great altar of sacrifice, over which the blood of victims is daily pouring in token of sin; and behind it, the laver for cleansing; and within the holy place, the altar of incense, symbol of prayer. This is the divinely-appointed order: atonement for sin, cleansing from sin, then homage sweet as incense. This great lesson of approach to God has been familiar to both men from their youth, and it is before their eyes now as they enter. One in their purpose, with a common meeting-place for their devotions, they have had very different courses of life, while their traditional places in the judgment of others have been far apart. The one is a Pharisee, the other a publican; the one has been marked for his profession of religion, the other at the least has not been noted for this. How they stand relatively in the midst of the class to which they respectively belong, is not stated; but they may be taken as fairly represented by the designation of these classes. A Pharisee and a publican are drawing near to God in the temple. And God is there to meet them, as He waits to receive all who come. He is there as the Hearer of what these men will say, and the Answerer, according to His sovereign and righteous pleasure.

In this narrative the Pharisee is allowed precedence as he claims it; but this is granted with ominous tokens that he may afford an example of the accuracy of that saying, "The first shall be last, and the last first." Advancing to a conspicuous position, as is obviously implied, he began as one who accounted himself a special favourite of Heaven.

Verses 11, 12.—"*The Pharisee stood and prayed thus with himself: God, I thank thee, that I am not as other men are, extortioners, unjust, adulterers, or even as this publican. I fast twice in the week, I give tithes of all that I possess.*"

The introductory words employed by the Lord in describing His position, seem to forewarn the reader of the want of reality in the prayer. He prayed *with himself*. He was in the house of prayer, his attitude was that of a suppliant, his exercise was in the form of prayer, but in reality he spoke only with himself. The prayer bears witness to unreality. His thankfulness that he is not as other men, is the centre and substance of the whole, what follows being only an amplification of this. He condescends on particulars that he may establish his claim to precedence, which is the one thing on which his heart is set. Comparison with others is so uncertain, and so often employed with varied extent of signification—at times implying comparison only with some, at other times with many, and often with most others—that the rendering hardly conveys the literal meaning of his words. He really says, "*God, I thank thee, that I am not like the rest of men.*" He too has a way of dividing men into two classes; but the division is such that he is the sole representative of the one, while all other men are crowded together, with wonderful facility on his part, and no misgiving as to his accuracy. So completely is he absorbed with the conviction that his own life presents a solitary example of perfection in the world, that he feels no compunction in placing the whole company of the Pharisees in the fellowship of publicans and sinners. How much of thought, and how much of mere pride of feeling, there is here, it would be difficult to estimate, unless we were to be satisfied with the conclusion that there is no thought, and that all is pride. But there is a kind of thought involved in the state of mind producing this prayer, even so much as seeks to establish the validity of its claim on some kind of evidence; and it is such thought as pride commonly rests upon. He seeks to establish innocence for himself by charging iniquity upon others. They are extortioners, unjust, and adulterers. This hideous charge he makes against all his fellow-men; he credits it with the testimony of his own belief, and then he lodges it in the presence of God as a buttress on which to rest his own claim to goodness. They all do wilfully injure their fellows in any way within their reach. If opportunity offer, they plunder by violence; if it be more convenient, they gain their own ends by deceit; and in their career of self-indulgence, they rob others of purity and peace, and of all that makes home precious. As if to show the intensity of self-exaltation in which he indulges, he catches at the case of the solitary worshipper whom he sees at the footstool with him; as if he would establish a rivalry between himself and this other suppliant at the throne, and, if possible, throw back some distance his prospect of approval, he says, "I thank thee, that I am *not even as this publican.*" The offensive character of the self-righteous disposition could not be painted in darker colours than in this typical prayer given by the Lord in this parable. Such a disposition seeking utterance in prayer is ever untrue as to self, unjust as to others, and dishonouring to God. So our Lord represents it. How different is true prayer as illustrated in Scripture! Its disposition is exactly the opposite, as exemplified in the utterances of David, such as this: "Search me, O God, and know my heart; try me, and know my thoughts; and see if there be any wicked way in me, and lead me in the way everlasting" (Ps. cxxxix. 23, 24). In contrast with these words, those of the Pharisee are so confident as to his goodness, that he feels as if no searching were needful, or could be even supposed to lead to another result. David, in the presence of God, always speaks as if his knowledge of his sin were enough to satisfy him that there must be much more iniquity in him than he has detected; this Pharisee speaks as if God's knowledge of his heart could involve nothing different from that to which he himself bears witness, whereas even if he were neither plunderer, deceiver, nor adulterer, the absence of these vices would go but a little way to establish moral purity.

But the absence of vice is never the only thing on

which a self-righteous disposition leans. Something more decided, in the form and clothing of righteousness itself, there must be. And so our Lord represents it here, although in such a way as to throw much discredit on the righteousness of the self-righteous, exposing to view its littleness when it testifies concerning itself in the presence of God. "*I fast twice in the week, I give tithes of all that I possess.*" The narrowness of this as a representation of a holy life is painfully obvious, the meagreness of it as an offering to God is still more so. In the eyes of such a man these things constitute righteousness; with such offerings God must be well pleased.

In estimating the significance of this prayer, its essentially parabolic character must be kept in view. It were easy to break forth in invective upon such a Pharisee as this; but invective were useless, and would miss the mark. This is a prayer of the Saviour's own sketching, drawn up in a manner so comprehensive and suggestive as to stand for an accurate representation of all prayer based in self-righteousness. In this light it must be studied. To catch our Lord's meaning, it will be well to mark off what is true and good here; then will the false and wicked stand out conspicuously. To render homage to the Deity, to acknowledge before Him the evil of sin, to render thanks for deliverance from it, and to offer thanksgiving for attainment in holiness—all these are good. To make God the sovereign of the soul, and to have "a conscience void of offence toward God and toward men," must be the very end of life. Thus far the Pharisee's prayer carries in it some acknowledgment of what is true and good. This admitted, we straightway come upon what Jesus condemns in the prayer of the self-righteous. Such prayer is not the utterance of need. Under the profession and form of the reality, it involves the reversal of every element of true prayer. Confession is perverted, the language of thanksgiving is used to cover self-adulation, and professed homage to God is turned to its opposite. There is confession, but it is only of the sins of others. Self-glorification is not concealed by the slim guise of thanksgiving thrown over it. Supplication there is none. The presumption of the whole, when regarded as a prayer, is apparent. The catalogue of his own excellences is presented merely as if for a formal recognition by the Deity. This is the general testimony against the self-righteous prayer, that it is in nature completely the reverse of prayer. The spirit of self-confidence cannot live with the spirit of prayer. The one is the contrary of the other. Hence it happens that the self-confident do only in appearance, not in reality, approach God as suppliants. They own that prayer is rational and dutiful, and yet act as if reason and conscience might be satisfied with a pretence.

This radical inconsistency is accompanied naturally with other features which give force to the condemnation of such prayer. 1. *The self-righteous spirit is harsh in its judgments of others.* Conscious of the weakness and falseness of its own claims, it does not shrink from injustice to others. The thing which could not be uttered in the hearing of fellow-men because of its falseness, is nevertheless assumed before God in support of the pretentious claims of self. Hence the comparison with others, who are represented as evil. It is not, "O God, I am what thou wouldest have me to be;" but, "I am not as other men." 2. *It is inconsistent in its utterances.* This is the penalty of falseness. It is always self-condemned. With truthfulness alone is it easy and natural to be consistent. The self-righteous man cannot utter his thoughts regarding himself without contradiction. With one breath this Pharisee declares he has no sin, and with the next he tells that he fasts twice in the week, as if he were laborious in his confessions. Either his profession of holiness is false, or his fasting is mockery. 3. *It is ever prone to magnify formal service.* Fasting and tithing are the symbols of highest excellence. Other virtues seem ordinary and commonplace. That man is thought to reach to unusual eminence whose life is greatly occupied with observing fasts, and calculating tithes to the fraction of a penny on the "mint, the anise, and the cumin" growing in the corners of his garden. This tendency to formalism is the natural fruit of self-righteousness. Fundamental virtues of character are assumed to be easy; multiplication of forms is voluntary subjection to difficulties, and wears a fictitious importance. God had appointed one day of humiliation annually—the great day of atonement; but if a man can fast twice in the week, what an addition to his holiness there must be! God required that they should give tithes of all their increase; and if a man should take reckoning scrupulously of the very flowers in his garden, how high his excellence must be! Thus it is that formalism, which first seems evidence of strong life, grows apace, until it chokes the better life. Where formalism reigns, religion becomes an affair of minute details. This appears from the Pharisee's prayer. Sincere prayer may, indeed, have parts tarnished in this way, for even genuine Christian life may have some admixture of the self-righteous spirit. Our Lord's parable, therefore, carrying condemnation of self-righteousness, has its warning for all His people, that they be not ensnared by insinuations of spiritual pride.

We have thus had an example of the prayer of the self-righteous. It is not indeed such a prayer as any man could be heard to utter. A prayer of this model is not to be heard even once in a lifetime. It is not on this account, however, unreal and inappropriate as a model. It is an illustration of the fact, apt to be forgotten, that the Hearer of prayer reads our utterance in the light of the suppressed thought and feeling cherished within the mind. In successive generations there may be no one shaping the utterance of his self-confidence exactly as we have it here, or thinking and feeling in all respects as is implied by such a prayer. And yet there is no man indulging in any degree the self-righteous spirit, who does not find his own thought in some measure embodied in the Pharisee's prayer. That men do not express themselves thus in actual form, is only because the spirit of self-reliance leaves still such a regard to truth, and such a dread of certain condemnation from others, that men can deceive themselves in the silence of thought, while they would be overwhelmed with confusion did the utterance of their thoughts fall upon their own ear. But here is the inmost thought of the self-righteous,—the accurate expression of his devotion,—and it is a clear sign that the suppliant is an alien from the covenant of Israel.

From this form of prayer, utterly unreal, and laden with sin, we turn to the example which our Lord sets forth as an illustration of true prayer. That it is a publican's prayer, is of no account; that he has not previously been esteemed a religious man, does not affect the worth of what he utters now; the prayer is real, befitting the man's past life, and as such it receives Divine approval. The description of his attitude and manner, with which the prayer is introduced, discovers the sincerity, the earnestness, and the lowliness of the suppliant. Verse 13.—"*The publican, standing afar off, would not lift up so much as his eyes unto heaven, but smote upon his breast, saying, God be merciful to me a sinner.*" It is not merely the appearance and demeanour of the man which present a contrast here. The attitude of soul in relation to God is different, placing the two prayers wide as the poles asunder. There is one thing which this publican needs, and longs after, and pleads for with all the earnestness of his soul at the footstool of the throne of mercy: "God be merciful to me a sinner."[1] His prayer is simple, concentrated, all-embracing. He is a sinner, hungering for mercy, asking provision where alone supply can be had. This cry stands in Scripture as the Saviour's embodiment of the prayer appropriate to a sinner. With such an example of prayer acceptable to the Deity, there is not a soul on earth which may not take courage in drawing nigh to God.

At the basis of this prayer is the *unqualified confession* of personal sinfulness. It is the perception of the dread reality of sin, and the sense of it as a mighty burden on his spirit, which give form and meaning to his prayer. Bunyan has exactly caught the ruling thought when he represents Christian as carrying a great burden on his back, until he comes in sight of

[1] This prayer might be rendered, "God be merciful to me *the sinner*,"—τῷ ἁμαρτωλῷ,—but the generic sense seems more consistent. The concentration precludes thoughts of comparison. As Stier has well said, "He thinks of no other person under heaven."

the cross, when it suddenly falls from his shoulders and is borne no more. The publican comes burdened in spirit to the footstool of the throne of mercy. His sinfulness absorbs his thoughts. In this he does indeed stand at the opposite extreme from the Pharisee. The self-righteous spirit is not only wanting; the soul recoils from it as untruthful. As a sinner he comes; as such he presents himself before God, pleading with the Holy One of Israel for pardon. This example our Divine Master gives as indicating the spirit in which men should appear before God. And in considering this example, it is to be observed that there is nothing in the prayer which indicates the degree or the aggravation of his sin. If these had been included, the prayer would have assumed a shape applicable only to his individual case, and would in this way have lost the universal applicability which our Lord desires to preserve, in accordance with the aim of parabolic teaching. Each suppliant can make mention for himself of the character, and extent, and aggravation of his own sins. But our Saviour here presents the basis of all true praying on our part. The publican says: "I am a sinful man, O Lord." He who takes his place at the footstool in this way, comes as he should into the presence of the Holy One, to whom all sin is hateful. It is a dark view of himself which the man has. He sees sin in his heart and life. The evil thing is everywhere present. He has wilfully done what conscience and Scripture alike condemn. The terrible evil now appears in its true character. He sees it now in some measure as God does. It is darkness without trace of light; evil without mixture of good. It is evil of his own working, which cannot now be undone, and for which no subsequent acts can atone. This is the view of his condition which deeply troubles his spirit. The one evil, which displeases God and ruins man, cleaves to his soul. Before God he appears to declare his sense of this, and his grief because of it. Such is true confession, having its foundation in truthfulness, humility, and penitence.

That which gives confidence to the prayer is *trust in the mercy of God*. In sight of personal sin all is fear; but when from self he turns to God, and beholds the Divine mercy, trust banishes fear. There is no inconsistency in a man seeing himself so low, and yet aspiring so high. It is the harmony of Divine mercy with the forgiveness of sin which lifts man's spirit beyond the cloud gathering thick and threatening overhead, even though he also perceives the harmony of Divine justice with sin's punishment. This suppliant does not expect that God will excuse his sin, or that He will do otherwise than he himself has done in condemning it. He expects that the Divine condemnation of his sinful conduct will be even more searching and more sweeping than his own. That he has often done what is right in the sight of God, this man knows; and he does not expect to be condemned for well-doing; but neither does he hope that God will find in such imperfect acts of well-doing even a small compensation for the sinfulness of his life. He has but one ground of confidence. The God of purity and of judgment is a God of mercy, and he will be a Saviour-God. This is the thought which the God-man, the Redeemer, puts into the minds of men when He sketches a prayer for a suppliant. God will be a Saviour-God. This is the thought soon to be made conspicuous on Calvary's Cross, when He, at once the High Priest and the Victim, shall present Himself as an offering for sin. Then, as now, will the mercy of God be the ground of hope; but thenceforth, as never before, shall the prayer for mercy be offered in the name of Jesus Christ, with reliance on His atoning sacrifice. Thenceforth the prayers of sinful men will ascend, freighted with the merit of the Divine Redeemer. The cry of sin shall still as ever carry its own condemnation; but the name of Jesus in the midst of the cry shall plead the merit of an all-sufficient atonement. Divine mercy is thus the ground of confidence in the prayer burdened with confession of sin. The God in whose hearing the suppliant speaks is "The Lord God, merciful and gracious, long-suffering, and abundant in goodness and truth, keeping mercy for thousands, forgiving iniquity, and transgression, and sin." The sinful suppliant has warrant from God Himself for the trust which inspires his prayer, for the Lord "delighteth in mercy."

The trust which encourages prayer, at the same time makes *prayer a necessity* in order to obtain forgiveness. The trust which warrants prayer is not such as to admit of our dispensing with prayer. Mercy does not go forth to vanquish sin with a conqueror's might, as justice may do: it waits the coming of the penitent, stretching out his hand that he may be rescued from perdition. "Therefore will the Lord *wait*, that he may be gracious unto you; therefore will he be exalted, that he may have mercy upon you: for the Lord is a God of judgment: blessed are all they that wait for him" (Isa. xxx. 18). God does indeed go forth in the exercise of His mercy to visit sinful men, but it is to call, to invite, even to entreat them to come to Him. All this has been already set forth in these parables with clearness and impressiveness. But what is now shown with no less vividness is, that men in coming to God must call upon Him for mercy. Here is the exposition of penitential approach. Prayer is the true coming;—such prayer as is here described, simple, earnest, and solemn. In this relation prayer is recognised not only as a rational and dutiful exercise, but further and more expressly as an exercise required by the urgency of deep personal need. This was entirely wanting in the Pharisee's prayer. He came as if to testify that he was in want of nothing; the publican comes to declare that he is in want of everything. From the depth this cry ascends unto the Lord, bearing witness that thence the suppliant must be lifted if he is to rise into the sunshine of the Divine favour. This parable holds in permanent representation the type of true prayer from one who would enter the kingdom of God, while, at the same time, the contrast between the true and the false is rendered conspicuous. Prayer has place in the Divine plan, not because God asks to be informed of our need, but because we ourselves must feel that need, and own it in the presence of Him who alone can supply the great want. He who prays thus, pleads on the warrant of the Divine pledge that mercy shall straightway have exercise.

With this representation of true prayer, the Lord who alone can answer prayer proclaims the result. With authority he declares the decisions given from the Mercy-seat. Verse 14.—"*I tell you, this man went down to his house justified rather than the other: for every one that exalteth himself shall be abased; and he that humbleth himself shall be exalted.*" The publican's prayer was answered; the Pharisee's called forth no response. This is implied, but something more is expressed. "Justified" is the term employed, in contrast with which stands the word "condemned." Something more than the result of the prayer is here announced. The condition of the man before God is decided. The one man is condemned, prayer and character at once. The other man is justified in his prayer with its confession, and in his person as a penitent. The one man is utterly abased, the other is exalted. The line which encompasses the kingdom of God runs between these two men, enclosing the publican and excluding the Pharisee. The teaching of the parable as to the nature of true prayer is explicit. There is a form of prayer which will never be answered, and had better be discontinued and changed for something more truthful. It is the prayer of self-righteousness. Such prayer strikes against a heaven of brass, and falls powerless to the ground; he who essays to approach Heaven thus is self-condemned, as he is most surely condemned of God. There is a prayer which is answered without delay. It is the prayer of the penitent pleading for Divine mercy. For the immediate answer of such prayer Divine provision has been made, and Divine promise freely given. To all those who thus ask, it is said, "Ask, and ye shall receive."

Division II.

THE PRIVILEGES AND DUTIES OF GOD'S KINGDOM.

CHAPTER VII.

STORES OF BLESSING WITHIN THE KINGDOM.

THE GREAT FEAST.

Luke xiv. 16-24.

By the representations of this parable we are guided within the kingdom of God on earth. The Wandering Sheep, the Lost Piece of Money, the Prodigal Son, and the Suppliant Publican, all represent men without; their recovery bringing to view entrance into the kingdom of grace. All who do enter appear as saved ones —rescued from their lost state, and secure within the kingdom which God has established as a home for sinful men. In all these parables, save the last, the joy which gains prominence is the finder's joy rather than the gladness of the saved one. God is seen rejoicing over the return of the lost. Now, however, we enter upon another division of the parables, revealing to us what is within God's kingdom. Here we see a great feast spread, and the guests gathered to partake of it. While there is joy over the saved, there is, as an accompaniment, joy among the saved. To those over whom God rejoices, He gives gladness of heart. Within the kingdom this is the first thing apparent to a beholder. There is a great feast; the preparation for it is made known even to those without, by the going and coming of the servants who bear the invitations. The kingdom is still represented by a house in which the Lord dwells, like the home thrice spoken of in connection with the finding of the lost; and this house is not separated and secluded, but is in the midst of the dwellings of men, so that there is a continual going forth with messages from the lord of the house.

Attention is first turned to the feast which God has provided; next to the invitations, given in order that the house may be filled.

Verse 16.—"*A certain man made a great supper, and bade many.*" This is our Lord's representation of His Father's munificence in the midst of the kingdom of grace. The feast which may supply materials for a parable must be on a large scale: it must be a great feast, to which many are bidden. In harmony, also, is the selection of *supper*, the principal meal amongst the people. With these particulars to guide us, we see that God's kingdom is not merely a house where He abides, and in the midst of which His people may dwell, but a house of feasting,—this being so essentially characteristic of it, that we may say, within this house the feast is continually spread. The story leads us to consider the provision for the feast, rather than the partaking of it. The feast of grace is one; but the experience of men in partaking of it may be as varied as the number of the guests. The variety of experience, however, is not here set forth, but the wonderful provision.

A great feast! Provision for man's spiritual nourishment and gratification has been made by God, with careful regard to the desire of those returning to Him in penitence from sinful wandering. It is "the feast of reason," in contrast with the revelry of licentiousness, in which the prodigal had vainly sought satisfaction in the far country. And it is more than "the feast of reason," as including ample provision for man's deepest moral and spiritual need, as well as the highest moral and spiritual joy, excelling the richest feast at reason's board. Truth is set forth, not only as to the unsearchable glory of God beyond what the wide revelation of Nature affords, but especially as to the mercy and grace which are in Christ Jesus. The provision is in varied form, for the satisfaction of the spiritually quickened, who "hunger and thirst after righteousness," who long for peace, and joy, and spiritual strength. Here are the treasures of mercy, "abounding mercy," however great the need of each, and however vast the number of guests. Here are the "riches of grace," giving strength, refreshing, and good cheer to all who partake of them. Here is "joy in God," and in all that belongs to God's kingdom. Here is fellowship with the King, and with those devoted to His service, by means of which the spirit of reliance, courage, and hope is roused and strengthened. And besides the provision spread out to view, there is evidence all around the banqueting-house of ampler and richer store yet to be brought forth, to the increased delight of the guests. But judged even by what is discovered to one whose eye scans the board, it appears as the prophet describes it when he says—"In this mountain shall the Lord of hosts make unto all people a feast of fat things, a feast of wines on the lees; of fat things full of marrow, of wines on the lees well refined." To the palace of the Great King men ascend when they are introduced to the feast of grace; and chief of all attractions of the feast is the presence of the King Himself in the midst of His guests, cheering all with the fellowship constantly afforded in His love towards them and delight in them.

Verses 17-20.—"*And sent his servant at supper time to say to them that were bidden, Come; for all things are now ready. And they all with one consent began to make excuse. The first said unto him, I have bought a piece of ground, and I must needs go and see it: I pray thee have me excused. And another said, I have bought five yoke of oxen, and I go to prove them: I pray thee have me excused. And another said, I have married a wife, and therefore I cannot come.*" He whose supper provides a basis for parabolic teaching has a mortifying experience just before the expected arrival of his guests. His invitations had been formally accepted; but when he sent his servant with reminders on the day appointed for the feast, those who had promised their presence one after another asked to be excused. His feast was to be despised, and his house, which he had counted on seeing crowded, was to be deserted. Delicate as such withdrawal is, and liable to give serious offence, they plead a variety of insufficient excuses, and do not show any concern though their conduct should occasion the loss of his friendship. Offended by such treatment, he sent out his servant to the streets and lanes to invite whomsoever he found there; and when this course did not altogether fill the house, he sent his servant to the outskirts of the city, that he might gather people from the highways, even though they were the poor and maimed, sitting to ask alms under the shelter of the hedges. In this way only was his house filled with guests for his great supper. That the occurrences are unusual we must allow. Such refusals as are here described are certainly not common: the most ordinary politeness imposes a check on personal preferences at such times. But when refusals do come, this mode of supplying guests is an expedient to which it would seem strange indeed were any one to resort. And yet this story, singular as it is, provides the requisite narrative for illustration: showing, on the one hand, the manner in which men act when favoured with the Divine invitation; on the other, the manner in which God acts when His invitations are refused. The significance of the story is most impressive. We can hardly hope to express the feelings of solemnity which creep over the spirit as we silently ponder it; but we must endeavour to gain at least a just interpretation.

God, who has so amply provided the feast of gladness for sinful men, has His invitations formally accepted, yet actually rejected. It is of necessity, under the figure employed, that a certain day is fixed for the feast, and that invitations are understood to have been sent out a considerable time before the day appointed. In this way some can be spoken of as previously invited. And if the definite time for the gathering to the feast be the appearing of the Saviour, as seems intended, it will be obvious that those formerly invited are such as had been prepared to expect the appearing of the Messiah. From the coming of Jesus, "a continual feast" has been provided; the invitations have been daily repeated; "*now* is the accepted time." The time for giving and accepting the invitation is now the same. We thus lose sight of the distinction as to invitations prior to the day of the feast; and for present application we are brought simply to contemplate the fact, common to all times, that Divine invitations are by many formally accepted, and yet actually rejected. Formally there is an expression of satisfaction with the goodness of God in the call to share of the riches of His mercy; and yet those who express the satisfaction are absent from the feast. To be reminded by a servant of the Lord of what is involved in the formal acceptance of his Master's invitation, is with such persons of no avail. With one consent they make excuse. An appearance of inconsistency they cannot deny, and their only course is to attempt some vindication. Of such self-refuting and unworthy defences, our Saviour gives us three examples. "*I have bought a piece of ground, and I must needs go and see it.*" "*I have bought five yoke of oxen, and I go to prove them.*" "*I have married a wife, and therefore I cannot come.*" In recording these three forms of apology, it is not meant that there were only three refusals. There were many such refusals, until at length the whole company had declined to come; but these three forms of excuse may be held to embrace all the explanations given. And to all these excuses there is this common, that a present good is esteemed above the blessing of God. There is no such longing after fellowship with Him while sharing with others the blessings of mercy and grace, as there would be if it were regarded as the most precious thing in life. Temporal good is esteemed above spiritual. For some earthly advantage a man is ready to risk the loss of the Divine favour, all-satisfying though that favour is admitted to be. The madness of this, and the dreadful impiety of it, we find it difficult to represent to our minds, so familiar are we with such refusals of Divine mercy. The best excuses which can be offered may be embraced under the three here given. The attractions which are allowed to eclipse those of the Divine banqueting-house are those of property and social enjoyment. These are represented under such examples as discover their advantages in the most striking manner. As to property, the pleasure of possession and that of acquisition are set forth; as to the attractions of social life, the marriage relation is taken as the closest of all, involving the most constant and powerful type of the influence of companionship. The two great antagonistic forces which gain ascendency over the mind are, love of money and love of friendship. Earthly substance and family relationships, which should appear as tokens of Divine goodness, we turn into hindrances, obstructing attainment of the higher good which God offers. The attractions of property are twofold. The delight of possession is seen in the case of him who has so prospered that he has bought a piece of land, and desires nothing so much as that he should just walk over it, and look upon it, and consider how he may improve it. The pleasure of acquisition is prominently indicated by the excuse of him who has been purchasing five yoke of oxen—a large number to be able to employ. He is thinking of his ploughing, and sowing, and reaping, and driving home the fruits of the field, rejoicing in his abundance and in the gains of a favourable market. For him it seems too much to give up a single day at the call of friendship. For fear of the loss of some expected gain men will thus risk their souls, and not hesitate to set slightly on the invitation of God. The power of companionship will sway others who are not blinded by pelf. The companionship of wife or husband—the reigning influence of the home circle, where brothers and sisters are apt to be governed by a common standard—the free fellowship of a favourite circle of friends, in the midst of whom the hours of the night sweep pleasantly on,—all these may prove a snare. It is better, no doubt, that we should be swayed by fellowship of valued friends, if the friends are good, than by the prospect or possession of gain. But it is unspeakably solemn and awful that any two, however closely knit, should consider nothing higher than themselves, agreeing that love should make their souls godless, instead of pointing their eyes upward, and inclining their hearts to walk in company to everlasting habitations. In such ways as these men spend their lives in ignorance of the joys which God has provided within His kingdom.

When the servant, in giving his reminders of the invitation previously made and accepted, found that all declined to come, he returned to communicate the vexatious result. Verse 21.—"*So that servant came, and showed his lord these things.*" This was essential to the story. But, in connection with God's kingdom, who is represented by this servant? As the Saviour Himself carries the message, it might be supposed that He is intended. In favour of this it may be said that He not only carried the invitation, but "took upon Him the form of a servant," and may well bear the servant's name. But, on reflection, it will appear that the Saviour does not in this parable hold the place of the servant, but rather that of the lord, unless we consider that in this He keeps His own special part out of view. He is not a servant who needs to go and come repeatedly, reporting unexpected occurrences and receiving new instructions. He is not a servant who knows not what His Lord will do, but is in His counsels. In this relation He may be regarded even as the Lord of the feast. Passing from the Lord Jesus Himself, it is plain that this servant represents all who bear the message of mercy to their fellow-men. The only difficulty is in the fact that there is but one servant; and indeed it seems strange it should be so, considering the structure of the story, which applies to a large house, a great feast, and many guests. But the representative purpose is well served. One servant may suffice to illustrate the fact, since the message is one by whomsoever it is carried, and the work is one by whomsoever done. The messengers are one, having their unity fitly represented in the one servant. Most attractive is the view thus given of their work. It is their part to say, Come! Their whole duty is represented in that one word. Wherever they go they have the same invitation, "Come, for all things are ready." They give the message, but cannot compel men to receive it. If it be rejected, they can but depart to repeat it to others. Disappointment they must have, which they will lay before their Lord; but they will still carry the invitation to others, exercising such constraining influence as they can by the earnestness and persuasive power with which, in the spirit of their Lord, they urge men everywhere to come. Knowing their Lord and the richness of the feast, the work intrusted to them is their joy ; and they have precious reward in the success of their mission, inducing others to come with them and share in the blessings of the great salvation. This servant in the parable thus stands as the representative of all who take part in the work of inviting others to come to the gospel feast.

The feast is ready ; but guests are wanting. What shall be done? Verse 21.—"*Then the master of the house, being angry, said to his servant, Go out quickly into the streets and lanes of the city, and bring in hither the poor, and the maimed, and the halt, and the blind.*" The reference to the master's anger may be passed meanwhile ; the allusion to it is thrown into the background, awaiting explanation in the last verse, while prominence is given to the measures instantly taken to gather a company. There is urgency in the command. The opening words of the commission run thus : "*Go out quickly.*" Whoever is indifferent, the master of the feast is in earnest. Thus it is with the Father who rules in the kingdom of grace. The King's work must not tarry ; His servants must not cease from effort by reason of discouragement ; when some refuse the invitation, others must receive it. The result of refusal is wider invitation, in some respects transferred invitation. So afterwards Paul and Barnabas at Antioch said to the Jews, " It was necessary that the word of God should first have been spoken to you : but seeing ye put it from you, and judge yourselves unworthy of everlasting life, lo, we turn to the Gentiles." Responsibility for carelessness rests with those who receive the invitation. But success is not wanting for the servant who carries the master's welcome.

As he goes out a second time, he does not turn aside to selected houses, but hastens along the streets and lanes of the city, that he may call the poorest he meets, not passing even the most miserable amongst them, but rather giving special heed to "*the maimed, the halt, and the blind.*" Wherever there is one to hear, the voice of the messenger cries, "Come." The most unworthy is not despised, but is selected for special assurance of compassion. The spirit of the master breathes in this message, "Whosoever will, let him come."

Even with invitations thus free, the guests are insufficient. Gladly have those come who were called from the streets and lanes of the city in which this generous householder dwells; but so great was the feast, and so many the guests first invited, that still there was room. The narrative is not delayed to tell anything of the experience of the servant as he went through the streets and more obscure lanes of the city. The purpose of the master is resolute. And the narrative, first burdened with the tidings of delay, cannot be detained to recount details as to the manner in which success is secured. It proceeds as if the whole had been done in an instant. The order is issued, and straightway the servant is before his master again. Verse 22, he says: "*Lord, it is done as thou hast commanded, and yet there is room.*" If the previous report occasioned displeasure to the master, this seems to give delight. "Yet there is room." The sound is pleasing in his ear. It is full of promise to many beyond the city, still ignorant of what has been going on within it. Grand is the interpretation of the words thus put into the lips of the servant! At every stage in the history of the spiritual kingdom, it is a joy to those within it, partaking of the rich feast which Divine grace has prepared, and a joy to the Lord Himself that it can still be said, "Yet there is room." How many there are even now in the world ignorant of the good to be enjoyed in it. They know not what a feast for spiritual strengthening and satisfaction has been prepared by God; they know not how many invitations have been given, and strangely refused; they know not how widely the messenger has travelled, making his circuit through the wide world, everywhere repeating the invitation. They know by sad experience that no such messenger has come to them. To us, familiar with the glad tidings and with the exceeding value of the feast, there is but one satisfaction as we think of those who are still excluded by no waywardness of their own: "Yet there is room." Here there is rational comfort, as there is stimulus to holy zeal. To every servant who shares in satisfaction because of the amplitude of God's house, the Master is saying, Go forth—bid others come in.

Thus runs the still widening commission,—now happily widened but not transferred: Verse 23.—"*Go out into the highways and hedges, and compel them to come in, that my house may be filled.*" The invitation must now extend to them that may be found in the less-frequented ways far beyond the city,—to them that are "out of the way,"—to the "strangers and foreigners" in more remote parts, that they also may become "fellow-citizens with the saints, and of the household of God." The command of this master to his servants sounds as the echo of our Lord's command, "Go ye into all the world, and preach the gospel to every creature." Further, let us mark what constraining influence is provided for them who are most out of the way. "*Compel* them to come in." Such words were not spoken concerning those who were first invited. When their formal acceptance was followed by a cold refusal, there was no such utterance as this: "Compel them to come in." It could not be. But in the case of those ignorant of the welcome, spending their days with few words of gladdening, and bruised under many sufferings, the Master expressly requires that there be some constraining earnestness in the endeavour to secure that they gather together to the enjoyment of the great spiritual feast provided. No marvel if such men need to be often entreated, scarce understanding the meaning of words strange to their ears, and scarce believing them when understood. And if, standing before them, the messenger oftentimes repeats his message, and that with increasing earnestness, which seems to say he can take no refusal, in this he acts according to the Master's purpose. "The first shall be last, and the last first." The first may have a reminder of what is implied in their professions, and righteously expected of them; but the last shall have their invitation pressed upon them with persistent earnestness. The righteous Lord has regard to the wants and woes of men, and makes compensating provision in wonderful adaptation to the disadvantages of those who are far from the centres of privilege. Many who have been far off, and have felt as if compelled to arise and come to the feast, when within the banqueting-house will sing—

> " 'Twas the same love that spread the feast,
> That sweetly forced us in."

The lord of the feast himself will rejoice over the

coming of these guests from all quarters. For this is the desire he expresses in sending his servant forth on the widest circuit: "Compel them to come in, *that my house may be filled.*" To serve the purpose of illustration, our Lord has taken the case of a rich citizen, whose mansion is large, with spacious halls, and who seeks that his house may be filled. Interpreted as applying to the purpose of the God of Salvation, the parable discovers, in a most striking way, the richness of Divine mercy with the freeness of Divine grace. The Lord, who has come to save, will gather into the house of rejoicing a multitude of saved ones. Even though there be many who refuse His invitation, His house shall be full, and He shall rejoice over all who are gathered together. The feast shall be great, the guests shall be many, His delight shall be complete.

But one sad accompaniment of the feast there is, and that remains to be thought of now. Passing allusion has been made to the anger of the master on account of the refusal of his invitations, but we have kept it in reserve, on account of the evidence that the narrative was really engrossed with arrangements for extending the invitations. But now we must return upon it, for the story closes with a solemn reference to the displeasure of the lord of the feast. He was angry, we have been told, when some had refused to come. And now, even when his house is filling, it is apparent that he has not forgotten the displeasure he felt, but rather expresses it with greater force, adding to the command to go out to the highways and hedges this by way of explanation: Verse 24.—"*For I say unto you, That none of these men which were bidden shall taste of my supper.*" This utterance, which comes so naturally from the master when speaking to his servant of his plans, becomes additionally impressive when set forth by the Saviour as a revelation of His Father's will. In the sight of God there is no offence so grievous as the rejection of His invitation to partake of the great salvation. This is the meaning of those closing words. In the midst of this universe, marked by beauty and grandeur, year by year yielding an endless variety of blessings for the use of man, the feast of spiritual good which God has provided for man, and to which He is ever calling men, is the most prominent feature in all the Divine arrangements for the benefit of our race. The invitation to come within His kingdom, is a call to escape from the range of condemnation beyond it; and, as it tells of a feast provided within the kingdom, it is a call to participate in satisfaction for the requirements of an immortal nature. To be content with the engagements, possessions, and companionship of this world, is to neglect the highest demands of our own being, and to fall beneath the friendship of God. Despising God's invitation to us to share the best blessings He bestows, is the most grievous sin, incurring His unchangeable displeasure. He will invite all to the feast; He will give a welcome to those who accept His call, however far they have been separated from Him and however deeply injured in their course of sin; but He must treat those who despise the message as the objects of His wrath. Anger with Him is no tumultuous passion, but something more awful. It is an unchangeable displeasure. Of such anger they become objects who despise His call. Those whom He excludes from the feast exclude themselves. And that absence which they voluntarily choose becomes a terrible penalty. The Lord saith of such : "None of these men shall taste of my supper." These words tell of a dread reality under the government of God.

In this parable we have our first view of what is within the kingdom of God on earth. We see how close is the relation between this kingdom and the sin-troubled state in which we all find ourselves. This kingdom, here represented as the home of our God in this world, His house in which the great feast is spread, to which men are continually invited, is the true Biblical intermediate state between the state of separation from God and the heavenly state in which there is enjoyment of perfect union with God in complete likeness to God. The kingdom is here shown to exist in the world even more for the sake of those who are still beyond it, than for the sake of those now within it. Between those within and those without there must be a continual going and coming, that multitudes more may be induced to enter, and that the house may at length be filled, in accordance with the gracious purpose of its Lord. By the aid of this parable we look within the gate; and there, as by the help of the parable of the Prodigal Son, we see the Father in the midst, rejoicing over those who are gathered around Him. Here, also, after the manner of the parable of the Prodigal, though more vividly, we see the rich feast of mercy and grace enjoyed by the guests, and the evidence of other blessings in store, richer than those of which they now partake. And here, as by the aid of no other parable, we obtain a survey of the large gathering of guests. They come from all ranks and spheres. None have been excluded from the invitation. Even the poorest of the people are there, and many who have wandered far in sin and been sorely maimed, all bearing still the marks of their trying experience. Indeed, as we examine the company, the poor and suffering seem most numerous. And this has come about under the testing power of the free invitation. For if God, of His own grace, and for the good of all, began with a selected people, and gave to them the first opportunity, gradually did the circle of invitation widen; and still as it extended, more were found to respond, so that many who were once far off are now brought nigh. In the great gathering where they now are, whatever marks distinguish them and tell of the sad past, all have this experience in common, that they honour the Master as the giver of all good, they rejoice in the shelter of His house as their home, partake of the blessings of His mercy and grace as His best gifts, and delight in fellowship with Himself as their chief good.

CHAPTER VIII.

UNION WITH THE SON IN THE FAVOUR OF THE FATHER.

THE ROYAL MARRIAGE FEAST.

MATT. XXII. 1-14.

THIS parable is in framework similar to that of the Great Supper. Our Lord returns to the same analogy in order to communicate further instruction as to God's kingdom. The whole truth cannot be conveyed in a single story. We are now taken round to a different point of observation, in order to gain a view of His kingdom not previously seen. That the two parables are not identical must be plain. We have only to consider what is additional to that presented by Luke, in order to be satisfied that there is here new truth as to the spiritual kingdom. We cannot assume that in the contrast between the two narratives we have an illustration only of diversity of recollection on the part of hearers, or greater or less fulness in reporting. The absence of all that belongs to royalty is marked in Luke's version, and is adverse to Meyer's supposition that Luke quoted from an imperfect version of the parable. What is additional in Matthew has a significance which could not be conveyed under the different construction of the story as it stands on the pages of Luke. And the additional significance is so clear and important as to afford ample explanation of a double use of the story. There is here at once richer grace and greater sternness—the latter being connected with a more open antagonism to the work of the Redeemer.

Both forms of the parable concern the kingdom of God. This kingdom Matthew always names the kingdom of heaven; for that which is God's kingdom on earth is in character and destiny a heavenly kingdom, —a kingdom belonging to a higher order of things. All that had been taught in the parables as to entrance into this kingdom concerns individuals. But looking within the kingdom itself, we see what concerns the people of God collectively. Guided by the earlier form of the parable, we behold a great spiritual feast provided, which is enjoyed in fellowship with God. As to the guests, we learn something about persons who are absent as well as concerning those who are present. Many who have been invited have refused to come; while the poorest and most miserable have been made welcome. These are facts of much significance as to God's kingdom. But there are many questions concerning the kingdom and its subjects which are left unanswered. Are those who refuse to come simply left to themselves? In giving a welcome to all, does God make no account of the character and conduct of those who seek to share in His favour? Is there any condition of their welcome other than their willingness to come? These are questions partially answered in the parable of the Pharisee and the Publican,—the condemned and the justified. To afford a fuller answer, the analogy of a feast is brought forward anew with needful additions. In turning attention to the distinctive features of the parable in its new form, those already commented upon may be passed almost without remark. The additions which affect the entire mould of the story are mainly these: What was formerly merely a supper is now a marriage feast; the marriage to be celebrated is a royal marriage, being that of the king's son; those who refuse to come are visited with punishment for their refusal; and those who are accepted in their coming are clad in wedding garments provided by the king. To these points it is needful to turn attention, remarking, as we proceed, any new feature affecting what has already come under review.

Verse 2.—"*The kingdom of heaven is like unto a certain king, which made a marriage for his son.*" In this parable kingly authority is made prominent. In the former it was, "A certain man made a great supper;" in this it is, "A certain king made a marriage for his son."[1] And if royal authority be conspicuous here, it appears in the arrangements for the marriage of his son. It is no longer an ordinary feast which illustrates what Divine mercy and grace have provided. A feast still affording the basis for illustration, the merely transitory aspect of such entertainment must be taken from it, and some conception of permanence secured. The abiding relationship of marriage, enduring while life lasts, is therefore introduced. Permanence of fellowship as well as gladness is foreshadowed. The marriage ceremonial itself is only anticipated. It does not form part of the parable, but is kept out of sight as a thing

[1] In the one case, ἄνθρωπός τις, a certain man; in the other, ἀνθρώπῳ βασιλεῖ, a man that was a king.

for which all the arrangements described are preparatory. The king is only here preparing for the marriage.[1] Thus the perplexity is avoided which should otherwise have been felt in adjusting our thoughts to the fact, that those who come are individually welcomed as guests, and at the same time, taken collectively, as a church, are represented as a bride. The complexity is escaped by treating the marriage ceremony as still in the future. Yet prominence is given to the fact that this is a marriage feast, and thus permanence of fellowship is in contemplation. This assurance of permanence runs as a soothing undertone through all the parable. You hear it sounding in the message as the servant says, Come! He says not, as the servant of even a rich householder must, For only a little time come! but as the servant of the king may, Come! accept a welcome to a place at the festal board of the king. As the king proceeds with the arrangements, everything is confirmatory of a permanence, of which no trace is found in the earlier form of the parable. Here it appears that this great feast separates all concerned into an inner and outer circle. To come within is to be permanently blessed; to continue without, or to be cast out, is to be permanently separated from what is satisfying. This thought we have far more vividly in considering that the guests collectively are represented by the bride—a fact always kept before us as an accompaniment of the parable, though the marriage ceremonial is not described.

[1] Not "made a marriage," as in our version, but "prepared for the marriage festivities." The plural is used throughout, τοὺς γάμους; except when the king speaks to his servants (verse 8) as of a prepared feast, when it is ὁ γάμος, "the marriage."

The marriage is that of the king's son. This additional aspect gives a large sweep of illustrative power to the parable, as it represents the kingdom of heaven, or God's kingdom among men. This reference to the son, rich in significance as it is, is meanwhile held in reserve. The king alone appears, making all the preparations, in the exercise of royal authority. We must also remark, without insisting upon it, that in this relationship of father and son, we have a parabolic indication of the relationship subsisting between Father and Son in the Godhead, differing from that relation in which God stands to us as a Father, as that had been set forth in the parable of *The Prodigal Son*. Passing this, however, it must be considered that it is the father of the bridegroom who is preparing the marriage festivities, and this quite in accordance with Eastern custom. It is the father who sends out the invitations, which are first refused and then widely extended, until the house is filled with guests. But the father engaged in these arrangements is a *king*. This introduces a large part of the additional force belonging to this form of the parable. He is a king, and those invited are his subjects. This completely alters the position of matters. The rich householder could only invite his neighbours, and if they refuse, he must be content to arrange for his feast apart from them. But there is here superadded the fact of regal authority over the persons invited. In that case, the invitations are in a sense commands. The authority of royalty is here. In this we are at once brought nearer the reality to be represented. It is the Sovereign of the earth who issues the invitations of mercy. His call to come is also a command. It appeals to our conscience as well as heart, and that with unquestionable authority. In neglecting or refusing such a call, we not only slight a gracious and most generous invitation, but violate the natural obligation under which we are laid to "the King eternal, immortal, and invisible, the only wise God."

Naturally, in the altered circumstances, the conduct of those who refuse the invitation is represented in a *worse light* than in the earlier form of the parable. In that their refusal appears as an ungracious and unkind act; in this, as a rebellious and unrighteous act. The difference of view springs from the structure of the story, and both are accurate, the latter, however, affording the most exact parallel. It is a painful reality, that the proffered love of God meets no kindly response from those who allow themselves to be engrossed with earthly possessions and friendships. But it is a fact, solemnising and saddening, that in thus rejecting the offers of mercy, men violate their allegiance to the Supreme, and bring themselves under just condemnation. Such neglect is a breach of loyalty to the Most High.

Very naturally it happens that in this form of the parable we have the strongest representation of *man's enmity against God*. The messengers were sent forth (verse 3) "*to call them that were bidden,*" and "*they would not come.*"[1] "Again he sent forth other servants," to say, "*Come unto the marriage.*" But those who were invited (verse 5), "*having made light of it,*"[2] went their several ways; while a remnant, more violent in their

---

[1] οὐκ ἤθελον ἐλθεῖν, had no willingness to come.
[2] ἀμελήσαντες, having slighted the invitation, or expressed their disregard for it.

antagonism than others, having seized the servants, "*entreated them spitefully,*[1] *and slew them.*"

The King who sends the invitations appears even more condescending than the householder described in the previous case. He sends his servants again and again to those who refuse to come. The forbearance and compassion of God thus find stronger representation here. But, in contrast, the conduct of men appears unspeakably worse. They appear not only engrossed with worldly interests, but strongly averse to acknowledge submission to the King. The growing urgency of the summons, carrying in it more of the indication of authority, gives occasion for the outbreak of enmity which really exists in the heart, venting itself in insults and injuries inflicted on the messengers. In the earlier form of the parable, we hear of nothing more than the slighting of the message. Nor could there, under the conditions, have been more. It is almost inconceivable that a mere invitation from a neighbour could have given occasion for an outburst of violence. But here, when regal authority comes into exercise, when appearance at the marriage is a test of readiness to do honour to the king, there is room for introducing those sadly common scenes of violence, in which the wrath of men is kindled against the messengers of mercy, whose message is resented because of aversion to the authority it implies. Authority may have sanctions of punishment to enforce it, and may therefore tempt men to resistance, and to such forms of violence as they can safely venture upon. Thus we read, "The remnant took his servants, and entreated them spitefully, and slew them." Such treatment of the mes-

[1] ὕβρισαν, subjected them to insult.

sengers, common as it unfortunately has been in human history, is a testimony against those who resort to it. But, as with the servants of this king, so with the servants of our Lord. Moved by the love of their fellow-men and by the desire to serve their Master, they have not been deterred by insult or danger. Having learned "not to fear them that kill the body, and after that have no more that they can do," they have courageously pleaded the cause of their Lord, the benefactor of all, believing that "if they suffer, they shall also reign with Him."

While, however, the servants yield themselves to spiteful treatment, and even to death, the king cannot know of such things and leave them unpunished. As God's long-suffering and gentleness are illustrated more clearly than in the parable of the Householder's Feast, so also Divine justice and judgment stand out more solemnly. Verse 7.—"*But when the king heard thereof, he was wroth: and he sent forth his armies, and destroyed those murderers, and burned up their city.*" The anger of the king was great. It was first manifested among the surviving servants, who brought tidings of the murder of some of their number. The king was wroth.[1] The servants who had borne the invitations to the marriage, now hear orders issued to the officers of the army. The tokens of the king's favour had roused active antagonism to his authority, thus disclosing an enmity which had been slimly covered over, and which needed only this special season of rejoicing in the royal household to make it break forth into scenes of anarchy and bloodshed. Such violence must be checked, and

---

[1] ἀκούσας δὲ ὁ βασιλεὺς ὠργίσθη : But the king having heard, was angered.

an expedition is sent out to punish the murderers. The invitations to share in the king's joy have not only been rejected, the messengers have been murdered; the avenging expedition next appears,—the murderers are slain, their city is burned up. This infliction of retribution by the king is the Saviour's illustration of God's way of dealing with persistence in wilful rebellion. Some have raised the question : Is there any historical event, or series of events, to which the Saviour is pointing ? Does Jesus here make prophetic allusion to the coming destruction of Jerusalem ? Such questions are apt to turn attention aside from the only true principle of interpretation. The parable sets forth what holds true of God's spiritual kingdom in the world. Our Saviour sets forth in parable the truth that God "would have all men honour the Son," and what are the consequences of this demand. This narrative discloses a uniform principle in the moral government of God. He who comes to us with messages of love as our best friend, also rules as a king, and visits with punishment all who resist His authority, and do evil to His messengers. According to the excellence of His nature He is just; and because His government is in accordance with that excellence, His exercise of power must be to the punishment of evil-doing as well as to the reward of them that do well. The narrative sets forth what legitimate reasoning must uphold. The message of mercy, uttered by the last breath of the messengers who are slain, is in fact the confirmation of this. For if there were no vengeance upon evil-doers, there were no need for a message to assure them of Divine favour, if they only repented of their sins. The martyred witness, falling beneath the stones which men in their rage hurl at him, may have faith enough, and sufficiency of the forgiving spirit, to offer the prayer—"Lord, lay not this sin to their charge." But such a prayer could be answered only on condition of repentance of the sin committed. Rebellion cannot be forgiven if it be still persisted in. The king must rule, or cease to be king; rebellion he must vanquish, else the order of the kingdom must be overthrown. Slaughter of the murderers and burning of their city affords such illustration as the analogy admits. The ruthless devastation of an avenging army presents but rough illustration, it is true, involving, as it always does, suffering for the innocent as well as the guilty, which can have no place under the Divine government. The one truth set forth here is, that certain penalty will follow upon wilful transgression. That death and burning are the forms of punishment in this case cannot warrant any conclusion as to the manner in which God punishes rebellion. These belong to the form of the parable, and point to the utmost penalty possible under earthly authority. Our Lord is speaking for all times, and not for any particular occasion, however important. If the words seem to apply to any historical event, it is because the occasion illustrates the general rule, not because the principle of government had been introduced for the occasion. The principle is unchangeable and eternal as the Deity Himself. The account of this work of judgment on those who slew the servants is described as following upon the deed, and preceding the celebration of the marriage, we may therefore interpret it as applying to that which precedes the celebration of the Lord's full joy in union with His perfected Church. The words may thus apply to what takes place in this world as

well as in the next. The forces of Heaven's King are
many, and ever at His command, embracing all powers
of nature, all actions of men and nations, working
according to His own decree. "None can stay His
hand, or say unto Him, What doest thou?" He may
destroy evil-doers, and remove them from their place on
earth, even as He must here and hereafter separate
them from His favour. This is the solemn truth set
forth in the parable before us, which could not have
been introduced under the parable of the Householder's
Feast. Its revelation is clear when the provision of the
kingdom is depicted as a feast prepared by the King,
to which his subjects are required to come in homage
to himself.

We turn now to the ingathering of the guests, and
the solemnities of the marriage. The words describing
the manner in which attendance was secured, seem
more to express what was to be expected by a king
than by a casual benefactor. Verse 8.—"*Then saith the
king to his servants, The wedding is ready, but they which
were bidden were not worthy. Go ye therefore into the
highways, and as many as ye shall find, bid to the
marriage. So those servants went out into the highways,
and gathered together all, as many as they found, both
bad and good.*" A reflection of royal authority is trace-
able in the doings of the servants. Distinct mention
of the gathering of *bad and good* is not found in the
instructions as reported, but it is present by implication. The mention of badness and goodness, always
having some moral colouring even in their most familiar
applications to men, seems to point, much more explicitly than anything in the earlier parable, to the exercise of sovereign grace in calling even the chief of

sinners. That there is a reference in these words to moral character, it is impossible to deny with any weight of reason, though it has been denied over and over again. In whatever way taken, goodness and badness concern in some measure the moral character. They are terms very different from "the poor, the maimed, the halt, and the blind," formerly distinguished as the objects of favour. All whom God calls are, indeed, sinners exceedingly before Him; but men differ so much morally, that some are accounted by their fellow-men as bad, and some as good. This distinction is a real one, of which God makes account. So the Saviour, without reservation, here uses the distinction as familiar. Those whom their fellow-men would shun as bad, God freely invites. If He visits with judgment rebellious subjects who refuse to come, it is not because they rebel, but because, in their rebellious spirit, they refuse offered mercy. But if any will come, however rebellious they have been, they shall find a welcome. Thus sovereign grace touches the worst of men. Most cheering it is for the student of the parables to find this record in close proximity, not merely with the threatening, but even with the execution, of Divine vengeance. The darkness of judgment is without, but the brightness of saving love is within.

"*And the wedding was furnished with guests.*" The guest-chamber was filled. Many who had been called were without, busy about their farms and merchandise, and those who had broken out into open rebellion were numbered among the dead. But the great guest-chamber was crowded. The reign of grace in a sinful world introduces sharp contrasts. There is grace rejected, and grace welcomed; worldly interests are preferred by some, the blessings of Divine love by others; there is open rebellion against Divine authority, and grateful submission to the beneficent rule. Such is this world when looked at from the standpoint of moral government. In the midst of this world is a kingdom of grace, whose courts are crowded. For all his guests, the king has provided wedding garments. This is implied, though not explicitly stated. Considering the social position of those who were brought together, and the circumstances in which they were summoned, it is clear they could not have appeared at the door of the palace in garments suitable for appearance at court, much less for taking part in the marriage festival of the king's son. Nothing more is required of those invited than that they should be willing to come.

The spiritual truth becomes clearer by the extension of invitations which has taken place. Men are asked who could not provide suitable costume; they are brought to the palace just as the messengers find them in the streets or on the highways; and thus it is clearly implied that suitable raiment had been provided by the king. That it was customary in Eastern nations to provide changes of raiment as a mark of favour, appears sufficiently evident. Thus Joseph, in making arrangements for his father and his brethren coming down to see Pharaoh, sent "changes of raiment" (Gen. xlv. 22); and Gehazi felt that he made no strange request in asking for his master, from the "captain of the host of the king of Syria," "two changes of garments;" while we read that when the king sent his captain away to seek a cure, he bade him go, promising to send a letter unto the king of Israel; and the captain took with him "ten talents of silver, and six thousand pieces of gold, and ten changes of raiment" (2 Kings v.) These examples are sufficient to prove that it was customary that the palace of the king should be largely supplied with garments, to be conferred on those who were objects of royal favour. The story may therefore be taken as in harmony with Eastern custom. And the interpretation is of deep interest, as illustrating the provision which God makes for sinful men whom He summons to the marriage feast. As each one enters the spiritual kingdom at the call of God, he is clothed in a robe which God has provided. Each one may exclaim, "I will greatly rejoice in the Lord, my soul shall be joyful in my God; for he hath clothed me with the garments of salvation, he hath covered me with the robe of righteousness, as a bridegroom decketh himself with ornaments, and as a bride adorneth herself with jewels" (Isa. lxi. 10). The prophet gives in these words the simple and obvious interpretation of the "wedding garment." It is a robe of righteousness with which God clothes the man whom He welcomes to His presence. He who cannot look upon sin sends His servants to invite even the worst of sinners to come to Him, and to come just as they are when the message finds them. But Jesus, the King's Son, has wrought a righteousness which may be given as a garment to all who seek the King's favour, and with that, as with a robe, is each one covered as he enters the palace of the Great King. This is the divinely-provided robe, in its richness and beauty suitable for a wedding garment, and in its amplitude completely covering the worn and soiled garments which betray the former evil condition of the wearer.

We have now a striking view of the assembled guests.

Gathered in the vast festive hall, they are all clad in robes befitting the palace of the king. In the earlier form of the parable the imagination is allowed to dwell on the mixed company of all classes and ranks, so strangely gathered that many have come even from the dingy lanes of the city, or from shelter under the hedges by the wayside. Conspicuous among them are the "poor, the maimed, the lame, and the blind." All these appear, taking their places at the royal board just as they have been found. And for the purpose of interpretation, it seems needful that such a view of the guests should be given. They are a gathering of good and bad—of those who have led a comparatively sober and rational life, and of those who have grown familiar with the haunts of vice, and have become polluted in their contact with all vileness. Under the parabolic representation of "The Great Feast," as we see the guests assembling, all this is conspicuous. Such a view, as it is accurate in itself, is needful for gospel teaching. But from the point of view now obtained the sight is amazingly changed. As the eye runs along the extended ranks of guests, all are clothed in robes of perfect beauty, and of a richness of texture befitting the palace and the greatness of the occasion. The interpretation is clear. The riches of Divine grace are before us. The immense differences of character are concealed from view, the poverty and maimed condition of the guests are not perceptible. They are clad in "robes of righteousness" supplied by the God who invites them to the feast, and provided only on account of the marriage of His Son. Here appears the essential importance of the Son, who is introduced in this parable. How plain it must have seemed to the eye of Jesus as He sketched the story. The spiritual significance of the marriage, though the actual celebration is held in reserve, comes at this point plainly enough before us by way of suggestion. But for the position of the Son, this rich feast, these free invitations, these royal garments, had not been provided by the King. And yet more must be added : shining through the parable, if not actually embraced in it, all are invited not merely to feasting and rejoicing, but to eternal union with the King, through union with the Son. Wonderfully different as are the two parabolic representations of the assembling guests, they are both essential to Christ's teaching, and both needful to meet the demands of the case. Salvation work takes men as it finds them, and makes them different from what they are when found.

Verse 11.—"*The king came in to see the guests.*" This introduces a feature unusual in the reception of guests. He comes to survey the guests, not merely with royal dignity, but for some exercise of judicial authority, as immediately appears in the expulsion of one of their number. Under the former parable, no ground for expulsion of any one accepting the invitation becomes apparent. But here, in the most awfully solemn manner, it is made to appear that those who have entered under invitation may be cast out. The king came in to see the guests, and the survey then taken was to judge of those present. Immediately his eye was arrested by one who had not clothed himself in the wedding garment provided for him. The question addressed to him carried the warning of his condemnation. Verse 12.—"*Friend, how camest thou in hither, not having a wedding gar-*

ment?" He has obtained admission, and meanwhile the king addresses him as an associate thus far, though not related to him in true friendship.[1] To address him even for this once as a companion implies much condescension on the part of the king. But to excuse his conduct is impossible. The man feels it, and is speechless. In some respects his conduct is worse than that of those who have refused to come. He has made his disrespect more offensive. The king has shown himself so generous as to invite all, however poor and unworthy; but he was not on that account so indifferent to the occasion and to the honour of his son as to be willing that his subjects should appear in any guise. He had provided for the company in a manner suitable for the celebration of a royal marriage. But this man has shown so little regard for the will of the monarch as to enter in his poor worn garments. He who acts thus cannot abide among the guests. Therefore, Verse 13, the king commands his servants to *"bind him hand and foot, and take him away, and cast him into outer darkness; there shall be weeping and gnashing of teeth."* His doom is sounding in these words: "Take him away!" He has been within the palace; he has seen something of its brightness and of the richness of the feast prepared; but he shall see no more; he shall not participate in the rejoicings of that day. Bound hand and foot, so as to make resistance impossible, he must be cast into the gloom without, mourning bitterly the loss which a stubborn spirit has to endure.

The interpretation of all this is very clear, and it is overwhelmingly solemn. Verse 14.—*"Many are called,*

[1] The word is ἑταῖρος, a companion or associate, not φίλος, which would have been quite inappropriate here.

but few are chosen." This man also must be added to the many who have been called, and nevertheless are left in the outer darkness. In his conduct and destiny, he is the representative of all who come within the kingdom of God in profession of friendship, and yet in heart and action belie that profession. While they are united in outward fellowship with His people, God may in condescension address them as associates, but not as true friends. Their certain exposure will come from their own sinful neglect of the offered merit of the Son. Refusing to be clothed in the robe of His righteousness, the shame of their sinful state shall appear to every eye. The want of the wedding garment is a thing conspicuous in the midst of the assembled friends of the Son. Before the joy of the marriage celebration has come, when the King looks around upon those who are met, He shall separate from the guests all who fail to appear in a robe of righteousness. In that hour there shall be no escape, for the servants are at hand who do the bidding of the King. There is no escape from the vengeance of God. As the words were uttered, "Take him away," so under the Divine command shall they be cast out who have not trusted in the merits of "the Lamb of God, which taketh away the sin of the world." By Divine strength, as has been touchingly shown in the parable of the Lost Sheep, men, helpless under sin, are carried into the kingdom; and by the same might, men, helpless under Divine condemnation, are cast out from the sacred circle into which, in a godless spirit, they have ventured to intrude. If we ask what is without the kingdom, the parabolic answer here given is twofold. The state is one of darkness, its experience is woe. The meeting-place of the guests is the *inner* circle; all beyond is the *outer*. Within is light; without is darkness: within is joy; without is bitterness of spirit. Into the outer darkness light does not come, for the light of God's countenance cannot shine upon evil. Those who are without are separated from Divine favour. Those who made farming and merchandise their absorbing interest, those who rose in open rebellion against Divine authority, and those who made false-hearted professions of allegiance, shall all be left in the outer darkness. "There shall be weeping and gnashing of teeth;" fruitless lamentation over what has been recklessly sacrificed; bitterness of despair, for that which has been lost cannot be regained.

Into the inner joys of the King's house we are not introduced. These joys are but foreshadowed. The gathering of the guests is conspicuous; the expulsion of the false-hearted is a painful and unexpected occurrence; and the doors are closed. But the feast within is the marriage festivity of the King's Son. In this the Son's relation to the whole is proclaimed. The number of guests coming from all quarters, and arriving at different times, involves multiplicity which renders it difficult to include in the same parable the marriage itself. But the union of Christ with His Church is declared. The Church is itself a unity, and lives in union with the Son,—a union which is life-long, that is, to everlasting. Throughout the eternity to follow, the Church's delight in the Saviour, and the Saviour's delight in His Church, shall be complete. In closest union they shall together rejoice in the midst of the glory of the Father of Lights, with whom is no variableness, neither shadow of turning.

Thus, then, these two parables, taken together, present

to view the provision made for those who are invited to be guests within God's kingdom. In the richness of Divine mercy and grace, a great feast has been prepared; all are freely invited—the poor, the maimed, the halt, and the blind; all who are welcomed are clothed in a divinely provided garment of righteousness; and all these arrangements are consequent on the marriage of the Son,—the favour which He has for the bride, which is His Church. The parabolic representation is complete. Questions unanswered when we had finished the study of the parable of the Great Supper are answered now. The feast of gladness in God's presence unfolds into marriage union with God's only-begotten and well-beloved Son.

CHAPTER IX.

THE PRIVILEGE OF ASKING FOR OTHERS FROM GOD'S STORES.

THE FRIEND AT MIDNIGHT.

LUKE XI. 5-8.

THIS parable springs from the midst of the most impressive lessons as to prayer. The Saviour Himself is seen at prayer; He afterwards teaches His disciples how to pray; next this parable is uttered; after which He presses the duty of earnestness in prayer by reiteration of the strongest assurances as to its answer. Thus the parable comes to stimulate the spirit of prayer. There is an obvious connection between this parable and the two which describe the spiritual feast. Those who are received into God's kingdom obtain a title to ask freely of God's stores. The fellowship with the king, enjoyed by the guests at the feast, leads into the further privilege of special requests according to individual need.

The purpose of our Lord in this parable of the friend pleading at the door of another in the middle of the night, is to illustrate the privilege granted to God's household of interceding for others. Verse 5.— "*Which of you shall have a friend, and shall go unto him at midnight, and say unto him, Friend, lend me three loaves."*

In the opening of the parable it appears as if our Lord meant only to enforce importunity in prayer, but afterwards we perceive that He has something more specific in view. The friend to whom appeal is made in extremity is first mentioned, but a friend in whose behalf the suppliant pleads is spoken of subsequently.

The foundation of the parable is laid in the following facts:—A friend in his journey comes in the middle of the night, seeking hospitality. On his arrival at the door, this friend stands without, seeking admission; he had lost his way—it is now well into the night—and he is exhausted, greatly needing food and rest. He is no stranger who is in this plight, but one well known, who has the claims of friendship. He is not merely on a journey, as our version suggests, and therefore far from home, but, as the marginal reading gives it, he is "out of his way." Besides, the time of his arrival is not an ordinary hour of the day, when he may readily find supplies somewhere else if not in the house of a friend. It is the middle of the night. In Eastern countries, the cool of the evening is often chosen as the time for travelling. But the cool of the eventide is past; the darkness of night has set in, when travelling is dangerous, and the weariness of the way is doubly irksome. A resting-place the man needs and craves, with nourishment sufficient to revive his sinking strength. By this representation our Lord suggests that a fellow-man—a friend—may have a strong appeal to make to his followers for help, in seeking to attain spiritual repose and nourishment when ready to sink on the journey of life. Appeal may be made for temporal aid, since this is a case clearly included. But our Saviour's teaching more particularly concerns the spiritual. So regarded, the representation here given of the case of one in spiritual perplexity, " out of the way," appealing to a Christian friend for help, is exceedingly striking. Life's journey is symbolically depicted as one which should end in the peace of a glorious home. But this traveller has lost his way, and having become convinced of this, he feels bewildered. Like one benighted, he knows not what to do. In this extremity he thinks of a Christian friend, and to him he turns. From him he craves help, desiring escape from his perplexity, and nourishment for his famishing soul. Jesus, speaking in all this to His disciples, is teaching them how to pray; He is warning them that they must expect to be appealed to in this manner, and that they will, therefore, find use for their privilege of prayer, not merely in offering supplication for themselves, but in interceding on behalf of others.

There is next presented to view the action of the Christian when appealed to in such a case. He is the friend at whose door one stands knocking in the middle of the night, who gives a ready and hearty response to the appeal made to him from without. To the friend within it seems a small thing to have his peace disturbed, if only he can render help to one who is in trouble. In answer to the knocking and the appeal, he not only gets up, but unbars the door, lights up the house, gives his weary, agitated friend a warm welcome, and sets himself to do everything he can for his comfort. Thus cordially should every disciple of Jesus prove himself the friend of any one, bewildered and agitated with the sense of being out of the way, who turns to him as one having a truer peace, and a better hope of reaching safely the destination where eternal peace is enjoyed.

But, however much can be done by a Christian at such a time in giving encouragement and comfort, he cannot do all that needs to be done. There is a want which he cannot supply; and the deficiency concerns what is essential. Another stage in the parable brings this into view. It is the representation of the host's perplexity. When he has given his friend a welcome, the necessary supplies are wanting. He has no bread to set before him. Sympathy and shelter will not support life; the famishing man needs food. In the absence of this, the generous host has put himself into an unexpected difficulty. His friend's wants must somehow be supplied, and that promptly, yet he has not at command what will suffice to set before him. In this way the Saviour indicates the limits of a disciple's power to help the perplexed. The disciple can sympathise with such an one, he can speak words of comfort, he can give him a welcome to his friendly regard, he can point him on the way; but he cannot supply him with the very bread of life itself. Sympathy, and love, and knowledge too, a troubled soul may find by turning to a disciple; but to the Lord Himself must supplication be made, in order to obtain the bread of life. As God gives life, and by His bounty provides the bread which nourishes it, so the Saviour-God must Himself give life to the soul, and, in the richness of His grace, provide the bread by which it is to be nourished. In harmony with this view of direct dependence upon God Himself for the nourishment of spiritual life, were the words spoken by the

Lord Jesus on another occasion, when He said, "My Father giveth you the true bread from heaven; for the bread of God is He which cometh down from heaven, and giveth life unto the world." Jesus, when received anew day by day as a gift from God, is received to the nourishment of the soul, and satisfaction of all its wants. Looking at the matter from this point of view, it would appear a serious difficulty to find any parabolic illustration suitable for indicating this inability on the part of the disciple of Jesus to supply to another that which is to be regarded as the nourishment of the spiritual life. But this difficulty is surmounted by bringing the wanderer to the door of his friend unexpectedly in the middle of the night, when it is not to be supposed that he could have supplies laid in for an unexpected arrival, and when it was impossible to obtain them by the usual channels. Verse 6.—"*A friend of mine in his journey is come to me.*" Thus the friend who has welcomed the wanderer is naturally without the store of bread required to supply his wants. The awkward position of this host serves as a fit illustration of the inability of any follower of Jesus to provide supply for the nourishment of spiritual life, however like to his Master in spirit, and however eager to benefit others.

From the contemplation of the host's perplexity, we pass to the scene which discovers his resort in extremity. The sight brings full before us the exceeding value of the warrant we have to approach our God with special supplication. Speaking to His disciples of going to His Father and their Father, He presses upon them, in substance, this inquiry: In such a case as that described, which of you having a friend near by would not go to him, even at midnight, making known your extremity, and asking the needful supply? This the Saviour contemplates as of all courses the most natural. What is the worth of friendship, He would say, if it cannot bear to be disturbed during the night watches by a plea for help in extremity? Thus the Great Teacher provides Himself with His parable. Beautifully does this scene illustrate the noble exercise of intercessory prayer. We must waive meanwhile the perplexity occasioned by such representation of the Hearer of prayer as is implied. The guest welcomed to his friend's house, and provided with such comfort as was at command, is left in the house, while the host hurries off to a friend of his own, to obtain, if possible, the loaves of bread required. Hastening along the street, he makes no scruple as to the disturbance of another family in the middle of the night. He is to occasion no disturbance which he has not himself most gladly submitted to first. He does not ask another to do what he is not himself willing to do as occasion may require. At length the door of the friend is reached. He knocks at once, and when inquiry is heard from within, he responds by narrating the circumstances which have led to his appearance at such an hour. But the friend within is not disposed to be troubled. He has many excuses, and as they come after one another in rapid succession, the burden of the whole is expressed in his first words: "*Trouble me not.*" The door is shut; it will occasion disturbance to undo the fastenings. I am in bed comfortable for the night; it will trouble me to get up. My children are asleep, and to rouse them by the opening of all the doors will cost me no small trouble before they are lulled to rest again. I beseech thee, trouble me not. "I cannot rise and give thee." Unwillingness easily magnifies difficulties; endurance of trouble seems an impossibility in the sight of a reluctant spirit. But the man of generous spirit who grudges no trouble in well-doing will take no denial from another, desiring to escape from a share in the sacrifice. Trouble falls to men as a condition of friendship. It is the strain which tests the strength of the bond uniting those who call each other " friend." What is the value of friendship if it be not ready to endure disturbance and discomfort for the sake of one who is daily saluted as a friend? The suppliant feels as if he would dishonour his neighbour who has spoken so unworthily, if he were to take him at his word and turn from his door. The man, he is assured, is better than might be supposed by a stranger, judging him by his hurried words. His friendship is strong enough to bear a heavier strain. Thus with better thoughts of his friend than his discouraging reception seems to warrant, he resolves to repeat, and even press, his demands until he obtain what he needs. Where friendship is genuine such resolution is already sure of success. The Saviour foretells the result. Verse 8.—"*I say unto you, Though he will not rise and give him, because he is his friend, yet because of his importunity he will rise and give him as many as he needeth.*" This is the natural result when genuine friendship is tested by honest, unflinching earnestness. Importunity gains its end, not on its own account, but because it works with the lever which true friendship provides. Importunity on the part of an entire stranger may not succeed. It may irritate rather than persuade. If importunity here leads to a different result, the difference is accounted for by this, that it works from the vantage-ground which friendship affords.

In this most condescending manner does our Lord commend to His disciples the free use of the warrant they have for His sake to draw largely on the friendship of His Father. And in full accordance with the form of the illustrative parable, which rests its teaching on human friendships, He points specially in this connection to the fact that the privilege of prayer is so extended as to embrace the right of supplication on behalf of those whose welfare is matter of deep interest to us. The benevolence of friendship cannot be more honestly and powerfully exercised than in our prayers. Many things friendship can do to soothe life's troubles and multiply life's joys. But friendship must often discover wants which it cannot supply. The deeper the friendship is, the oftener this painful discovery must be made, and the more important must such wants appear. The most urgent wants of man are those which the best earthly friend cannot satisfy. To this it is that Jesus here points. But "there is a Friend that sticketh closer than a brother,"—there is a Divine friendship with men;—some at least have been named "the friend of God;" such there may be amongst men still. Yea, says this gentle Master to these His disciples, ye yourselves are the friends of God; use your friendship in behalf of others, plead for them that they may receive the bread of life—that they "may eat thereof and not die."

With all this soothing, encouraging, and ennobling truth concerning the believer's privilege, the "Good Master" shows that He does not shun uncomfortable truth. He does not hide the trials attending on privilege; nor does he avoid what may seem unaccountable in the ways of God. While directing notice to the reward which will crown the effort, He does not hesitate to tell of stumbling-blocks in the way. The privilege of intercession may be freely used, yet the fruits of the intercession may be long delayed. But even then this parable stands as our encouragement to believe and persevere. Here we must take into account the seeming incongruity of the representation of the Hearer of prayer, and the condescension of the Divine Teacher in employing such analogy as the unkind delays of men can afford of those wise delays in answering which cannot be fully explained to us. The hindrances in the way of intercessory prayer are not such as those encountered by the man pleading for a supply of bread from a friendly neighbour. The Friend to whom we go "neither slumbers nor sleeps;" there are none in His house who will be roused from their slumbers by our calling; no time can prove to Him untimely; we cannot by our continual coming weary Him. All these things are sure, nevertheless intercessory prayer may wait long for its answer. Nay, the suppliant pleading at God's throne on behalf of another, *is likely to have long to tarry*, and will have need of patience in the work he has undertaken. But if his friendship for his fellow-man be true, he will deem the drafts on patience not too great a cost for gaining his end. The attainment of everlasting life by another,—or even of fuller spiritual strength,—is a result so grand, that it will seem but a small thing to the disciple to continue waiting at the footstool in expectation of an answer. Perseverance will in such a case appear a necessity, even more urgent than that which summons all the energy at command to save a life in danger. And if there be confidence in the Divine Friend to whom the petitions are addressed, there will be assurance that the answer shall be granted when it is fit it should be, and in the manner which to unerring wisdom is the best. With such confidence to sustain patience and perseverance, the suppliant will find many reasons for delay in answering, and as many for perseverance in praying. He will reverently own that it may be a needful thing, because merciful in its result, that the friend who has wandered from the way, and is in want of the bread of life, should still be left perplexed and famishing for a season, while another stands pleading in his behalf. This is the lesson coming from the period of waiting on the part of the guest, while the host seeks supply of bread. As it does not seem strange to him who seeks bread at a neighbour's door, that the wanderer is meanwhile left in hunger; so to the suppliant who asks from God the blessing of salvation for another, it must not seem strange that the other is left for a season in trouble. God, who encourages intercessory prayer for the highest spiritual blessings, taking measures for providing an answer long before fulfilment of his desire is apparent to the suppliant himself, requires of the disciples that they do not marvel, and certainly do not weary or become despondent, if the object of affectionate interest be left for a season in suffering. The answer to intercessory prayer must at the same time be answer to prayer from the object of our regard. The intercessor and he for whom he intercedes must both be suppliants for the same thing before intercessory prayer can be answered. At this point we have an example of the impossibility of one parable conveying the whole truth on a subject. This parable as to intercessory prayer needs to reduplicate on that of the publican. He for whom his friend intercedes must become a suppliant for his own soul's good, as the publican did, crying, " God be merciful to me a sinner," before the intercessory prayer long offered on his behalf can be answered. Nothing under God's government is more certain than this, that intercessory prayer in behalf of the Pharisee can never be fully answered as long as the Pharisee spirit remains in the man, inclining him to say, "I thank thee that I am not as other men." But if, while others intercede for both, the publican be brought to mourn his sins, and the Pharisee be abased to own that his self-righteousness is false and wicked, the first results may be disturbing, yet intercessory prayer is being answered. Not till such results are reached can it be answered. But God, who values intercessory prayer, and acts in accordance with it, has many measures which He can employ in a manner quite beyond the observation of the suppliant, which shall contribute towards the answer, long before the thing desired is effectually accomplished.

Here the full beauty of the parable opens to view. When the ultimate result is gained, in the salvation of the friend for whom intercession has been offered, there is constituted *a threefold friendship*, which shall not be broken. In the structure of this parable every individual finding a place in it is described as "friend." It is a friend who has been travelling, and, having lost his way, comes to the door of his friend for shelter and help. And he who welcomes him goes in to turn to his friend for aid to entertain the other. The truth thus conveyed is exceedingly attractive. The wanderer from the way of life, when he seeks deliverance from the position to which sin has brought him, will find a friend in the disciple of Jesus. And though this friend cannot supply his need, he knows a Divine Friend who can. To Him he will go in his behalf; to Him the penitent may go also in secret prayer. The double prayer will be answered, and these two suppliants will find their highest joy in a triple friendship, both being now friends of God, and God the Friend of both. They will together rejoice in the feast supplied from the stores of Divine grace.

CHAPTER X.

ENCOURAGEMENT TO PERSEVERANCE IN ASKING.

THE IMPORTUNATE WIDOW.

LUKE XVIII. 1-8.

IN this parable the duty of continued prayer is enforced. Verse 1.—"*And he spake a parable unto them, that men ought always to pray, and not to faint.*"

The parable has been very commonly named "The Unjust Judge." And no doubt the judge appears first in the narrative, and on this account may easily be allowed to give a name to it. But to designate it thus is misleading, for the widow is the conspicuous figure in the story, and by constant reference to her we find the key of interpretation. This view is confirmed if we look at the whole group of parables concerning prayer, with reference to their relations to each other. Their unity is apparent at once when we contemplate the several suppliants: the penitent,—the friend whose willingness to help outruns his power,—and the injured one.

Here the judge is apt to attract, if not engross attention; and it is, indeed, a great marvel that God should be willing to liken Himself to an unjust judge. As expositors have almost uniformly said, we could not on our own responsibility have ventured on this form of illustration. Only because it has been supplied by the Lord Himself, do we escape a feeling of discomfort in instituting a comparison with one who has become notorious for injustice. Great as this marvel is, however, we must be content to hold it in reserve, lest the main features of the parable be obscured.

The avowed object of the parable is to teach that men ought always to pray, and not to faint. Verses 2, 3.—"*There was in a city a judge, which feared not God, neither regarded man: and there was a widow in that city; and she came unto him, saying, Avenge me of mine adversary.*" The history of the suppliant affords the designed instruction. Everything discovered regarding her position gives force to the illustration. She is a *widow.* Whether she has any family, who may afterwards grow up to help her, is not said. All such considerations are left out of account, and attention is concentrated on her widowhood. Under the providence of God, this is her first and great trial. She is bereaved of her husband, and is now facing life's cares without her companion, supporter, and protector. In the loneliness and helplessness of her state she stands as the representative of the suppliant.

Giving additional force to the illustration, she is *an oppressed widow.* According to a turn of events sadly common in the world, weakness meets oppression in its path. Helplessness is easy of attack. On the other hand, selfishness is ever mean, and is apt to be cruel. Experience of this is a bitter trial for the widow. Within the neighbourhood of the city in which she lives, there is one who is mean enough to take advantage of her weakness, in order to secure gain for himself.

Bereaved of her husband, she is afflicted yet more by the injustice of one whose knowledge of her case does not move compassion, but whets cupidity. The nature of the wrong inflicted is not explained. The indefiniteess in this respect is designed, making her case more easily applicable for illustration. Endurance of wrong at the hands of another is set forth to view, and every one who thus suffers may here find analogy with his own experience. God, who has promised to be a husband unto the widow, permits this further trial to come upon her. Doubly tried—bereaved and wronged—she stands before us as the representative of the needy and distressed who bow at God's throne.

To complete the view, we must see this bereaved and wronged woman *pleading in vain for redress of the wrong.* Suffering injustice, her only resort in her adversity is to turn to him who is the dispenser of justice in the city. She must appeal to the judge set in the place of authority. Well it is that such a tribunal is set up, if only the administration of justice is pure and prompt. Otherwise, the good is turned to evil, and under the fair name of justice there is a curse in the city. From such perversion of justice fresh trouble breaks on the devoted head of this afflicted widow. The judge is unworthy of his position. Speaking in name of justice, and professing homage to her authority, his reckless decisions violate the sacred principle of equity, according to the impulse of the hour. He does not concern himself with the feelings, rights, or sufferings of those appearing before him, though he is capable of being moved by largesses unrighteously presented, but with needful secrecy. He even makes light of the name and authority of God. Expressions of irreverence come freely from his lips, and he is even pleased with himself as he jests with sacred things, which fill others with awe. "*A judge, which feared not God, neither regarded man.*" This is the vivid portrait as sketched by a Divine hand. To such a dispenser of justice it is that this widow must turn. What hope can she have in making her appeal before such a tribunal? Here is an increase of her affliction. God is permitting manifold trials to close in upon her path. She looks for protection where she has a right to claim it; but her weakness makes her the object of mockery, and her burden is bound more closely about her shoulders. She has come to the final resort, but her appeal is treated slightingly. She is disappointed in her hope. The star which cheered her has set behind a dense cloud. Now she may feed upon her sorrow, throwing open the door of her heart, before which despair stands knocking for admission.

But no; she would not surrender in this way. She had urged her plea, saying, "*Avenge me of mine adversary. And he would not.*" But she resolves that her plaint shall not be thus lightly treated. She will renew her demand—she will persist in claiming justice at the hands of the judge—she will not cease, even though her efforts seem useless. Here is the praying spirit exemplified. This woman supplies a model for Christian suppliants who bow at the footstool of the righteous and compassionate God. With them, the occasion for importunity is different; but the spirit of earnest determination to seek, even when the answer is withheld, must be the same.

How impressive is the parabolic representation of the suppliant's place and experience! The weak pleads with the mighty for help; the oppressed one flees to the shelter which sovereign power has provided for the injured. As illustrating the experience of those who wrestle anxiously for deliverance, and receive no answer to their prayer, she is foiled in her effort to gain redress. The mighty one refuses aid to the weak petitioner. The refuge is closed by the hand of him who has been set to keep open door for every one who hurries thither in flight. The judge refuses to hear, says remorselessly that he will not avenge her, and impatiently requires her to be gone. In the brief period granted for a hearing, not a word of encouragement falls from the judge's lips—not a glance of compassion steals from his eye. Again she comes, hoping for a more favourable opportunity, but with no better result. Once more she returns, but the same cold indifference and relentless mockery are all she experiences. Morning after morning she wends her weary way through these familiar busy streets, to the place where the courts of justice are situated. Patiently she waits the hour when the doors are thrown wide, and immediately she hastens within. The court attendants, now familiar with her appearance, glance at each other with a faint smile as the rueful face and worn garments of the widow reappear, accounting of her persistence as if it were evidence that reason had been there dethroned by the crash of heavy calamity. Her experience is the repetition of what has grown familiar to her. The sad, dejected face reappears as she issues from the court-house, and once more she returns with a heavy heart to her desolate home. Into such details as these the imagination is left to enter, that there may be some appreciation of the difficulties which this widow encountered in pressing her demands. How hopeless is the search for justice in her case! We are almost ready to conclude that it were better for her to desist from those efforts which are putting patience to a painful strain, and adding fresh bitterness to the cup of gall which she is daily constrained to drink. Nevertheless, she will not cease. What is it that nerves her purpose? It is simply this, that she pleads for justice. Weak as she is, in this she feels that she is stronger than the cold, imperious judge. She can conquer him. Strong as he is in position and authority, he can be made to feel a treacherous weakness when justice cries out against his verdicts, even though it be the feeble, faltering lips of an oppressed widow which utter the cry. The strongest becomes weak in attempting to defend wrong; the weakest receives strength in pleading for right. Yea, in such a case as that before us, there is strength in weakness itself, if there be only steadfastness in pressing the claim. The commanding simplicity of justice is made more apparent in the absence of accompanying supports, which might conceal its majesty and strength. This conviction nerves the widow's heart, as in the stillness of the night, under renewed disappointment, and again in the freshness of the morning, with its new opportunity, she ponders the course to be taken. She will not desist. With fixed determination she encounters still the ordeal of reappearance to press the oft-rejected suit. Her persistence is at length rewarded, for she prevails. Her determination, sustained by the justice of the claim, to which even injustice must yield homage, at last forces the judge to relent. Verse 4.—" *He said within himself, Though I fear not God, nor regard man ; yet because this widow troubleth me, I will avenge her, lest by her*

The Importunate Widow. 153

continual coming she weary me." Thus is he defeated, while he vainly attempts to persuade himself that this is simply an exercise of his power. The whole legal force of the city is won to the widow's service by her own quiet determination. Our Lord discovers to us the secret thought of the judge, seeking to delude himself and others with the belief that he is disinterestedly performing a pure act of justice. The Lord accounts it a tardy act wrung from a reluctant judge at the close of an unrighteous and cruel delay. Our Lord adds, in solemn appeal for reflection from the reader, "*Hear what the unjust judge saith.*"

This parable our Lord uses to encourage persistence in prayer. The condition, conduct, and experience of the suppliant carry a large part of this lesson. She is weak, she is bereaved, she is oppressed, and under all she cries in vain to him who is on the judgment-seat to dispense justice. The selection of such a case as this is a cheering testimony to those who are overwhelmed by distress, that they are not overlooked by God, but are tenderly cared for. Their prayers are heard, and "are had in remembrance," though the answer is not yet. As this widow returned daily to repeat her request, so would God have all who trust Him to continue untiring in supplication, even though the answer be long delayed. Though we are weak, and the weakness is appointed by God; though we are wronged, and that wrong permitted by God; we are to cry to Him for deliverance from the wrong, for defence from the oppressor. Yea, even though our prayer appear to be unheeded, we are to continue in prayer, never fainting in this exercise.

Under all this, however, lies the lesson, that our plea

must have the support of justice, and God's warrant for expecting the granting of our petition. These things are essential to the example presented in the parable. Neglect of these things defeats prayer. An unrighteous petition receives no heed from God, however perseveringly offered. But it is the will of our Father, in answer to our prayer, to deliver us from wrong, even though there be long delay in working out deliverance. Verse 7.—"*And shall not God avenge his own elect, which cry night and day unto him, though he bear long with them? I tell you that he will avenge them speedily.*" Thus while persistent prayer is one of the established privileges of the kingdom of God, His people must exemplify in this world patient endurance of wrong. There are, all around, those who are willing to injure others, and God does not shelter those who trust Him from experience of the painful consequences. Continuance of injury they may expect, long after they have begun to cry to God for deliverance. He permits such suffering, and we are to bear it as of His appointment. Nevertheless we are counselled to cry unto Him for defence; yea, to "*cry day and night unto him.*" He is our refuge; waiting upon Him in faith is our privilege; and though there be no sign of reply, our prayers shall be treasured in His presence, and in due time have their answer. "Though we believe not, yet he abideth faithful; he cannot deny himself." He owns our plea as just; He will have regard to the earnestness and faith which our prayers discover, but having regard to other things besides, He may hold in reserve the deliverance which He has prepared and promised. Our continued suffering is, indeed, continued subjection to injustice, carrying with it serious responsibility on the part of the wrong-doer; but, for wise reasons, which will yet commend themselves to our own judgment when the suffering is past, He will "*bear long.*" The turn of this phrase shows the direction in which the thought points. He who has regard to the oppressed has regard to the oppressor as well, and ever as He listens to the cry of a confiding child for escape from anguish, thoughts of mercy are directed towards the oppressor. There is a striking peculiarity in the form of expression with which our Lord closes His question. *Though He bear long*, is the rendering we have in our English Bibles. The passage may be read either in this form, And shall not God avenge His elect, also bearing long with them? or thus, Shall not God avenge and bear long? It is not mere waiting that is implied, but exercise of forbearance towards those who have no claim to consideration. The reference is clearly to the wrong-doer, for even towards him God will exercise forbearance, while His own believing people may be called to wait for a time. All their best possessions are beyond the reach of harm, and for them there is discipline in the trial while it lasts. While His people bear much wrong, God bears long with their oppressors, that space may be given for repentance.

This gives us the key to the delay so often experienced in obtaining an answer to the prayer which seeks escape from evil inflicted upon us. If the answer to our prayer involved personal experience alone, there might be little delay in the response. But in the case under consideration it is otherwise. There is another responsibility intertwined with the suppliant's, and God has regard to this in the delay to which He subjects him who waits at His footstool. The prayer is heard, but God, in the exercise of mercy and forbearance, has dealings with the oppressor, rendering necessary delay painful for the sufferer. It is thus that those who have obtained mercy do, by patient waiting in prayer, make an offering of their own continued anguish that their enemy may share in mercy. At the hands of others they become "partakers of Christ's sufferings." Waiting in faith, and patiently enduring their wrongs, they wait to this end, that their adversaries may be blessed. It were easy for God to grant an immediate answer, by instantly visiting the oppressor with judgment. But this is not in accordance with the plan of His government, nor has He, at any time in the world's history, acted in this way. He did not act thus even when the cry of a whole people rose to Him from the midst of Egyptian bondage. He bore long before His judgments were sent forth. So it is in personal history. The whole race is under a reign of mercy; the worst of men share the advantages of forbearance, even though they employ the space given for repentance in injuring those exercising a humble trust in God. With this exercise of forbearance on God's part, there must be an exercise of patience on the sufferer's part. This is the grand lesson which the parable teaches, running parallel with the direct command of the Saviour—"Pray for them which despitefully use you, and persecute you" (Matt. v. 44). God in His mercy has to do with them also. Pray for them. Such prayer will not stay your own cry for deliverance, but will save you from bitterness in that prayer, and aid you in patience. Yet must we continue to pray for escape from oppression. Content to wait God's time, we must nevertheless continue to plead, in full persuasion that He will have regard to the earnestness and constancy with which we turn to Him, who is able and willing to help.

The grand perplexity of the parable now rises full before us. Why, in teaching us such things, should the Redeemer compare the Father with an unjust judge? There is an incongruity which cannot be disguised, and which is apt at first to awaken painful emotions. By way of relieving the mind of difficulty, it is first to be noticed that *the character and conduct of the judge are expressly condemned.* As our perplexity is occasioned by the fact that the character of the man is evil, it is of consequence to note that the evil occasions severest blame. To read the parable without seeing and feeling this would be puzzling. To attempt to escape the perplexity, by seeking for ingenious excuses for the judge, as has often been done, is to ruin the parable. Such interpretation not only injures the story, but breaks it into fragments, which no skill can cement. Look at the judge as he is sketched by the Saviour's hand. The colours in which he is depicted are exceptionally dark. He is described as one who neither fears God nor regards man, and who is even so hardened as to make a boast of this. And when he utters his "lest she weary me," the Lord, expressing wonder and blame, exclaims, "Hear what the unjust judge saith!" Then, by way of complete contrast, He adds, "And shall not God avenge His own elect?" The immeasurable distance between the two is conspicuous. It is the irreconcilable difference between righteousness and wickedness. The perplexity as to the comparison may remain as before, but it is not heightened by a single touch which blurs moral distinctions.

If, then, the purity of God is not obscured by the manner of the comparison, His glory is untarnished. While with wonder and awe we regard the Divine condescension in constructing for illustrative use such a narrative, we are led to accept this as the only solution of the perplexity, *that our Lord, in His eagerness to instruct us, does not shrink from the use of an available comparison, even though it be drawn from a corrupt life.* He does not hesitate, if with the lesson to be taught, the condemnation of the judge be expressed. If a judge's authority may symbolise the authority which is Divine, he will not refuse to compare God with the merely human judge, who arrogates to himself absolute sovereignty, and wickedly presumes to settle the claims of others according to his own caprice. This judge is deserving of unqualified condemnation, yet Jesus does not hesitate to stoop so far as to employ for illustration his reckless assumption of sovereignty, that he may by contrast present to view the mysterious unsearchable reality of absolute disposal of all events by the Great Ruler of the universe.

This being the explanation of our Lord's use of the example of an unjust judge, it is needful more particularly to mark the points of analogy in the case of this judge. As, in civil affairs, the judge is the last resort in the appeal for justice, so is God the final resort for the supply of every want. In close connection with this, but still more important for the end in view, follows another point of analogy, obtained only by taking for illustration the conduct of an unjust judge. This judge, expressly by reason of his evil character, assumes the prerogative of Deity, claiming by his own sovereign will to dispose of the destinies of men. In the *manner* in which he assumes this he misrepresents the Deity. This judge would exercise a self-seeking sovereignty in violation of justice; God exercises a wise, holy, and beneficent sovereignty, upholding justice, yet showing mercy. In *result* also they are sufficiently like to serve the end of illustrative teaching, and sufficiently unlike to make clear the excellence of Divine sovereignty. In both cases the answer of the petition is by sovereign decree refused, inflicting suffering on the suppliant; but in the one case it is an act of cruel injustice, in the other an act of fatherly discipline, with aid of sustaining grace, accompanied by opportunity for the repentance of the oppressor. At length, in both cases, the petition is by sovereign decree granted; but in the one case it is an act of tardy justice at the call of a languid, profligate self-indulgence; in the other, it is an act of justice lovingly and joyfully granted, with evidence of personal gain in the exercise of faith and patience during the delay, and with accompanying result in the history of the adversary, either good or bad, according as he has valued or despised the opportunities of repentance which mercy has afforded. If, by the importunity of one who pleads for right, an unjust judge be constrained to decree tardy justice, how much more shall the Holy God satisfy the just demands of those who trust in Him, though He tarry long in His dealings with their oppressors? Thus saith the Lord (verse 8), "*I tell you that he will avenge them speedily.*"

This singular parable our Lord closes with a startling question. "*Nevertheless, when the Son of man cometh, shall he find faith on the earth?*" It is the Son of man Himself who throws this question before our minds, leaving it unanswered, that we who expect His appearance may ponder it against His coming. It was needful the Master should leave it unanswered, for the practical good is dependent on our pondering it, with acknowledgment of uncertainty as to what the answer shall be. Let us make sure of *the real meaning of the question as put.* The reference to the coming of the Son of man may be left in its double signification, the one more immediately connected with the departure of individual believers, and the other, more prominent and glorious, connected with the close of this world's history. He who aims at gaining an answer to the question, will not err by regarding the coming of the Son of man in both of these relations. The main inquiry must be, What is the Saviour's allusion in thus referring to faith, as He points to His anticipations when He shall reappear? What will He seek for, and rejoice in finding? Will He find *faith* on the earth? The nearest and simplest answer is this: If He find a people on the earth whom He can call His own, He will find faith, for they are His by faith, and by that alone. Faith in Himself as the Saviour of men He shall doubtless find. Hence, we conclude, it is not to such simple faith His question points. And if not to that, there seems but one answer to the question. He has in the parable sketched the rare faith He wishes to see in His people; such faith as He once found when He tested the Syrophœnician woman, and in admiration at the result exclaimed, "O woman, great is thy faith!" Faith in God's goodness while He continues to afflict; faith in His willingness to answer while He seems for a time to refuse; faith in His justice and in His love even while prosperity is granted to those who injure us. Will He find such faith among His people? This is a faith most difficult to maintain, when sight is no help but altogether a hindrance. To trust that when we pass hence and come into the presence of God, He will save us, is comparatively simple. Then we shall pass away from all that assails us here, and be in the hands of God Himself. But here we are in the midst of evil; our adversaries afflict us most grievously, so that we cry out in our distress, yet no help comes. We must believe that God is here, though we see no token of His presence; we must believe that He is ruling in the midst of these things, while evil is prevailing; we must believe that He is attending to our prayer, though there is no token that He hears, but temptation even to fear that He has cast us off. There is no servant of God who does not find such faith extremely difficult of attainment. David experienced this difficulty. He tells us of his own failure in the attempt to exercise such faith. "As for me, my feet were almost gone; my steps had wellnigh slipped. For I was envious at the foolish, when I saw the prosperity of the wicked. When I thought to know this, it was too painful for me, until I went into the sanctuary of God; then understood I their end" (Ps. lxxiii. 2, 3, 16, 17). The difficulty with David has been a sore difficulty for all who have cried for deliverance from the wicked. To walk by faith and not by sight is hard; but it is still more trying to walk by faith when all the evidence of sight is directly against it. Our Lord, contemplating the possible attainments of His people, asks if He will find such faith in the world when He appears. At His coming He shall search for this; will He find it? His work at that coming shall indeed be one of judgment and heart-searching. In prosecuting His search for spiritual excellence, He shall seek for a faith which is stronger than sight, a faith which has been steadfast, while blessings were refused and trials multiplied. He will search, not with the view of making any discovery on His own part, but for the purpose of discovering the reality to ourselves, and pronouncing special approbation on them who have excelled. And here it is to be noticed that *our prayers will be the test of our faith.* The whole force of the Saviour's question is experienced here, fastening attention on the great lesson of the parable. To whatever wrong we are subjected, He would have us "always to pray and not to faint." And with the utterance of this desire, He gives warning that at His coming the history of our prayers will discover the measure of our faith. This is a thought of high practical importance to all who account it their honour to be His disciples, and to gain His favour. It is a thought which admits of wide illustration. It is essentially connected with "praise, and honour, and glory at the appearing of Jesus Christ." At His coming He shall pronounce a blessing higher than that uttered upon those who excel the doubting Thomas, " Blessed are they that have not seen, and yet have believed." A greater blessing shall then be given to those who in patience have waited under sore wrongs, and have not ceased calmly and joyfully to trust. "These are they which came out of great tribulation."

CHAPTER XI.

THE SERVICE OF THE KING.

THE TWO SONS.

MATTHEW XXI. 28-32.

IN this parable we enter upon a new department of instruction. Attention has been turned, first to the outflowing of Divine mercy for the salvation of the lost; and, next, to the privileges of the kingdom. Now, advancing a step further, we are taught how the penitent, after being brought into the favour of God, begins to render a willing service, finding in this a further privilege.

There is wonderful proof of the love of God to our race in the first breaking of this thought upon us : that we, who are unworthy, and whose doings are all so tarnished with evil, can render service to God, who has performed so great a work for us as to deliver us from destruction. We can do Him a service, and He stoops to ask it of us; but it is only after penitence has brought us to the footstool, and our Father has given us His welcome as penitents, that we can understand the blessedness and honour of being asked to serve Him. When a man makes this discovery, he is quite past the dark and troubled place where the prodigal son, sitting in wretchedness of heart, wondered if his father would receive him and let him be even a hired servant. All the surroundings are changed when God, as a reconciled Father, speaks as one who asks a service at our hands. This is the point reached now in our study of our Lord's parabolic teaching. By the avenues of grace we are advancing into the sphere of service. Beyond the house with its scenes of rejoicing, is the vineyard with its scenes of labour. We have the windings of the way which have brought us to the vineyard gate. First, we have seen a place of humiliation and penitence; next, there has come full in view a place of pardon and peace; in close proximity with that, a place of fellowship with God, where we may have free approach to Him with our petitions; and now we are on the confines of the vineyard, where work is to be done.

The true aspects of this work are now to appear, introducing the dark side as well as the bright side of human conduct in reference to it. God, who has been the wonderful benefactor, comes now as if willing to be benefited. He to whom all supplication has been offered, comes to us as if He would be a suppliant, asking a favour of His own children. The parabolic view of this truth is simple and impressive.

Verse 28.—"*A certain man had two sons; and he came to the first, and said, Son, go work to-day in my vineyard.*" A certain man had a vineyard. It is under this guise that our God appears to us. He is as the holder of a vineyard, who is dependent on help for securing increase. This allusion to a vineyard is in striking harmony with the figurative teaching of revelation. This form of similitude abounds in the sacred pages. The Psalmist, addressing God in the interest of His people, speaks of the kingdom of God thus: "The vineyard which thy right hand hath planted." (Ps. lxxx. 15.) Very specially does the allusion here call to mind that exquisitely beautiful parable in the fifth chapter of Isaiah, beginning, "My beloved hath a vineyard on a very fruitful hill," and closing with the explanation, "The vineyard of the Lord of hosts is the house of Israel, and the men of Judah his pleasant plant." In the course of the Saviour's own teaching, we cannot forget the reference in the fifteenth chapter of John's Gospel, "I am the vine, and ye are the branches." It is, then, in harmony with favourite imagery of Scripture, when God is here represented as the owner of a vineyard.

The particular aspect in which God here comes into view is not that which discovers His wealth in the possession of the vineyard, but, if we may say it, that which implies *dependence* upon others for help in its cultivation in order to secure the vintage. The vineyard needs to be irrigated; the soil must be loosened about the roots of the vines; weeds must be struck down on their first appearance; over-luxuriant shoots of the vines must be pruned. Using this similitude, God comes condescendingly with illustration of the fact that He asks service from His people.

That God cannot be in any way dependent on us is a truth to be kept in view in this connection. Our regard to this fact may be appropriately quickened by the impressive utterance of Scripture: "If I were hungry, I would not tell thee: for the world is mine, and the fulness thereof" (Ps. l. 12). Besides, if God could be enriched by any means, it could not be by any effort of ours, since from Him we have received all we have. Even did we render to Him a perfect service, we should be constrained to say, "We are unprofitable servants: we have done that which was our duty to do." Even at the best, our God could in reality be no gainer by our service.

And yet God, possessor of all, in the plans of His grace concerning us, not only comes to pardon us and to listen to our cry, but to address to us His own request for help. He has so ordered the affairs of His kingdom, that, as a vineyard, it depends upon the service of labourers in the midst of it, in order that it may yield fruit which shall be to His joy and glory. In accordance with this need, there is established a form of voluntary dependence upon His people. God asks of them service, that, when "the harvest is past and the summer is ended," the wine-presses may be full.

This owner of the vineyard, who needed help for its tending, had *two sons*. As these two sons are introduced to view within the home of a certain man who had a vineyard, we are arrested by another proof of the unity of the parabolic teaching of Scripture. Are not these two the younger and elder of the parable of the Prodigal,—the Penitent, and the Alienated? Are they not still the same as the two suppliants in the parable of the Pharisee and Publican? As we proceed, we shall find ample warrant for an affirmative answer. The consideration which is here before us once more, in restricting the number to two, is, that in very many points of view affecting our relation to God it is seen that men are really embraced in only two distinct groups. There is a close connection between the several views of our relations to God presented in the parables where the persons appearing are only two in number. For it is to be observed that while the parable now before us has express reference to service, there were also important references to service in the parable of the Prodigal Son. The younger son not only bewails that he has transgressed, but underneath his thoughts of return, there is a desire to serve; while the elder son claims approval as if he had all along been serving his father. In a light very similar, there is here a twofold failure as to service, presenting the dark part of the picture, which fills in the background.

The owner of the vineyard asks his two sons for help in its cultivation. With a father's authority, he says, "*Go work to-day in my vineyard.*" This use of authority in desiring the service is befitting in a father. By its introduction, the parable more adequately represents the position of the Deity, who only in condescension, and in His desire to bless us, comes to ask service at our hands. Well does it befit Him, coming in such a way, to use words of command, and say, "Go work to-day in my vineyard."

Much additional effect is here given to the instruction as to our part in serving God, by introducing an explicit reference to time. *To-day!* The demand is for immediate service, and that throughout a definite time of short duration. The time of service is now, as the call reaches us; the sphere is "God's vineyard," near by our own home. God asks our service all the day long. The work to be done needs instant and constant attention. If we cherish filial love, we shall joyfully respond, and shall not grieve though that response involve much self-denial. How natural it is, besides, that our Father in heaven, with whom a thousand years are as one day, should describe our present opportunity as *a day of service*. If we bear the burden and heat of this short day, a gracious Father places in prospect, at the setting of the sun, a reward, glorious and satisfying, which shall spread through the long course of an Eternal Day.

The poor beginning made by both sons on that day when their father's demand for service came upon them, must first have attention. Verses 29, 30.— "*He answered and said, I will not; but afterward he repented, and went. And he came to the second, and said likewise. And he answered and said, I go, sir; and went not.*" The result of the father's demand for service is sadly disappointing in the case of both of his sons. The one said, "*I will not;*" the other, "*I go, sir; and went not.*" The record is shortly and sharply put, giving full effect in the reader's mind to the completeness of the refusal. This is the Saviour's view of the manner in which men treat God's call for service. There is little wonder that in contemplating it, He should ask men themselves to judge of it in light of what is due to a father. "What think ye" of this? When a father looks to his own sons for help in cultivating his vineyard, he receives a direct refusal from the first; and though the other makes a promise of help, that promise is not kept. In the account of the disobedience of these two, there lies before us a representation of the conduct of our whole race in disobeying God's demand for service. The first prominent point of the parable is discovered here. When God calls to men for service, there is *universal disobedience* to the call. There are indeed two distinct aspects of this disobedience, but only two. The one is open and defiant. The other is not without some evidence of a disposition to obey; and a promise of obedience is actually made, but the promise is not kept. A general view of human service, painted in colours so dark, is apt at first to be staggering to us. All the more is this so on account of our being constantly prone to excuse ourselves for shortcoming, in consideration of our meaning to do well. Yet there is no ground for doubting the accuracy of the colouring. Nor does there seem to be any hope that a longer study of the picture will soften down in our estimation its intended meaning. The most careful and renewed study will not detect any modifying touches, at first unobserved on account of the darkness of the general effect. There is, indeed, candour in the very directness with which the first refusal is given; but candour is no credit in evil-doing. There is in the case of the second a manifest wish to avoid blunt refusal, and even an inclination to stand well with his father; but this does not lessen the blameworthiness of subsequent disobedience, burdened as it is with the additional sin of unfaithfulness to the promise. The substance of the teaching of the parable at this point is, that all men fail in rendering to God the service required of them. There is no one amongst us who begins as he should. No doubt there are great differences in the manner and extent of disobedience; but the spirit which leads to disobedience is the same in all, and the manifold varieties can be reduced to two classes. If there be any difficulty in acknowledging the completeness of this twofold classification, it must be connected with the attempt to include, under the example of the second son, all who are not openly rebellious. And this difficulty would be serious if we were shut up to interpret the parable in such a manner as to regard the second son as designedly hypocritical. If the story could not be otherwise read than as conveying that the second son deliberately intended to deceive his father, then would it be impossible to take the twofold classification here given as all-inclusive. But there is really no warrant in the structure of the story for pronouncing the second son hypocritical. Indeed, if the story be pondered, it will appear that the statement of the case of this second son is intentionally short and vague, so as to leave the state of his mind undescribed. In this way it is left in such form as quite successfully to include the mere hypocritical promiser, who in his heart does not mean to obey, and at the same time those who honestly mean and wish to serve God, and yet, under a variety of inducements, turn aside. If due account be made of the restricted nature of the description of the conduct of the second son, there can be no difficulty in admitting that under it may be included all who are not openly defiant against God's authority; for it will be seen that nothing more is said than that he made the promise and did not keep it. How the failure came about is not told. Such reserve, practised intentionally in the structure of many of the parables, is far more appropriate to the end in view than a fuller narrative could have been. The son made the promise, but in some way that promise was left unfulfilled. How many cases are covered by such a restricted statement! An honest wish to serve, but a mind pre-occupied with designs of its own, which speedily regain the ascendency. A desire to please God, but a pliable nature, easily swayed to please men rather than God. A genuine assent to the voice of rightful authority, but inertness of nature, slow in passing from purpose to action. As we go on with the enumeration, we can see that the classification may indeed embrace all the cases of an honest intention to serve, which is followed by failure in action. The result in all such cases is that God is not served; the work of the vineyard is not done; all become transgressors.

Though this is the sad account of the beginning—for it must be owned that we all begin badly—this is happily not the end. While universal disobedience is the first result which God beholds, He is not left altogether without service on the earth. But that service comes after disobedience, being in all cases a recoil from it, brought about by the working of God's own grace, in a manner already explained in the first group of parables. And now, under the operations of that grace, there are ever some repenting and turning back upon the way, that they may at length enter upon a willing service. Of these two sons, the first, who said in reply to his father's command, "I will not," *afterwards repented and went.* Here we reach the second prominent feature of the parable. We first see universal disobedience among the children of men; now we discover that in the case of many there is at length entrance on service by the gateway of repentance. That this is the lesson meant to be taught at this point, it seems impossible to doubt. It follows as a necessary consequence from the first feature of the parable. If disobedience be universal, obedience can be only by turning again from the way of transgression. The repentance which turns from sin and leads to pardon, guides by the next step to the beginning of a life of holy service. This is according to God's plan when He shows favour to the guilty. He does not pardon because He sets lightly on sin, or would excuse it. No man can look at Calvary with the slightest appreciation of the scene there witnessed and continue to think so. God pardons in order that He may lead men back again to holiness. This is the lesson before us. The picture of this penitent son quietly entering the gate of the vineyard to set about his father's service is, in the direct line of personal history, the picture which meets the eye as we turn the page from that which depicts the joyous welcome of the penitent prodigal in the midst of the father's household. That scene of rejoicing is not by any means a closing or even a permanent scene in family history. It is only the first scene in a new course of life for the son whose return is gladly celebrated. His new life is not to be one of never-ending festivity, which would certainly become tame and tiresome. Its noblest feature is a return to filial obedience. It is an entrance upon service which is thenceforward to be continued unremittingly. The passing sight here given us of this son entering by the vineyard gate, with all the signs of preparation for work, is the parabolic representation of an essential feature of Christian life— true service following on repentance. It is not thereby implied that the work thereafter done is perfect of its kind, but it is honestly and faithfully done; and while all its imperfections are observed and owned, there will no more be abandonment of the task, but in its steady continuance there will be acquirement of new experience, by which a still better service shall yet be rendered to God.

As we look thankfully upon this son entering the vineyard after the first hours of the day have fled, there remains one ground for lamentation. This concerns the other, whose state of mind at first seemed more promising. His brother is not there before him. Answering in a manner quite different from the answer given by the first, he had said, "*I go, sir.*" But he went not. All through the vineyard his brother may look for him now, but he will not find him there. It is not that his work has been done. It has never been begun. Here stands before us the final lesson of the parable. The defiant sinner is the first penitent. He is first within the vineyard, bending his energies to the service of his father. Those who do indeed feel a wish to serve God, and who shrink from high-handed rebellion—those who mean to obey God's voice, and are continually promising to do so, yet are ever coming short,—are apt to be slowest in coming to repentance. Rebellion is not so manifest a thing in their case as in the life of those who go openly into sin. Thus the disobedience which is not so extreme is liable to be longer continued. Reluctance to take a place of penitence along with the worst of transgressors deters many from humbly acknowledging that in all things they have sinned and come short of the glory of God.

Whether the second son did afterwards repent, we are not told. In this, as in other points, there is intentional reserve. The same course is here followed as was previously taken in the account given of the elder brother in the parable of the Prodigal Son. The references in both parables are quite plainly to the same type of character, only seen from different points of view. The son not to be found in the vineyard when his brother enters it in penitence, is one who has been thinking well of himself, and contrasting his case favourably with his brother's refusal. He has not been so bad as the other in the form of his disobedience. This he can say truthfully. But there is a snare in this supposed superiority. And now it happens to him that he must be blamed more than the other. Thus it is that God, who condemns the life of publicans and harlots much more than the life of scribes and Pharisees, points, with all the solemnity of a warning, to the fact that He is dispensing the blessings of salvation first to those who have been the worst. While they are being pardoned, those who have shown most wish to serve Him are less earnest, or rather are wholly indisposed to take their place before Him with humble confession, and with sincere desire to have a share in the work to be done in His vineyard. What their future shall be depends upon themselves. God waits to be gracious; His service waits to be done; and it is left with them who know these things to determine what their lot shall be under their Father's government. Those who study the parabolic teaching of Scripture, must be content to have this parable break off suddenly as it does, and must await the future for the completing of the record.

CHAPTER XII.

SERVICE TO GOD IN SERVICE TO OUR NEIGHBOURS.

THE GOOD SAMARITAN.

LUKE x. 25-37.

THIS parable presents a more advanced view of Christian service than that given in the parable of the Two Sons, to whom their father said, "Go work to-day in my vineyard." In the latter the glimpse of the actual service is very slight; we have the history only of its beginning. We see a son who had refused obedience repenting as the day advances, and entering the vineyard to begin the work required of him. In the parable now before us we are shown how Christian service works for the good of mankind generally. A scene on the highway illustrates the truth that love is the fulfiling of the law—the love of God flowing forth in love to man.

The picture is in itself an impressive one. A man, stripped of his clothing and seriously injured, lies by the wayside in a half-dying state. Those who have robbed him and nearly murdered him have hurried from the spot, giving themselves no concern though the morning's sun should rise on a countenance stiff in death. Down the highway, beyond the panting sufferer, two figures are dimly traced, the one considerably in advance of the other. Both of these men are near enough the scene to indicate that they must have passed since the robbery had been committed. In the foreground is a man who, having alighted from his ass, is kneeling by the prostrate figure, engrossed in the attempt to revive the sufferer. This man illustrates how love to God is shown on earth, and how His service is done.

Some consideration needs to be given to the circumstances in which the picture was sketched. A teacher of the law, whose duty it was to read and expound the Scriptures in the hearing of the people, approached Jesus with this question: "Master, what shall I do to inherit eternal life?" The question had often been present to his mind, and by putting it now, he wished to test this public Teacher, of whom the people said that He spoke "with authority, and not as the scribes." Jesus, knowing that by profession he was familiar with the Scriptures, said, "What is written in the law? how readest thou?" Having the question thus turned upon himself, the teacher of the law answered in the words of Scripture: "Thou shalt love the Lord thy God with all thy heart, and with all thy soul, and with all thy strength, and with all thy mind; and thy neighbour as thyself." The answer had the approval of our Lord as in every respect worthy of one whose duty it was to be the instructor of others. Jesus therefore commended it. "*Thou hast answered right.*" But seeing that the lawyer inclined to trust in *doing*, the Lord said, "*Do this, and thou shalt live.*" Life on such a standard is life with God, and it is eternal life. A perfect love is a perfect fellowship. The teacher of the law felt the emphasis thus laid upon the actual *doing* of what is here enjoined. When the doing of the law is made the testing-point, the uneasiness of self-condemnation springs up. The inquirer felt this, but sought to shelter himself by requesting an exposition of the passage in its last clause. "Who is my neighbour?" The directly personal application of the matter is shown in the form of this query. How shall I be taught and guided by this passage? Who is neighbour to me? The picture sketched by the Master's hand is the answer to this inquiry. Look upon that poor sufferer, and upon this man who bends over him with all-absorbing compassion, and the answer lies before your eye. "Who is my neighbour?" was a question apt to be made matter of casuistry. It offered a variety of nice distinctions, on which cases of conscience might arise. The lawyer wishes therefore to see how Jesus, the prophet of Nazareth, will disentangle these perplexities. If He clear up one difficulty, a multitude more can be raised.

But the Great Teacher takes an unexpected course, which suddenly clears off the perplexities. The cases of conscience are at once disposed of by an extreme illustration including all cases of a more ordinary type. The lawyer said, "*Who is my neighbour?*" To him it seemed that there must be some limitation. Perhaps the limit might be found in their own countrymen. Surely it could not take into account the Samaritans, "for the Jews had no dealings with the Samaritans." At least, it could not go so far as to include the Gentiles, from whom they had been separated as by an impassable wall. What a fruitful source of debate

M

was here, sheltering all the casuistry of the lawyer! But when Jesus speaks, all these distinctions between Jew, Samaritan, and Gentile are put out of sight. Verse 30.—"*Jesus, answering, said, A certain man went down from Jerusalem to Jericho, and fell among thieves, which stripped him of his raiment, and wounded him, and departed, leaving him half dead.*" Here is a man who needs help, as he lies by the wayside ready to die. His wounds, his groans, his blanched face—all plead for speedy assistance. As you look upon him, the Divine word says, "Love thy neighbour as thyself." Is he a neighbour? Are you a neighbour to him? Has a suffering man a claim on his fellow-man standing by him in his suffering? The whole question is a matter of nearness, or neighbourhood. Can it be anything more than this? If it admit of discussion whether the law of love requires you to help such a man, it must somehow seem doubtful whether love may not willingly see a man die in neglect without stretching out the hand to save him. The suggestion refutes itself. Love must help when help is needed. The law is explicit. In substance it is this, Love another as thyself, and neighbourhood or nearness is that which determines who the object of regard should be. Nor is it more doubtful how love works, than who is to be its object. Love *as thyself*. Suppose yourself in the place of the sufferer, and suppose him the onlooker. Would you turn to him for help? If you had breath and strength, would you not ask aid of him? And if so, your duty is clear as noonday. This is what the Saviour teaches. *A certain man* is a sufferer, whose condition calls for help. The absence of other description than that which tells of the injury he has sustained, and the danger to which he is now exposed, is to be remarked. Whether he is Jew or Gentile—whether he is rich or poor—yea, even whether he is good or bad in moral character—are considerations kept out of view. He is a suffering man, and as such his claim to help is unquestionable. The neighbour is the man who needs help, and finds you near enough to give it. Thus beautifully the law of love clears away perplexities. In its view social distinctions bring no exceptions. Before that Love which serves God, as before the Saviour who brings us to the love and service of God, "there is neither Jew nor Greek, there is neither bond nor free, there is neither male nor female." Duty is the same everywhere, knowing no respect of persons. This lawyer is like Peter, desiring to have a definite limit put on the application of this same law of love in the matter of forgiveness of injuries. "How oft," said the apostle, "shall my brother sin against me, and I forgive him? till seven times?" How noble is the answer, how satisfying to conscience, how beneficent in its practical application! "I say not unto thee, until seven times, but until seventy times seven." And so the answer runs now. Thy neighbour is thy fellow-man, when thou and he are near. The Saviour, who has a gospel for "every creature," imposes a service which carries the influence of love no less widely.

The meaning of the law being thus made clear, we revert to the difficulty of keeping it. This is the real perplexity. It is not hard for a man to settle who is near to him, claiming aid in a time of trouble; but it is difficult to prove a neighbour indeed on all such occasions. The beauty of the course of action enjoined is evident; but it is a severe test of love between man and man which is required in daily life. The world is full of examples of the opposite. As we journey down the highway of life there seems more of transgression than of obedience. A picture of a part of this highway is before us here.

There lies on the road between Jerusalem and Jericho—long a favourite resort of banditti—a man who has been stripped even of his raiment, seriously wounded, and left half dead. Our Lord is illustrating the application of the law of love; and we see first the bitter fruits of cruel selfishness. Such a murderous career as these men lead is the furthest removed from the service of God. Disregard of God is not only disregard of man, but leads to most cruel maltreatment of others for personal gain. The robbers are not to be seen near; but in their bleeding, panting victim there is evidence of their doings. They have done their cruel part; they have wrenched by force some booty, including even the garments of this defenceless solitary traveller; and they have fled from the scene, as such men must flee, for it is the penalty of evil-doing that it is done in fear. These are "far off from God;" "citizens of the far country." Life with God and service to Him are both embraced in the single word "love:" the extreme opposite is before us here. "He that loveth not his brother abideth in death. Whosoever hateth his brother is a murderer; and ye know that no murderer hath eternal life abiding in him."

The victim of their attack lies helplessly where they left him; fortunately he lies on the highway, and between Jerusalem and Jericho there are many going and coming. As we look down the road so far as it is presented to view, there are two figures visible, travelling away from the spot. These two have passed since the attack was made. We need some explanation of their connection with the occurrence.

The first statement given concerns the one who is farthest down the way. Verse 31.—"*And by chance there came down a certain priest that way; and when he saw him, he passed by on the other side.*" The connection between the two events is not well conveyed in the phrase "*By chance.*" The word employed is the same in structure as our word *concurrently*. By concurrence of events, such as determines nearness to one who needs help, making him the neighbour of the sufferer, a certain priest, as he travels along, finds himself at the place when the man's wounds are still fresh. There is here, as elsewhere in the parable, avoidance of what marks the individuality of the man. His profession only is discovered. He is a priest, one of the sons of Aaron, accustomed to minister at the altar of God, standing in "the holy place" where incense is offered to the Most High. By the order of his office he is trained to reverence and love. How fortunate it seems that one of his position should be the first to arrive! And yet, as the event proves, anything less favourable could hardly have been. He passed by without even taking time to ascertain the condition of the prostrate man. This priest's thoughts may have been more or less excusable. The main fact in the case is that love to God was not so strong in his heart as it should have been; and love to man wanted that force which would have made him instantly the helper of the man ready to perish. It is not merely such men as are at the extremes of antagonism to God's law who fail to keep it. This priest, brought into comparison with the robbers who have done the wrong, is far removed from them in character and life; and yet he leaves the man to die whom they in their violence have nearly murdered. This priest knows that the law of God is love; but it is not in his heart to keep that law. Even the forms of religion, however regularly performed, are not a security for the development of love in the heart; they are not even a sure defence against hardening of the heart. A man's heart may wither even at the altar of God: he may minister in the services of religion, yet fail in the ministry of life.

There is still another who in like manner has been content to pass this perishing creature. Verse 32.—*"And likewise a Levite, when he was at the place, came and looked on him, and passed by on the other side."* Why should there be in this parable two examples of similar conduct? Though the result is the same, the actions are different. By concurrence of events, as in the case of the priest, this man also has his faithfulness to the service of God put to proof by the claims of the sufferer. The result is not exactly as in the former case. This is a subordinate officer of the temple, less directly in contact with the more awful solemnities of its service. He is in a position more analogous to that of the teacher of the law who has raised the question under consideration. The priest saw the man, and yet deliberately held on his way; but this Levite stopped at the place, and took time to look at the man before he passed by. Whether he was better than the priest, since he at least stopped at the sight, cannot be determined, as there is a manner of looking on the sufferings of others which is in no respect better than passing them by. But his conduct is certainly worse when, having taken time to see the sad condition of the injured man, he cruelly turns aside, and gives himself no concern lest he should perish, or at the least lie for hours in anguish. If every passer-by act either as the priest has done, or as the Levite now does, the man so maltreated by banditti must die where he has fallen.

A scene of a very different kind comes now under observation. Verses 33-35.—"*But a certain Samaritan, as he journeyed, came where he was: and when he saw him, he had compassion on him, and went to him, and bound up his wounds, pouring in oil and wine, and set him on his own beast, and brought him to an inn, and took care of him. And on the morrow, when he departed, he took out two pence, and gave them to the host, and said unto him, Take care of him: and whatsoever thou spendest more, when I come again, I will repay thee.*" A different rule of conduct seems to sway the next traveller along that highway. And who is he who acts so much more satisfactorily, representing the life of true godliness? "*A certain Samaritan.*" His nationality is indicated, and not a word more is uttered. A Samaritan! The furthest removed among the dwellers in Palestine from influence of the temple service. He is beyond the circle of rites and privileges belonging to the Jewish Church; and, in common with his people, he is despised by the Jews. But he believes in God; he worships Him; and, as the result shows, he gives himself to the service of God with devoutness of heart. Immediately when he beholds the wounded man, he makes it his special business to attend to him, and that with an overflowing benevolence. With a gentle hand he examines his wounds. Carefully moving him to ascertain where he has been injured, he takes of his oil and wine to anoint these wounds, and then binds them up. Having eased the poor man's pain and revived him, this benefactor lifts the bruised one on to his own ass. He thus carries him to an inn, where, with appliances at command, he ministers to him as a brother. On the morrow the Samaritan must go in prosecution of his own business, but before departing he gives to the host payment for two days' longer attendance. He does not expect that the host will do what he has done, taking on himself the charge of the injured one. The Samaritan has brought the sufferer to the inn, and he will not cast his self-assumed burden on another: he himself will bear the charge to be met in a place of public entertainment. He even shows such completeness of sympathy and of brotherly care, that he takes upon himself the charge not only for the immediate wants of this man he has found by the wayside, but even for demands which may still arise before he can be able to depart. He undertakes to make up to the utmost for the injury which cruel hands have inflicted.

Here, then, are three men, all of whom, by the same concurrence of events, have been brought into the neighbourhood of extreme suffering. Verse 36.— "*Which of these three, thinkest thou, was neighbour unto him that fell among the thieves?*" The question is thus put on the converse side. The lawyer asked, Who is to be loved by me as a neighbour? That the Saviour has answered by saying, Every one who needs and seeks your help. And now the Saviour in turn asks, Who is he who loves as a neighbour? Is not the true neighbour to a sufferer the man who helps him in his suffering? Is it not he alone who performs the neighbourly part? What sayest thou, as a doctor of the law? To that question the teacher of others could give only one reply (verse 37): "*He that shewed mercy on him.*" And with such reply, it was acknowledged that his difficulty was solved. There only remained practical use of the teaching for which the hearer must be responsible, "*Go thou and do likewise.*" This is the real difficulty in the case; and the intention of the Saviour plainly was to press this difficulty on the mind of his questioner, leaving it with himself. The doctor of the law seemed to fancy that life could be obtained by rendering a perfect service. Now, however, that the real demands of the law are discovered by the light thrown upon them in this parable, he must feel self-condemned. To love God with our whole soul, and to love our neighbour as ourselves, are requirements most obviously righteous. But who can endure their test? We come so far short, that we are constrained to own that we have lost eternal life, if these are the terms on which it is to be gained. To such service we must, indeed, bend all our energies; however far short we come, we must still strive to reach this attainment. Pure love is the law of life in God's kingdom; it is the law by which Christ's teaching tests all service. As a law of obedience, it is a law of love; and as a law of social life, it is the same. Thus all Christian service is reduced to these two aspects—service to God, and service to man for God's sake; the motive power leading to performance is the same in both—supreme love to God, carrying with it love to our fellow-men as to ourselves. In this parable both of these aspects of Christian service are presented to view, as the lawyer had quoted the whole law. By this means a connection with the parable of the Two Sons is maintained, that indicating what is due to the Father, this what is due to our brethren. That parable gave prominence to the failure of men in rendering service, except by the way of repentance; this brings failure and success into contrast, leaving the way of escape from failure undetermined, and the way towards complete obedience undiscovered. This is done intentionally, that the lawyer, and all who think as he does, may deal with the question, How then shall we be saved, and helped to a perfect obedience? To this question the Saviour has an explicit answer. He is Himself the answer— "I came that ye might have life, and that ye might have it more abundantly." He came that He might lead us again to the Father's favour, establishing in our heart that love by the power of which we shall be enabled to serve Him more fully and more joyfully. The necessity for this union to Him, in order to render a true service to God, He has elsewhere presented in metaphorical illustration, analogous to that of the parable. He urges that without Him we can do nothing; and that true life must show itself in fruitfulness to God, and in love to one another. Under the image of a vine, He represents Himself; while His disciples are the branches (John xv. 1-12). To Him we must be united, as the branches to the vine, that from Him we may draw our life, and be capable of rendering fruit to God. Thus living in Christ, we must continually lift our hearts to God, even as the branches spread themselves towards heaven, receiving the light and warmth of the sun, and being refreshed by the dews of the night, and by the showers which water the earth.

Division III.

RELATIONS OF GOD'S KINGDOM TO THE PRESENT STATE OF THE WORLD.

CHAPTER XIII.

SOWING OF GOSPEL TRUTH FOR AWAKENING OF SPIRITUAL LIFE.

THE SOWER.

Matt. xiii. 3-9.

With this parable we pass to the world-wide aspect of the work of the Lord of the kingdom, all whose subjects work under His guidance, according to His great plan for the world's regeneration. The unity of design in this work is made apparent in parabolic teaching, as well as the various phases of work required for accomplishment of the Divine purpose.

The need for sowing seed in order to reaping in harvest time affords here the first form of illustration; after which, the leaven and hid treasure are selected as illustrating the deeper results accomplished by the extension of the Kingdom of Grace.

Verse 3.—"*Behold, a sower went forth to sow.*" Thus the Son of God depicts His own appearance on earth to change the face of our world into a fruitful field, yielding plentifully the fruits of righteousness to His Father's glory. "He that soweth the good seed is the Son of man; the field is the world" (verse 37). There is great gain in illustrative force by the appearance here of a single sower rather than a multitude of sowers far apart from each other over the world's surface, acting under the direction of their Lord. The Son of man Himself is the greater sower. It is thus made impressively conspicuous that the ingathering of fruits of righteousness is dependent upon the exercise of Divine grace. He who comes to save the world— He who comes as a lamb to take away the world's sin —comes also as a sower, bringing with Him stores of seed, preparing for a great harvest. This is the explanation of all that has since happened in the history of the world, in the growth and ripening of the fruits of righteousness under the sway of the Lord Jesus Christ. Without this interposition of Divine grace, the field of the world had lain waste, yielding only mixed results, nowhere the golden grain of true righteousness. The selfish life with rank growth would have spread out on every side, yielding briars and thorns. The best life of humanity would have proved feeble in the earth, doing little to encroach on the reign of selfishness, rather finding itself constantly encroached upon by noxious weeds. The struggle after a better life would still have been the struggle of the weak against the strong. Testimony from the leaders of thought, witnessing against self-seeking, and pleading for a universal benevolence, would have proved little better than an ineffective protest,—a dragging of the ploughshare through the soil, without casting in fresh seed.

Jesus comes as one who has stores of seed, enough for the requirements of the immense field over which it is to be scattered. He Himself undertakes the work of sowing, spreading the good seed on the right hand and on the left as He moves over the fields. It is the very work of His life, until the appointed time draws on for yielding Himself a sacrifice in our stead. He dies, leaves in His "finished work" the seed of gospel truth, which may be scattered to the ends of the earth, and when lodged in any heart, may be quickened into life by the Spirit of God. He withdraws from earth, and ascends to the throne of His glory in the heavens, but the sowing, as it proceeds, is still His sowing —carried on in His name, and with His blessing, by those whom He has awakened to self-consecration after His great example. If, in the midst of His suffering, we say, Behold the Man of Sorrows ; in the midst of His toil we say, Behold the Sower of the seed of righteousness.

The seed is "*the word of the kingdom*"—the truth proclaimed by Jesus, the Prince of Peace, the Revealer of the Father. This is God's *word* to sinful men.[1] In a sense all truth is as seed, bearing fruit after its kind. But the highest example of this is found in the word of God, which, taking root in the heart, yields the fruits of righteousness in the life of those who receive it. Gospel truth has to do with the very sources of action in the mind ; it cannot be received without having constant application to the life ; and its only fruit is the fruit of righteousness. All this is clear from the nature

---

[1] Very fitly, as showing the unity of gospel revelation, *Jesus himself* is the word.

of the truth discovered by the Lord Jesus. It is a message of love and mercy from God; a discovery of pardon through the atoning death of the Son; an assurance of newness of life by the work of the Spirit. ' The word of the kingdom is thus the word of life, whose quickening in the soul of man is the awakening there of a life of righteousness, in the love of the Father and of the Son. (The Bible is to us the storehouse in which the Lord has laid up the treasures of seed. As the sowers in spring-tide bring their grain to the field, and set it down there, to obtain fresh supply of corn as they continue casting it abroad, so do the sowers of the kingdom bring forth their supplies from the storehouse of Scripture, and cast abroad the sure word of the kingdom.

Such truth as that described the Son of God Himself casts upon the minds of men. A God-like exercise! The God of Truth brings to man the truth most precious. The God of Salvation scatters among men that truth which, when believed, proves the beginning of life eternal. But such truth is as seed which, unless it be lodged in the soil, remains dead—unless it go deep into good soil, has its vitality wasted in a brief and fruitless growth. Thus it is with seed, and not less so with truth. Even the Son of God Himself, when He goes forth as a preacher of righteousness, goes as the sower, who loses some seed as it falls from His hand, finding by and by that much of that which was safely covered has contributed nothing to the harvest. The Lord of the universe is like to His creatures in this, that He casts abroad much good seed which yields no return. In this relation there comes out to view the main practical lesson of this parable.

The Sower.

Verse 4.—"*Some seeds fell by the way-side, and the fowls came and devoured them up.*" The scene is familiar in every land. The birds of the air hover on the path of the sower, ever ready to alight and pick up the seed not fully covered. That which falls on the pathway is their sure portion. In vain are the harrows dragged joltingly over the beaten track; to no purpose does the heavy roller lend its weight to crush the seed into the ground—still it continues exposed, and the fowls find an easy repast. This, the most unsatisfactory result, is that which is soonest seen. For the best results there needs to be the longest waiting. In this case the seed is scarce fallen from the hand until it is lost to the sower. It is even so with the truth communicated to men. But why should the sower thus lose his seed? Why should he cast any part of it on the pathway through which the opening ploughshare has not passed? It is not for the sake of feeding the hungry fowls which may eat of something less valuable. He casts away his seed with so free a hand only because of his wish that no part of the tilled land may want its share. And thus it is God acts in casting abroad the seeds of truth. His dispensation of the word of the kingdom is with unstinted hand, as appears from the case of those who have often received it without profiting. It is done in love and mercy to all. That the prepared souls may have no lack, there is much toil spent and much seed lost in communication of truth to them who understand it not. This is after the manner of God, and it is repeated at every sowing-time. The truth is by Him ever scattered wide of the prepared soil, well knowing that the spirit of evil has many emissaries hovering around, ready to snatch away the truth, though they do not appropriate it. For while the sower of corn may with some large-heartedness console himself for the loss of his grain by the thought that he is at least feeding the fowls, God casts abroad His truth in vain, knowing that the emissaries of evil, in snatching it away, only seek its destruction. Jesus, as the Sower of truth, goes His way mourning the loss, and in sadness of spirit says with Himself, in hearing of His fellow-workers, "If I had not come and spoken unto them, they had not had sin; but now they have no cloak for their sin." But how comes it that there are any whose minds are so closed against the truth that they understand it not, even when they hear it uttered? Part even of the corn-field may with good reason be given up for a footpath; but why should the hearts of any of the children of men be hardened as a beaten track? Where a pathway now is, the soil was once soft as that around; but now, having been long trodden by the foot, long untouched by the ploughshare, it has become hardened, causing the seed to roll as on a surface of stone. There is such hardening in personal history for minds long familiarised with the passing and repassing of evil thoughts, and long unacquainted with the penetrating power of conviction, which, like a ploughshare, pierces the soul, become hardened, not even understanding when they hear the words of eternal life. Yet even here there is hope. The present disappointment of the sower may not always continue. The pathway is not stone, but trodden soil, which, if it be only torn up by the ploughshare, may yet receive the seed, and yield a harvest.

Verses 5, 6.—"*Some fell upon stony places, where they had not much earth; and forthwith they sprung up, because they had no deepness of earth: and when the sun was up, they were scorched; and, because they had no root, they withered away.*" The loss in this case is longer in being discovered, because of a false promise satisfying the eye for a time, before failure becomes visible. Experience of this is common to every husbandman, and no less common is it with those who communicate to others the Divine message. All seed covered by the soil does not grow to maturity, so all truth, even when understood, does not lead to practical results. It finds entrance into the mind; but more than this is needful in order that it may yield spiritual result. Though the truth effects a lodgment, there may not be much depth of interest in it; if beneath the open soil there is great hardness of heart. At times this condition of things is laid bare, as when a cutting through the soil discovers its meagre depth, with hard rock underneath, there being but a turf and little more, the rock stretching for many feet downwards. This is the divinely-chosen illustration of a class of hearers described with much minuteness. Their mental condition is indicated by antithesis: pliableness of surface, with great hardness underneath; willingness to receive, but aversion to have the depths of the nature laid open to the influences of the truth; clearness of intellect, with hardness of heart. The successive stages of experience to one in this condition are carefully discriminated. The seeds fell into a thin surface soil, "and forthwith they sprung up, because they had not much deepness of earth." Quickness of growth is a first characteristic in the case, for there is emphasis on the *forthwith.* It is not the strongest growth which pushes fastest above the surface. The early appearance of growth is the reverse of satisfactory. Because of the impossibility of striking root downwards, the life has been forced quickly up, to an exposure for which it was ill prepared. There is in like manner a superficial readiness to receive the truth, and that with joy; delighting in its beauty, in the Divine compassion it discovers, and in the blessing it promises. Such appreciation of the truth, and delight in it, appear to give great promise; but the promise is deceitful. The interest fails for want of depth. The man has understanding, and joy too; but he has "no root in himself." The truth has not struck downwards into the mind, so as to gain full possession of it. Even a tree is easily laid low whose roots are spread only along the surface of a sandy soil. The seeds cast into the ground are here all represented on the field, but only as by withered straws, from which no harvest shall come. With little depth of soil from which to draw moisture, they are scorched by the sun, and wither away. If a man have not root in himself—if his mental state offer an effectual obstacle to the practical application of the truth,—we may be assured that weakness will appear when the strength of inner life is tried. When growth of the truth requires practice of self-denial, with endurance of reproach and suffering, he cannot submit to such things. He will surrender truth itself, rather than become, even in a small way, a martyr for its sake. Here also is lost seed, more disappointing than the former, because of the better promise. Yet is not even such a case utterly hopeless in prospect of another seed-time. The result must indeed be the same if the rock beneath continue as before; but there is a word of Scripture which asks these pertinent questions: "Is not my word like a fire? saith the Lord; and like a hammer that breaketh the rock in pieces?"

There is still another form in which failure appears, when the seed has been cast into the soil. Verse 7. —"*Some fell among thorns; and the thorns sprung up, and choked them.*" Wheat and thorns cannot both prosper. What holds true in the field, holds also in mental life. The soil can give only a limited measure of nourishment. When several plants draw of the nourishment sufficient only for one, all must be weakly; or one gaining the mastery, the others must die. The stronger growth will choke the weakly. The roots striking deepest into the ground will draw the most moisture. The growth raising its head highest will overshadow all below, and obtain for itself most of the light and warmth of the sun. Weeds grow rankest. Thorns grow more quickly than corn, and as they grow apace, they crowd and close in upon the corn, and then choke it. So it is with a mind where Divine truth has not room to grow. Disturbing cares multiply, as business absorbs thought; present difficulties, and hazards which the future may bring, add more to their power, until the mind's strength and interest are so absorbed, that religious life has not room to flourish. Or the state of matters may be such as prosperity occasions, and then riches engage the mind with deceitful promise of satisfaction, so alluring the mind that spiritual attractions seem feeble and unsatisfying. The heart is deceived, and the growth of the seed of the Word is stopped, choked by a stronger growth feeding on the same soil. For in mind, as in nature, it is true that weeds grow quickest; the evil flourishes rather than the good; fair promise is unfulfilled, because an evil growth has come more quickly to maturity.

Verse 8.—"*Other fell into good ground, and brought forth fruit, some an hundredfold, some sixtyfold, some thirtyfold.*" This is the true harvest, and is the result longest of being reached. The failures come first, the successes last. What distinguishes good ground we learn from the negative aspects already passed in review. It is broken up, not trodden down; it is deep, well-tilled soil, not soft surface-earth, with the flinty rock a few inches below; it is ground well cleared of weeds, not pre-occupied with thorns. The soul which offers good ground for the word of the kingdom is a mind in which the understanding is active, the heart is open to the sway of the truth, and cares and pleasures are kept subject to the requirements of religious life. When the word of the kingdom is received into such a soul, that word, like good seed, has sure and steady growth until the time of harvest. There is depth of soil to draw upon. Weeds there are even here, for the best soil is not altogether clear of them, but there are no weeds so rank as to choke the growth. Upon such souls the sunshine and the rains of heaven descend freely, and the harvest is sure. But while the seed is the same in all cases, and the favouring influences from above the same in value, the results are such as to show considerable diversity,—some an hundredfold, some sixtyfold, some thirtyfold. If we ask how this can be, the answer is already given by implication. Growth is according to depth. The more nearly the truth approaches toward a full possession of the soul, the more nearly does it come to the yielding of an hundredfold. The great Husbandman desires the largest return. Thus said the Saviour,—"Herein is my Father glorified, that ye bear *much* fruit." Yet whatever the measure, the Father shall be glorified in the increase. The "fruit shall be unto holiness, and the end everlasting life." Those who produce fruit thereby produce *seed* for new sowing. It is thus, and only thus, that men become sowers with Christ. In this way all become sowers who receive the truth indeed. Thus is it apparent that the whole growth of the fruits of righteousness is the result of the interposition of Divine grace. Such grace it is which provides the seed, casts it into the soil, and nourishes it in its growth, until the fulness of harvest is brought in amid great rejoicings.

"Who hath ears to hear, let him hear." There are here solemn lessons for gospel hearers, and for all who possess God's word. They have need to take heed how they hear, that their hearing be not with mere understanding and joy, but also with heart-searching and faithful application. And here are precious lessons for all sowers. They must not be discouraged though much seed be lost. It is ever so where the work of sowing goes on. But in order that sowing may not be in vain, the fallow ground must be ploughed up; the hammer of the Spirit must break the flinty rock; the thorns of selfishness, care, and evil desire must be uprooted; the good seed, "the word of the kingdom," must be cast into the soil, with prayer to the Lord of the harvest for favouring sunshine, that the fruits of holiness may be ripened. These things are all provided because of the gracious purpose of our God concerning this world. He works for the perpetuation and extension of righteousness on the earth. He is continually extending the area over which the life of righteousness is made to flourish, thus continually encroaching on the region where the growth of evil is favoured. Whether, therefore, we contemplate God's purpose, or the task He has assigned to His people as fellow-workers with Him, we must recognise that all progress is by sowing "the word of the kingdom,"— making known the truth concerning mercy and grace provided through Jesus.

CHAPTER XIV.

PROPAGATION OF A GODLESS LIFE IN THE WORLD.

THE TARES.

MATT. XIII. 24-30.

THERE are two sowers. The Son of God now throws light into the darkness of night, and upon the evil done in the midst of it. A sower is thus discovered who "cometh not to the light,"—one skulking to deeds of evil while men slumber. He is the Evil One, whose sowing is evil, seeking a harvest of evil. There is an Adversary of righteousness in the world. Though invisible to us, intelligence and deliberate purpose are at work for encouragement of the growth of wickedness.

There is an intimate relation between this parable and that of the Sower. The opening words of this seem to be the commencement of the former parable in a slightly varied form, a recommencement for further explanation. Verse 24.—"The kingdom of heaven is likened unto a man which sowed good seed in his field." The sowing of the good seed is still the first and most prominent fact; without this, the Enemy would have wanted occasion for the exercise of his malignity. On the other hand, this parable is needful in order that the parable of the sower may be completed. After the sower has sown his good seed, the full measure of unfavourable result is not told by mention of the fact that only some of the seed yields a harvest. We need explanation of the additional fact that there is seed he did not sow, which is springing up, and yielding a harvest after its own kind. The parable before us is introduced as the sad but necessary supplement to the other. In comparing the two parables, for discovery of the continuity of teaching involved, we observe a change in the structure of the second parable. In the former the seed represents the Word of God, the truth of the Gospel; in this, where a comparison between good seed and evil is introduced, "the good seed are the children of the kingdom," and "the tares are the children of the wicked one." The identity of thought is easily seen. The transition from the truth received to the person who receives it, and who moulds his life under its guiding power, is natural. The seed—the germinal principle, out of which the whole result springs—is, in the one case, the truth of God; in the other, falsehood, or an evil principle of life, which repels from God. The seed is thus contrasted as the true and the false, the good and the evil becoming operative within the moral nature of men. According to the character of the seed received and vitalised within, so is the man who receives it as to the principle of his life. Practically, the unity of teaching is secured. The sole difference in the two cases is this, that in the one case we speak of the germ, in the other of the plant in its developed state, with root, stalk, and fruit-laden head. As in the first parable, the Great Teacher makes the "seed" apply to the truth; and, as in the second, He makes "seed" apply to the persons, both views are taken, thereby making parabolic teaching more complete. We now, then, take the seed as representing the results, using it as applying to individuals,—living seed, germinating in individual life. There are good men and evil in the world—children of God and children of the Wicked One; and we are to consider how the evil life is propagated as well as the life of holiness,—how the kingdom of wickedness encroaches on the kingdom of righteousness, in retaliation for the encroachment which God is ever making on the dominion of evil.

Verses 24, 25.—"*The kingdom of heaven is likened unto a man which sowed good seed in his field; but while men slept, his enemy came and sowed tares among the wheat, and went his way.*" The field is the world (verse 38). Here is the kingdom over which God rules; but the world is a divided kingdom, for there is an enemy within it who has sway over many willing subjects. The presence of this *adversary* (Diabolos) is now to engage attention. He is the enemy of Jesus, the Son of God, the Saviour of the world; the cherisher of enmity to Him whose work it is to renew the life of righteousness on the earth. Enmity is the motive force urging him to take the position of Adversary. This Enemy not only refuses personal subjection; he scatters evil seed over the world, like thistle-down floating on the autumn breeze. This he does in wilful wickedness. It is not so much that he wishes to sow and gather a harvest from ground not his own, as that he wishes to injure the growth of the wheat, and lessen the value of the harvest to be reaped by the owner of the field. He comes designing mischief against the Lord of the kingdom, and as each one must who has evil intent, he comes stealthily. He is evil in heart, and defiant on that account; but he is timid withal, and would conceal himself if he could. Cowardice dwells in the heart of even the strongest evil-doer.

As the sowing of evil seed is what a man would not allow on his field, if he were aware of the purpose to do it, the due form of the parable is maintained by representing *the time when the mischief was done* as the time when "men slept." The story thus naturally harmonises with the ways of men; and, at the same time, by appropriate analogy, represents the deeds of the Wicked One as works of darkness, yet done under sufferance of God. If an adversary covets the shelter of the night, there is nothing surprising in the circumstance that he is not discovered either by owner or servants. The natural time for sleeping gives a safe time for mischief-working to those whose evil nature is strong enough to rouse them by night, that they may gain the opportunity they desire. The night-watchman has his lonely round in the great city, in acknowledgment of risk of ill-doing while men slumber. But natural as all this is according to the life of men, we need interpretation of it in relation to the Lord of the kingdom, for "he slumbereth not, nor sleepeth." So far as He is concerned, nothing can be done secretly. And, on the other hand, so far as the life of men can be perverted by evil counsel, this cannot be effected while men slumber. What, then, is conveyed by this introduction of sleeping-time as the season when the evil is done? Something, obviously, in reference to the feelings and designs of the Enemy; and something also as to the Lord, who has already sown the good seed. These two references lie in this marked introduction of intentional secrecy as to the sowing of evil seed. We see, first, how this sowing is thought of by the Adversary while he is engaged in it. He does it *as if he were successful* in concealing his agency in the matter. This fancied secrecy, leading to a fancied security, strengthens him in his evil course. He accomplishes his purpose and goes his way, as if he had never been there. With the devil success is the test of power. When at length the sun breaks over the scene, all is peaceful, as if the echoes of the night had not been awakened by the footsteps of any wanderer. The mantle of the night has covered the plot. It will take many days until the results discover what has been so secretly done. The Adversary thinks well of his evil work. The deceiver is self-deceived. The Lord of the field looks forth on the scene; He slumbers not; the darkness and the light are alike unto Him, and He marks what is done, not needing to wait later discovery. Yet there is no hindrance,—no utterance of wrath,—no infliction of vengeance. He sits still in quietness, not even calling His servants to interfere. Instead of sending them out to prevent this grievous mischief being done, He lets them take their rest. Here is instruction as to the moral government of God. The facts are familiar; their meaning needs pondering. Liberty of action is granted to the Adversary. Men are exposed to the influence of evil while occupied in the regulation of their life, and may even be reckoned among the children of the Wicked One. Their double liberty —liberty of influencing, and liberty of opening the mind to influence—is granted, even to the subversion of God's gracious purpose; because he who exerts the influence, and they who yield themselves up to it, are equally moral beings, for whom there must be such liberty. This is the answer to the question, Why does Jesus permit the sowing of the tares? It is part of the wider question: Why does God permit moral evil? The Son of Man casts the good seed into hearts ready to receive it. They who do so with willing mind themselves become sowers of this seed under His guidance. But, in contrast, freedom of action is allowed for sowing evil seed; and they who receive the evil into their hearts, in turn become sowers of evil. An active agency for propagation of evil thus exists in the world under sufferance of the Lord Himself. This dark side of the truth was for a moment discovered even in the previous parable. There were thorns in the field, which were suffered to grow, and even to choke the growth of good seed. As weeds grow in the ground, occasioning to the husbandman continual struggle with them in his preparation for harvest; so moral evil works in the universe, opposing the Lord as He provides for the fruits of righteousness to His own glory. The moral significance of this will appear before the parable is brought to a close.

Having considered the conduct of the sower of the evil seed, attention must next be directed to the seed itself, as a representation of *the children of the Wicked One,—* those whose life is a life of ungodliness. *Tares* are sown amongst the wheat. There is very general agreement as to our Lord's reference when speaking of "tares." The word does not apply to the tares or vetches, often sown by our farmers along with oats, as fodder for their horses. There could be no propriety in such a reference. The word rendered "tares" applies to a poisonous weed, a species of wild grass, usually known by the name of "darnel," and not unfrequently described in common language as bastard wheat. In view of the moral purpose of the parable, this last designation most aptly describes the thing selected. This bastard wheat is so like to wheat in the earlier stages of its growth, that it is difficult to distinguish between the two. At a later stage, the difference is so great that a child sees it at once. And this bastard wheat is really a poisonous herb, needing to be carefully separated from the wheat before it is put to use. The fitness of the analogy in all these points is obvious.

The mischief done is incalculable when this bastard wheat is scattered over a field already sown with good seed. It is indeed impossible at once to detect the mischief, though a time of discovery comes at length, but only when it is hopeless to guard against the mischief, or to prevent the progress of the poisonous growth. The Enemy sowed the tares among the wheat, and went his way. Verse 26.—"*But when the blade was sprung up, and brought forth fruit, then appeared the tares also.*" This description is exactly suitable to the darnel, so similar in appearance to the wheat, that it is only when the head appears that the complete difference between them is apparent. When, however, the blade brings forth fruit there is no risk of mistake. The analogy here is important. The Lord Himself observes the sowing; He easily recognises the distinction in the growth from the bursting of the germ. But His servants, as they are without the earlier knowledge, are also without the later. In watching the promise of early life, we know not what may be the result. The good and the evil may be wonderfully alike in youth; only when character is formed in more mature life, are we able to say of it, that it is in its very nature either the one or the other. The only certainty granted us, in the first instance, is that of sowing. There is no power of discriminating the type of life to be unfolded. In so far as we are workers in the matter, if we sow good seed, and watch its growth, we may have assurance as to the result. "Train up a child in the way he should go, and when he is old he will not depart from it." But if we are only observers of those not directly under our influence, we are left in uncertainty for a season. Until the blade spring up, and bring forth fruit, we can have no certainty. The result must declare.

The time surely comes, however, for discovery of the mischief. The ear is formed, and then it becomes clear that disaster has befallen the crop. There is not merely here and there a stalk of bastard wheat, which might have been accounted for by the condition of the ground; but all over the field the darnel is growing to an extent which can be explained only on the supposition that it has been regularly sown. Either the seed has been bad, or wilful mischief has been done. What shall be said of this? The servants are in perplexity. Verse 27.—"*So the servants of the householder came and said unto him, Sir, didst not thou sow good seed in thy field? from whence then hath it tares? He saith unto them, An enemy hath done this.*" The servants are in doubt; their master is sure. He knows the quality of his seed, and the state of his ground; and to his mind there is only one possible answer, even though his servants should think it hardly probable that any one could deliberately go over the whole field to scatter evil seed amongst the good. The perplexity and the certainty are as readily found in the spiritual world as in the natural. The power of evil in the world must occasion great perplexity to the disciples of Jesus Christ. How is the evil there? and how does it grow so plentifully? The disciples raise the questions as these servants did, and feel disturbed, as the servants were. The disciples cannot answer the questions. Naturally, they turn to their Master for explanation; but even thus they do not altogether escape their disturbed feeling. Their Master could not have done it. He is good, and would not sow evil seed. And is He not sovereign? How, then, did He suffer it? The statement of the parable is: Verse 28.—*An enemy hath done this.* The answer is good and complete for the natural world. It is good, but incomplete, for the spiritual world; and He who teaches by this parable leaves it incomplete, as all teaching on the subject is left. The mystery remains. In the management of our fields there is no marvel in the case. The owner of the field must retire to his house, and take rest in sleep; even when awake and watchful, he cannot always prevent the doing of the mischief, if an enemy watches for an opportunity of inflicting it. But the Lord of the spiritual kingdom can prevent it, at least by destruction of the Adversary. Yet He does not destroy. Thus mystery hangs over the question, *Why* is the Enemy *suffered* to do this thing? Our Lord is, however, quite explicit in replying to the question, *How* is evil so quickly, so quietly, and so widely extended? "An enemy hath done this." This answer occasions concern. There are, indeed, multitudes of men sufficiently at enmity with God to use their influence for the increase of evil in the world. The very same difficulty lies in this familiar fact.

But there is some additional perplexity in the existence of an unseen Enemy,—an Adversary of our race, an Enemy of God, as he is the enemy of righteousness. The parable expressly deals with this acknowledged difficulty. No new difficulty is discovered when we say that such an Adversary is never *recognised* by us. This belongs to the very nature of the case as stated. It is difficult to obtain direct evidence of the presence of a skulking foe. But the question of his agency is raised by observed facts. How is the darnel in the field? How is evil in the world? Making even the most liberal allowance for the natural wickedness of the heart, do we not find a power for evil not to be accounted for by the evil purpose of men? Is this not the very thing we wish to have explained? If so, when we are told that the facts to which we point are explained by the working of an invisible foe, it is of no account to reply that neither we nor our fellow-men have seen such an Adversary. If we had, we should not have needed to ask the question, nor seek its answer. We may object to invisibility, but such objection carries no force of reason with it. When shot is flying, it is of no account to say that no riflemen are within sight. When we are told that an unseen Adversary walks the world, it is enough that we are pointed for evidence of his agency to the effects of his working. The only objection open is objection to the inference drawn from recognised facts. Our Lord tells us of the existence of an enemy, and we have evidence painfully abundant of the evil work he does on the earth.

In this grievous state of things, the servants of God are concerned as to what should be done to subvert the design of the great Adversary. This concern finds expression in the parable. "*The servants said unto him, Wilt thou then that we go and gather them up? But he said, Nay; lest while ye gather up the tares, ye root up also the wheat with them.*" Evidence of genuine devotion to their master's service appears in this readiness to do the first thing occurring to their minds as proper to be done. The devotion of these servants has had its counterpart in the Christian Church. But the servants need guidance of their master, who restrains their eagerness, and shows the risk of acting on their first impulse. The evil is effectually done, and the only course now is to abide the harvest. The significance of this as applied to the kingdom of God in our world is far-reaching, and deeply solemnising. On the part of those who have committed themselves to a life-service for God, there is a strong desire to root out the evil from the kingdom. "Uprooting" is the term most adequately expressing the work they long to see accomplished. They would destroy evil everywhere, even if it were by destruction of the wicked. This indiscriminating desire to destroy evil is most characteristic of an early stage in discipleship. The apostles gave some evidence of subjection to it. But in the service of their Lord they had to learn to temper their ardour. It is a leading feature of the Gospel that it destroys this uprooting disposition, and trains to patience, supported by faith, in face of abounding evil. That there must be separation between the evil and the good, the Lord allows. But the time for that separation is not yet; it does not belong to us to effect it. To foster the life of righteousness is our present work. By and by separation will come, and then it shall be complete and final; but for the present the good and the evil must grow together. Wisdom and love are displayed in our Lord's determination. In the midst of that field, where the tares and the wheat are growing hopelessly intermingled, there is unseen a fountain of mercy, welling up from the depths, and quietly sending forth its waters for the nourishment of the weakest life there. There is, what the parable can only hint at,—cannot formally include,—some possibility that what appears to be darnel may yet prove to be good wheat. What is impossible under laws of nature is possible under laws of grace. Even if those delighting in evil draw encouragement from Divine forbearance, growing stronger in their iniquity, there are tender plants which are being nourished, in prospect of a richer harvest at last. The servants of the Lord must share the spirit of their Master. Christian zeal, if it burn as a flame, must not be a consuming fire. A hand quick to pluck may do grievous harm, while the hand diligent in the work of cultivation may promote unexpected growth of righteousness.

The significance of the owner's words as applicable to God's kingdom now demands attention. The determination as to both growing together is only temporary forbearance for the sake of increase of righteousness. A striking contrast is thus introduced. The Enemy sows tares in order to destroy the wheat: the Owner spares the tares in order to increase his harvest. There is deeper truth underneath, which is only indirectly hinted at, for no parable is sufficient to convey the whole truth. We must wait for a later parable—that of the Leaven—before the spreading power of the life of righteousness can be clearly introduced. Meanwhile, guided by the present line of illustration, we are led to contemplate from afar final separation of the evil from the good. The provision for this really begins here, for sowing of good seed into hearts ready to receive it, is effectual separation of them from others, as sowing evil seed separates by its development in the life. The seed determines the nature of the harvest; tares must yield according to their kind. The Gospel is a spiritual test by which separation is begun. But there comes into view, far in advance, complete separation, such as takes place at the harvest, when the tares are separated from the wheat. The reason for separation lies in the difference of the two. It is because they do so completely differ now, that they shall be separated at last. The word now is, "*Let both grow together;*" but it is only "*until the harvest.*" For the owner of the field adds: "*And in the time of harvest I will say to the reapers, Gather ye together first the tares, and bind them in bundles to burn them: but gather the wheat into my barn.*" This foreshadows the great future awaiting our race. It is, indeed, presented under cover of analogy, but analogy employed on account of the accuracy of its teaching. And it is to be remembered that wherein the analogy differs from the reality, it differs by conveying so much *less* than the reality, not at all by transcending it. Lest, however, there should be uncertainty attaching to the use of analogy, Jesus Himself interprets in words which leave no room for doubt: "The harvest is the end of the world; the reapers are the angels. As therefore the tares are gathered and burned in the fire; so shall it be in the end of this world. The Son of man shall send forth his angels, and they shall gather out of his kingdom all things that offend, and them which do iniquity, and shall cast them into a furnace of fire : there shall be wailing and gnashing of teeth. Then shall the righteous shine forth as the sun in the kingdom of their Father." The completeness of separation at the time of harvest is explicitly declared. All things that offend, and them which do iniquity, shall be gathered out of the kingdom. The poisonous shall be parted from the wholesome. The sovereignty which suffers the growth of an evil life, and that with designs of mercy, travels onwards to a time of judgment. Separation is inevitable, on account of the holiness of the kingdom, and the evil nature of them which do iniquity. The whole dread reality cannot be told. Figurative language flows over from the parable into its interpretation. The "fire" of the parable is a "furnace" in its interpretation. We can reach but a faint conception of the reality of Divine condemnation. Of the dark side of destiny, as of its converse, distinguished by exceeding brightness, we must say, "Eye hath not seen, nor ear heard, neither hath it entered into the heart of man to conceive." We leave the parabolic, coming here in view of personal responsibility in man and absolute purity in God. God's holiness is here manifested. His own people have indeed suffered by growing up in companionship with the evil; but they have also gained. If the marks of the trying ordeal are upon them at the end, there are also the proofs of greater strength gained in the struggle for existence. Hampered here, they shall be set in a large place hereafter. The Saviour's words now break away from the restraints of analogy. "The righteous shall shine forth as the sun in the kingdom of their Father." The golden grain gathered in the heavenly kingdom shall shine as a sun in the firmament. And again we must say, God's holiness is manifested. Personal responsibility is brought to light; they who have refused the Gospel, and have preferred to do evil, are condemned according to that which they have done. Not in hard defiance, but in overwhelming woe, do they meet the issue. There is "wailing and gnashing of teeth." The Enemy himself, the sower of the tares, does not here come into view, though his condemnation, his utter defeat, is clearly involved. He sowed the tares seeking to destroy the wheat, yet the wheat harvest is gathered. The terrible contrast remains; the furnace into which the tares are cast is that "prepared for the devil and his angels." In the storehouse of the husbandman there must be separation, and when that is complete, there remains only the burning of the poisonous darnel. The significance lying in this analogy may be most surely reached by keeping before the mind the contrast between wheat and darnel. The one is to be preserved as the treasure of the husbandman; the other is to be separated from the wheat with scrupulous care, and cast out as not only useless but injurious. The harvest of poison is appointed unto the fire of judgment,—a judgment which shall be conspicuously the condemnation of "the devil and his angels."

CHAPTER XV.

THE BENEFICENT INFLUENCE OF GOD'S KINGDOM IN THIS WORLD.

THE MUSTARD SEED.

MATT. XIII. 31, 32.

IN this parable the Great Teacher shifts the point of view from which to contemplate the spiritual kingdom. A completely distinct aspect of God's kingdom is thus presented. Under the similitude of a true and a false wheat, we have been shown first how men grow up in the favour of God, yielding fruit to His glory; and next, how wicked men grow up, introducing confusion into the kingdom, and yielding an evil fruit, which God must separate from the good. In their relation to God's kingdom, men have been distinguished into two classes, subjects and aliens. The individuality of the members of the kingdom thus received prominence, for they are as thoroughly distinguishable as separate stalks of wheat waving in the breeze.

In the parable before us, the unity of the kingdom becomes conspicuous, the individuality of its members subordinate. The figure is changed accordingly. Verse 31.—"*The kingdom of heaven is like to a grain of mustard-seed, which a man took and sowed in his field: which indeed is the least of all seeds; but when it is grown, it is the greatest among herbs, and becometh a tree.*" The kingdom is a tree; its subjects are as birds sheltering under its shadow. As it grows and spreads out its branches, it is shown that it has been planted by God for the spiritual good of men. The kingdom here appears as an organic whole, a source of blessing for all who come under its shade. Taking the illustration at its earliest stages, we must have regard not only to the "*grain of mustard-seed,*" but also to the presence and action of "*the man who took it, and sowed it in his field.*" That the agent in sowing this grain of seed is the Son of Man admits of no doubt. The Saviour is not here represented by the tree; for then would His disciples be the branches, as in the fifteenth chapter of John's Gospel. He is the man who sowed the seed in his field. Our Lord having thus a distinct place in the parable, we are precluded from thinking of the tree as a symbol for Christ Himself, and afterwards for His people collectively, as His representatives on the earth. Further, we are prevented from seeing here any allusion to the lowliness of the Saviour's birth, or the feebleness of His infancy, understood by some to be implied in the image of the little seed. The incongruity of the description, verse 32,—"*the least of all seeds*"—as attributed to the Divine Redeemer, is so glaring as to warn us against such methods of interpretation. The kingdom is here represented as something to which men come, and in coming to which they receive shelter and comfort. At first sight this might seem to point to the Church, as the outward manifestation of the kingdom,—a view which might have been accepted had the branches of the tree represented the members of the Church. But when the members are not the branches, but are sheltered among the branches, something distinct from the Church seems intended. Both in this parable and in that of the Leaven, the reference is clearly to the truth of the kingdom, as in the parable of the Sower the seed is the word of the kingdom. This parable is concerned with the outward exhibition of the truth; the Leaven, with the inward and hidden application of it. The kingdom of heaven is a kingdom of truth; this truth is displayed to the world in outward manifestation, and also applied to the souls of men as an unseen influence. We have accordingly two parables, the one representing the visible, the other the hidden operation of the truth revealed in Jesus.

The truth of the Gospel—the truth as to the pardoning mercy and renewing grace provided in Jesus—was as a very little seed, planted in the earth by the Messiah, and that so quietly that the act hardly attracted the attention of the world. The significance of the act was not understood even by those who observed it. To the future was intrusted the discovery of the importance for the world of this little seed. It was destined to spring up and attain a great stature, spreading itself forth on every side, attracting attention all around.

That *the mustard-tree* was selected in preference to the olive, or the sycamore, or the cedar, or the fig, or the vine, merely by accident, or because it was seen growing near, no one will imagine who has minutely studied the teaching of the Lord Jesus. In His discourses careful selection of details is so obvious, and the end to be served by the selection is so plain, that we are deterred from glancing superficially at any distinctive term. Jesus has selected a tree whose seed is small, as compared with the height it attains—a fruit-bearing tree, and a tree whose fruit is remarkable for its pungency. These features are not affected by disputes as to whether the plant intended is the common mustard plant, or the mustard-tree, known by the name of khardal (*Salvadora persica*), as Dr. Royle has maintained. The dispute concerns only the matter of height, and not the properties of the tree—the difference between seven feet and twenty-five; and on the ground of height alone we prefer Dr. Royle's view. But the properties are the same in either case. The mustard-seed was proverbial for its smallness; and in this fact was found one of the required elements of analogy. But in its fruit there is, no doubt, something additionally important for the pupose of illustration. It is not the cedar which is chosen, for the Lord seeks a tree which will yield fruit, and not merely timber; He takes a tree whose main use is found in its continued growth, and not in its being cut down and divided asunder. The vine is not selected, for that has been otherwise appropriated, that the branches may represent believers yielding the fruits of righteousness unto God, whereas this is taken to indicate the yielding of fruit for the use of man. If, then, we are correct in understanding the tree to represent Gospel truth, we find clear analogical teaching. All truth is fitly represented as a tree—a germ planted in the world, showing its vitality by shooting up and spreading forth its branches. The truth made known in Jesus, constituting a kingdom of God on earth, is properly represented as a tree providing shelter and yielding fruit.

We must, however, dwell on the special features of the mustard-tree having illustrative value. First and most prominent among these, is *the smallness of the seed* in proportion to the greatness of the tree. The mustard-seed is spoken of as "the least of all seeds." This is not meant as an absolute statement, but is introduced as a proverbial one. "Small as a mustard-seed" was a current expression among the people to indicate anything insignificant. The Saviour accepts this as representing the seed of truth He was then planting in the earth. In doing so, He does no more than indicate what most of the people thought of the revelation He had made. To many of them it was insignificant indeed. To some it appeared as no seed, but a mere dried and withered husk; something of so little worth, that if once put in the ground, it should be buried for ever and no more remembered. But He who brings it, and leaves it in the earth, says it is indeed small, but it is a *seed;* it has vitality, and needs no more than to be left in order to live and grow apace. Few gave heed to the sowing of this seed, and few of those who did had much prospect of its growth. But the Lord Himself had no misgiving. That which finds only a hiding-place in Palestine will spring up, and shoot forth on every side, until it occasion worldwide interest. This is the confidence of the Great Teacher who proclaims the truth, which finds small acceptance. He is like the man who has hid a mustard-seed in his garden, and has set a mark at the spot. He is content to wait, and when the first feeble signs of growth appear, he knows well to what extent that plant will yet expand. The reality is greater than the analogy. The God of creation draws from nature illustration of His procedure in the kingdom of grace. But to understand aright such illustrations as are employed in this way, we must rise from man's part in tilling the field to God's part in ruling the world. The man who sows mustard-seed in his garden must acknowledge uncertainty as to its growth. Many adverse influences may obstruct it. But it is otherwise under Divine procedure. The God who gives the seed provides the sunshine and the rain to nourish its growth. And so the God who gives gospel truth supplies the Spirit's quickening power to make that truth extend its range of influence all over the world. Men may cut down the tree to its very roots, but it will sprout again, and grow strong as before. Men may despise this truth hid in the midst of the earth—they may in their heart dislike it—they may scorn those who receive it, and attempt to banish the truth from the earth by persecution. All these forms of opposition have been tried; but all with little effect. Scorn has not withered it— the weapons raised against it have not prevailed. He who planted the seed has looked down from heaven's height, beholding the attempts to injure the tree of His planting. He Himself has provided the sunshine and the moisture by which it has been nourished. That which is false may grow quickly as thorns do, yet soon disappear; while that which is true may grow slowly, yet be of sure continuance. Error begins to wither at the top; its development proves its destruction. Truth has strength to sustain the most extended growth, becoming stronger and firmer in its roots the higher its branches rise, and the wider they spread.

If, then, the growth of the tree be certain, we have next to consider *the outspreading of the branches*.

Expanding growth means extended shelter for men throughout the world. "*When it is grown, it is the greatest among herbs, and becometh a tree, so that the birds of the air come and lodge in the branches thereof.*" This history of growth is in accordance with the natural development of the mustard-seed. The plant becomes great, even the greatest among herbs. This growth is simple organic development, such as belongs to every shrub or tree. It is the unfolding of the plant towards maturity. So it is with the living power of gospel truth, shooting upwards and spreading outwards, widening its influence over the nations. Its unfolding is its outspreading amongst the tribes of men. From its native soil it springs, advancing till it spreads out its branches on all sides, reaching forth towards all Gentile nations, while men of all climes gather under its shade. The growth here meant is thus plainly the extended discovery of the truth, accompanied by extended experience of its comforts. These two go together, and are essential to each other. There is an outstretching of gospel truth, and an ingathering of men under its shelter. As birds find a retreat among the branches, so do men find that the truth of God provides under its cover a soothing rest. This is of the very essence of the parable, showing how certainly growth of Christ's kingdom must involve at once a wider revelation of the truth, and a wider acceptance of it. Each believer reaps the benefit of his faith by reposing under the assurance of Divine mercy and grace discovered in Jesus.

But the significance of the parable is not exhausted, when we refer to the refuge for men provided in the kingdom of God. The branches and leaves of any tree may suffice to symbolise shelter. Our Lord, however, selected *a tree which yielded fruit* of a very distinct kind, and of which many of the birds of the air were particularly fond. So strong was their liking for its fruit that numbers made this tree their favourite retreat, being attracted thither not merely by its pleasant shade, but also by its seed. This was, indeed, their chief attraction. The pungent and stimulating power of the seed was so relished as to induce them to prefer it to other kinds of fruit within their reach. Here a wider analogy comes into view. A fruit which, in its influence on the body, is pungent to taste, stimulating to vital energy, and healing in sickness, well represents the spiritual effects of the word of the kingdom. The truth of the Gospel is capable of producing varied effects on the mind which receives it. There is in it that which condemns, and yet, while condemning, quickens the whole activity of the mind, and exercises a healing power within the moral nature. God's word to man is in its first phase a word of condemnation, having such pungency as readily to occasion disrelish. Dealing with men as transgressors, who, on account of the disordered state of their nature, persist in their evil course, it denounces unsparingly all moral evil. Its first influence,—what we may describe as the tasting of the word,—is disturbing in its pungency. If it carry a blessing, it begins by causing uneasiness. This form of disturbance, which in its outward aspect had been represented by the sweeping of the house in the parable of The Lost Piece of Money, is here presented in its deeper aspect as a personal and inward experience. But, in advance of its condemning influence, the word of the kingdom also stirs spiritual energy, and awakens new hope. It is the great stimulating influence for spiritual life. Divinely revealed truth as to abounding mercy, present grace, and future glory, animates the whole spiritual nature, rousing it to the higher activity of which it is capable. Thus by combining sternest condemnation with loftiest encouragement, it exercises at once a healing and a quickening power.

The truth of the Gospel, growing and spreading as a tree in the world, is as the mustard-seed in its influence upon the spirit of man. God's condemnation of all sin is so stern in itself, and so powerful in its influence, that when the soul is thrown open to its penetrating force, tears of penitence flow freely from the eyes, and a fountain of strange sorrow is opened. Yet, painfully searching as this is, the soul once moved by it, so far from being repelled, is attracted, finding a new stimulating power in the truth which so pierces at its entrance. The mind is roused to spiritual exercise previously unknown. The more clearly its own condemnation is recognised, the more fully does the mind rest in saving grace, and cherish ardour of devotion to the Saviour, whose troubling of the soul introduces peace. Here one paradox of God's kingdom is explained—how trouble and peace dwell together—how grief of soul gives strength, and fits for joyful service. And here, too, we see the crowning result, in the fulness of praise ascribed to God by the members of His kingdom in every land. The birds of heaven not only nestle in the branches of the tree, and pick freely of its seed, but warble their sweetest songs under its shade. So men, rejoicing together in the gospel of love, burst forth in praises to the God of Heaven, who has discovered Himself as the God of Salvation. They are blessed who enjoy the shelter, taste of the fruit, and join in the praises of the kingdom of God. Doubly blessed are they who promote the growth of the sheltering branches of this tree of life, that others may share its shelter, and that the praises of God may be more widely extended, in anticipation of the expected day of universal praise.

CHAPTER XVI.

THE ASSIMILATING POWER OF GOSPEL TRUTH.

THE LEAVEN.

MATT. XIII. 33.

In the parable of the Mustard-Seed we have the outspreading of the kingdom of God as a tree sheltering men and yielding valuable fruit. In this parable the kingdom of God is represented as silently and secretly extending in the world. This discovers an inward influence, gradually bringing men to perfection otherwise unattainable. In both parables the kingdom is a kingdom of truth. In the one, it is an outward revelation, manifesting Divine love to all men; in the other, an inward power, touching, subduing, and elevating the souls receiving it.

The two parables are companions; but companions by contrast, and for the sake of contrast. The parable of the Leaven, so far from being a slightly varied repetition of that which preceded it, is essentially different. Embraced in a single verse, its brevity may at first tempt the reader to regard it as slight and simple; but study of it will satisfy the searcher of the Scriptures that it needs more than usual carefulness in exposition. In it there is little of narrative, but the absence of this is more a source of difficulty than a means of simplification. Verse 33.—"*The kingdom of heaven is like unto leaven, which a woman took and hid in three measures of meal, till the whole was leavened.*"

The fundamental thought is clear. It is this: Gospel truth in its influence upon the hearts of men is like the working of leaven which ultimately pervades the mass. There is much to be unfolded, however, before we can reach a definite conception of the whole kingdom of God on earth, as described by means of this figure. The kingdom of our Lord is a kingdom of truth. It is not by an exercise of authority that God subdues us to Himself;[1] nor is it by a mystic influence, without use of means; it is by the instrumentality of truth, which first gains admission to the soul, and then permeates it.

We have, then, to consider the influence of truth as it resembles the working of leaven, and afterwards the spiritual dominion obtained through means of the truth as it may be likened to the ultimate dominion of leaven in a mass of flour.

Leaven is the familiar agent for production of light, palatable bread. Microscopic investigation has quite recently shown that the leavening process results from the rapid growth of a plant, propagating cells in the midst of surrounding material brought into a favourable condition. It involves a species of fermentation, which makes the dough porous, exposing it more readily to the action of fire. Leaven was originally obtained

---

[1] As Luther, in his own strong way, has said: "I can drag no man to the gospel by the hair of his head; I cannot drive any man to heaven. It must be faith which gives God the glory."

by the decaying process in dough itself, now more commonly it is taken in the form of yeast generated in brewing. Leaven is thus an agency obtained in the process of decay, which nevertheless contributes towards preservation of the mass pervaded by it. Out of the evil comes forth good. By use of that which is offensive, there is obtained that which is most palatable.

Reference to the nature of leaven sufficiently explains the circumstance that earlier Scriptural usage represents it as an evil agency; the advantage gained in the preparation of bread by use of leaven sufficiently explains how, in later Scriptural usage, leaven becomes an agency for good. Acting in the midst of decay, it will accelerate it. Introduced amongst good flour, which has been moistened and brought to a favourable temperature, it will originate a species of vital action, which, when taken at the proper moment, will produce wholesome bread, if the mass be worked up and subjected to the action of fire. The natural action of leaven is evil, tending to corruption. The second and applied action is good, producing the finest of bread. There is thus in leaven singular fitness for being employed as a type of the mysterious blending of evil and good in human life, and the power of self-propagation belonging to both.

In turning to the symbolic teaching of Scripture, it is at once apparent that the symbolism is twofold, in harmony with this double action of leaven. First, leaven is used to represent evil. This occurs in connection with the rescue of the Israelites from Egyptian bondage, the type of escape from evil. At the institution of the Passover—an ordinance commemorative of special deliverance granted to the people of God—it was required that they should put away all leaven, and eat only unleavened bread. "Seven days shall there be no leaven found in your houses" (Exod. xii. 19). As symbolic of the moral corruption which is offensive to God, it was to be cast out. Old Testament Scripture, warning against evil, takes leaven as the symbol of its influence. In harmony with this, leaven was generally excluded from the offerings presented to Jehovah. There is, however, a notable exception, introducing the other side of symbolic usage. As the Passover represented deliverance from Egypt, the Feast of First-Fruits represented introduction into Palestine. Passing into the land of promise, there is transition from the symbolism of evil in leaven to the symbolism of good in the same. In the time of harvest, a sheaf of the first-fruits was presented as a wave-offering before God; and at the close of fifty days after the gathering of the first sheaf a new meat-offering was presented, consisting of two loaves of *fine flour baked with leaven.* "Ye shall bring out of your habitations two wave-loaves of two tenth-deals: they shall be of fine flour; they shall be baken with leaven; they are the first-fruits unto the Lord" (Lev. xxiii. 17). Leaven, producing the finest bread, is thus offered to the Lord in thanksgiving.

Passing from the Old Testament to the New, the same double usage appears. Our Lord bade His disciples beware of the leaven of the Pharisees, which is hypocrisy, an evil acting quickly in a corrupt nature; and when the disciples misunderstood His meaning, He told them He spoke not of the leaven of bread, but of the leaven of doctrine. So also in Paul's First Epistle to the Corinthians (v. 6-8), leaven is used as the symbol of evil: "Purge out therefore the old leaven, that ye may be a new lump." This is a continuance of Old Testament symbolism; while the descriptive term "*old* leaven" is acknowledgment of the introduction of a *new* leaven. If there is a leaven of malice and wickedness, there is also a leaven of love and righteousness. When, therefore, among the parables we come upon one which likens the kingdom of God to leaven as something good, there is nothing perplexing; there is only a recognition of the double action of leaven in conformity with Old Testament usage. In the one case, we have the putting away of leaven, that the heart may not be corrupted; in the other, we have the reception of leaven, that the heart may be invigorated. In the latter case, the soul leavened by righteousness is presented in thankfulness to God, in analogy with Old Testament practice, which made the leavened bread a thank-offering for Divine goodness.

The symbol of leaven implies *more than diffusive power*. Diffusion through the flour is as characteristic of water where no leaven is used, as of leaven itself. Both moisture and some degree of heat are needful in order that leaven may permeate the mass. Leaven hid amongst dry flour will not act upon it. The flour must be brought into a suitable condition by moisture, in order that the energy of leaven may manifest itself. Thus it appears that more is involved in the action of leaven than diffusion through the mass. There is an *expansive power* at work, altering the character of the material on which it operates. It must therefore be taken into account that the leaven of gospel truth has a marked adaptation to the moral nature of man. The Word of God has energy which will act upon the whole nature, if only that nature be not as the dry flour, but be brought into a state of intelligent interest suitable for the free action of the truth. Spiritual susceptibility is, however, needful in order to experience the assimilating power of practical truth. There is a law of application for truth, in neglect of which the presence even of gospel truth in the world is altogether unavailing to man. Hence the call to hear,—to take heed how we hear. And hence also the frequent allusion to the outpouring of God's Spirit as water upon the dry and thirsty land. In connection with the leaven, there is need for both the water and the warmth, that the latent energy may become operative. There is power in the word, but there must be intelligent appreciation, and the influence of God's Spirit, in order that the energy may become efficient.

The Word of God is *hid* in the souls of men who receive it, as leaven is hid in meal.[1] It is hidden; and like the leaven, its action depends upon certain conditions favouring its influence. As the leaven gives no sign of its power except by being placed within meal moistened and brought up to a certain temperature, so is it with gospel truth, which is powerful only when received and applied in a heart warm with spiritual interest, under the quickening of the Holy Spirit. When gospel truth is thus lodged in the soul, it at once becomes practically operative, and thenceforth continues, after the manner of the leaven, to exert a transforming influence. As leaven changes the character of the bread, expanding its substance, and preparing it for the action of fire, so spiritual truth, beginning to operate

[1] Lisco is surely wrong in making concealment the prominent feature of both the mustard-seed and the leaven.

in the soul, changes its character, expanding the heart by awakening new and lofty desires, laying open the whole soul to the favouring influences of the Holy Spirit. In all this the analogy is strikingly exact. Truth permeates and changes the soul as leaven does the dough in which it is placed. But, in order to this, truth must be intelligently received, must be treasured by the receptive power belonging to mind, and must be applied in regulation of the motive forces, so as to form the character anew, thereby bringing the heart completely under its sway. Thus only can the soul become a kingdom of truth—a kingdom which is righteousness, and peace, and joy in the Holy Ghost.

Having considered the action of truth on the mind, we must observe the *instrumentality* employed to bring about the desired result. "The kingdom of heaven is like leaven, *which a woman took and hid* in three measures of meal." This plainly points to human agency, "*took and hid*" being a double phrase, indicating the bringing of the leaven, and the covering of it up within the meal. Does all this belong only to the circumstances connected with the use of leaven, or is it meant to carry parabolic significance? *The woman* is introduced in accordance with the customs of domestic life, the three measures of meal being mentioned as a quantity commonly used for a household. The woman is sufficiently conspicuous here, though not so prominent as in the parable of the ten pieces of silver. There the woman is introduced first, as are the shepherd and the father in the other two parables of the fifteenth chapter of Luke's Gospel. "What woman having ten pieces of silver, if she lose one piece, doth not light a candle, and sweep the house, and seek diligently till she find it?" In this parable, however, the woman is subordinate: "The kingdom is like unto leaven." There is a distinct reference to her instrumentality as performing an important part, nevertheless it is kept in a secondary position. Human agency may come into exercise, and commonly it does much in this matter, therefore the woman has a definite place in accordance with the work belonging to the Church. But human agency may perform no conspicuous part, on which account it happens that the woman is not here introduced as the central feature in the parable. Since, however, there is a constant, if not an invariable, use of instrumentality in disseminating the truth, the woman's part is definitely referred to, and so is the quantity of three measures, indicating that human agency in this matter can influence only a limited area.

Taking now a general survey of the parabolic representation, there is brought into view *a hidden kingdom steadily advancing*, though it "cometh not with observation." Contemplating this, we advance beyond individual references. There is, indeed, a kingdom in the soul of each believer,—a kingdom greater than the whole realm of nature. But a larger kingdom is introduced to notice—a kingdom of many souls—a kingdom hidden in the world, yet advancing to occupy the whole earth. By the operations of His grace God has a hidden kingdom of truth and righteousness in the world. Its existence is a marvel. Leaven is hid by a woman in meal previously unleavened, but ready for household use. But here the good leaven is hid in that which has already been permeated with an evil leaven. A kingdom of spiritual truth is silently extending through a kingdom of spiritual error; a kingdom of righteousness is advancing upon a still wider kingdom of evil. This conflict of two leavens, the evil and the good, makes the action of the spiritual leaven doubly marvellous. Gospel truth acts as a leaven of righteousness, not upon good material, but upon evil. And so effectually does this spiritual leaven work upon the springs of action within the soul, that it gradually gains ascendency over the evil leaven which had corrupted it. Secretly and silently is the internal change wrought out, so that the evidence of its progress appears only slowly, as its effects come upon the surface of life. Men being taught by God as to His love and mercy towards the sinful, trust rises up within their souls, and with this is stirred a deep and ardent love to Him. By the growing power of this love the evil leaven of wickedness is slowly expelled from the heart, thereby throwing open the whole nature more effectually to the action of truth and of all heavenly influence. The process thus begun is progressive. It does not, indeed, advance with equal rapidity at all times. Progress here, as elsewhere, is dependent on fixed conditions. The action of leaven is retarded or quickened by the degree of heat applied to the mass. In like manner the action of Gospel truth on the soul is according to the warmth of the love maintained in fellowship with God. On this condition progress is continuous. The power of truth is not lessened by its diffusion over a wider area. While widening the range of its action, it seems to multiply its original energy. Applied here to one mass and there to another, the action of the leaven of righteousness is still the same. Distinct examples of its operation may seem as if they were only isolated occurrences, having little connection with each other.

But they are not. Separated by a wide interval, they are working towards a more extended influence over the human race. They have important relations to the world as a whole, and also to the world's history. "The kingdom of heaven is like unto leaven, which a woman took, and hid in three measures of meal, until the whole was leavened."

This kingdom, though advancing secretly, is preparing for a glorious revelation. It is not a kingdom of mechanical force, but of something greater; for force were the mere overwhelming of human weakness. It is not a kingdom gained by enticing men to enter on irksome service, but a kingdom of grace, where subjection is esteemed by the subject to be highest privilege. It is a kingdom of truth, begun in the manifestation of truth, and extended by its acceptance among men. This truth, moving within the hearts of men, is the grandest of all truth; it concerns the glory of the Divine nature, carrying in it provision for the glorifying of the sons of men. This truth, when accepted, harmonises the whole nature of man, convincing the intellect, satisfying the conscience, elevating all the motives. By its increasing influence "the kingdom of heaven" is extended in our sinful world, as a kingdom of purity over which God shall reign with joy, and upon which the light of His favour shall continue to shine through eternal ages, when the confusion and corruption of earth have passed away.

CHAPTER XVII.

THE EXCEEDING VALUE OF SPIRITUAL GOOD FOUND IN GOD'S KINGDOM.

HID TREASURE.

MATT. XIII. 44.

UNDER the analogy of "hid treasure" another aspect of the concealed condition of God's kingdom is pointed out by our Lord. The truth of God is hid as *seed* in the field, developing first beyond observation, afterwards before the eyes of men. In so far as received by men, it is hid as *leaven* in their minds, spreading its influence in a manner which cannot be checked even by those most opposed to it. This placing and spreading of gospel truth in the world is the doing of the God of mercy, seeking deliverance of men from evil, and restoration of a kingdom of righteousness. But, in addition to these representations, the good of God's kingdom is as *hid treasure*, concealed from common observation, which men must eagerly seek if they would make it a personal possession.

In the parables of the Mustard-Seed and of the Leaven the spiritual kingdom appears as a Divine possession in a corrupt world. The one illustrates the external growth, the other the secret spiritual expansion of the kingdom; both apply to it as a whole, discovering the gracious love of God to man. In these parables there is little trace of individual relations to the kingdom. In this parable, however, and in its companion, The Pearl of Great Price, it is shown how the kingdom becomes the possession of man, so that an individual member of our race may say, "The kingdom is mine." We thus obtain *a twofold view of proprietorship* in the kingdom, Divine and human. We are now to consider how the kingdom of God may become the personal property of men. "The kingdom of heaven" in this world is the kingdom of righteousness, which is the highest manifestation of Divine sovereignty. In the laws of nature there is a subordinate manifestation of Divine power, an indication of the Divine *will*, operating for accomplishment of temporary ends, and in directions liable to be changed. Judicial sovereignty over the rebellious is a natural accompaniment of the Divine relation to moral beings; an expression of the Divine *nature*, and unalterable accordingly. But God's highest sovereignty appears in grace. This is the marvellous expression of His *good-will* as He interposes for deliverance from a sinful condition otherwise doomed to inevitable condemnation. Here also is man's most precious possession—the true riches of men. Material substance is subordinate as a possession, so also is the higher property acquired in growing acquaintance with nature's secrets. Of that which belongs to our personality itself, righteousness is the noblest possession. The gospel of God thus provides us with a scale of values, offering great treasure, in the acquisition of which man becomes possessed of the highest riches.

The kingdom of heaven is like unto treasure. In this

utterance of the Saviour we have a marked feature of Bible teaching, insisting that man's highest property is that which belongs to his own being. Scripture uniformly leads a man to this reflection: Of all that I have, that which I am is not only the most enduring, but also the most important. How then shall we contemplate "the kingdom of heaven" so as to regard it as a human possession? If we reach the proper point of view, we shall easily discover how truly it is of all human property the one treasure. RIGHTEOUSNESS is the grand feature of the kingdom in which the proprietorship of God and of man plainly meet. The kingdom is mercy and grace, these belonging exclusively to the Sovereign. It includes peace and joy, belonging exclusively to the subject. But RIGHTEOUSNESS is that which is God's while it is man's, and is man's while it is God's. The standpoint for observation is thus secured. Righteousness is treasure for man; human righteousness, as a form of life, distinguishing man's own being. Moral purity may, by God's grace, be reckoned in the sum of possible possessions, and "the kingdom of heaven" has been established by the Lord Jesus Christ to the intent that it may be secured by men. Such moral purity does not consist in mere absence of sin. It is a possession—a treasure—the highest human treasure. Among the possessions belonging to man as part of his own being, the intellectual is more in value than the physical, but the moral is still higher than the intellectual. By moral purity, then, is meant right principles of action, harmonious dispositions, perennial stores of holy energy. Within this the largest sum of human treasure falls to be computed. In its possession the worst poverty is escaped, the highest wealth is secured—wealth valuable in itself, and procuring the greatest blessedness. If this possession be once lost by man, lowering him in the scale of being, it may seem impossible that it should ever be regained; it may appear more hopelessly lost than that which has sunk to ocean's vastest depth, or been consumed by fire. But the gospel comes proclaiming the possibility of that which we fear to be impossible, presenting a practical solution of the great mystery of moral life, though leaving the problem beset with many perplexities. By God, moral purity is made conspicuous in the circle of human possessions, and any member of our sinful race who attains it, finds the kingdom of heaven. The sovereignty of this kingdom is exercised to this end, that special privileges may be conferred on all who would escape from sin and account righteousness their chief treasure. On all such the Sovereign bestows peace, strength, and gladness in their most valuable forms. This kingdom is thus a form of life; and such life, as is true of life in all forms, is the gift of God. The present parable guides us in inquiring how this life, as a treasure, is acquired.

Spiritual good is like *treasure hid in a field*. This saying seems at first difficult of interpretation. The blessings of salvation are openly proclaimed in Scripture, their exact nature and the precise means of reaching them are made known. Acceptance of the gospel is even pressed upon men as a free gift from God. And yet, from the structure of this parable, it is clear that in some sense the kingdom of God is really hid from men, notwithstanding the proclamations so freely made, and the invitations widely circulated. To be convinced of the accuracy of this description, we have only to inquire if the existence and value of the treasure are apparent to all who hear the gospel proclaimed. So far is this from being the case, that the worth of the treasure becomes known only as men make the discovery for themselves of the real nature of the blessings of Divine grace, as possessions which they are warranted to call their own. On this account the gospel, even when preached, is still said to be hid from some, whose eyes are blinded, and whose hearts are hardened. The gospel which makes known the existence of the treasure indicates the need to search for it. Thus it appears that the treasure is really discovered only when men lay hold upon it and appropriate it. Without this, its existence remains concealed—buried out of sight. The Saviour is, indeed, clearly revealed, all His work is set forth in detail, and everlasting life is offered through His name; but each man needs to discover for himself the gift of God which lies within this great revelation. No one can find it for another. Each man must search for himself, must dig in the field where it is concealed. He must, by penitence, by prayer, and by appropriating faith, accept Jesus as a Saviour, thereby receiving the gift of God, even eternal life—the life of righteousness.

What, then, is *the field*, which is the hiding-place? When the revelation of truth is likened to the scattering of seed, "the field is the world." But another and more restricted view of the field must be taken here, when its boundaries mark the scope of personal search for salvation. By a few simple steps we shall reach confirmation of this. Eternal life is to be obtained through acceptance of God's offer of reconciliation. "This is life eternal, to know Thee, the only true God, and Jesus Christ whom thou hast sent." And this knowledge is to be found in the Scriptures. Here we must dig if we would find Divine treasure. "Search the Scriptures; for in them ye think ye have eternal life : and they are they which testify of me." The Bible is that field in which lies hid the treasure which is the most precious of possessions attainable by men. In the field of nature is hid the treasure of scientific truth; in the field of mind is concealed the store of philosophic truth; but in the field of Revelation is hid the treasure of spiritual truth, in personal discovery of which man becomes the possessor of everlasting life. Gospel treasure is for all. Whatever treasure may be secured in other fields of toilsome search, men must come to God's Revelation for the treasure which must be reckoned the highest. This treasure, like all other, is hid beneath the surface, and is not to be found without searching. As we must pierce far beneath the surface to discover where the coal seam lies buried—as we must dig deep to find the gold ore imbedded in the soil,—so must we, with earnest effort and patient toil, dig beneath the surface of the field of revelation in order to find the treasure stored there. "Search the Scriptures." Nowhere else can the spiritual treasure be found. To dig deep and patiently is needful, for the treasure is not lying openly in sight. To visit occasionally the field of Revelation, only turning up the surface, may end in disappointment, leaving the searcher to go empty away. Nevertheless the treasure is there, and the mine is inexhaustible.

Two distinct aspects of hiding thus come to view in the history of the spiritual kingdom. There is hiding of truth in the hearts of men in order to provide for its diffusion; and there is hiding of spiritual blessing so as to require effort for its finding. These two are so different, that in the one case the field is the World; in the other the field is the Word. God begins a spiritual kingdom, hiding it in the world, that as a seed it may grow quietly and become a great tree. In its beginning, the spiritual kingdom is but a seedling among the full-grown trees of the earth. But viewing the advancement of the kingdom through society by the ingathering of individuals, it becomes plain that this can be accomplished only by personal knowledge, conviction, desire, and choice. A Revelation must, therefore, be provided, and its use must be left to men themselves, in accordance with individual responsibility. The revelation, while plain enough to all, must nevertheless require labour for its understanding and application. God calls for earnest search from men who would become possessed of the highest spiritual good.

There is, however, *a further hiding*, which is man's doing, having its explanation in himself. "The kingdom of heaven is like unto treasure hid in a field; *the which when a man hath found, he hideth.*" First perusal of these words is apt to favour the view that this concealment was designed to hide from the owner of the field the existence of the treasure, so that the field might be bought at a cheaper price. This, however, is not the case. The hiding has plainly a regard to others who do not know of the existence of the treasure. The buyer is represented as selling all that he has, in order to give the utmost which may be required. Thus is it implied that the motive for purchasing the field at a high price, is the admitted discovery of the treasure. When men for the first time make a discovery of spiritual good in the Scriptures, they tend to conceal the fact. Whether before familiar with the teaching of Scripture, or ignorant of it; whether previously leading a life inconsistent with its requirements, or in comparative harmony with its precepts, the result is the same. There is that in the first discovery of the great treasure, which makes the discoverer incline to silence and secrecy. A sense of sacredness favours silence. This impulse to secrecy does not concern God but men, who, sooner or later, must come to know of the discovery which has been made. The desire of the heart to keep its own secret arises in part from the exceeding grandeur of the discovery, in part from the wish to feel quite assured of actual possession of such treasure. Hiding from God is not contemplated. There could be no motive for it, even if it were possible. The finding of the spiritual treasure necessarily sends the soul to God with grateful acknowledgment. He placed the treasure there, He invited the search, and at His call the searcher becomes rightful possessor. The discovery implies fellowship, with which there may well be a deep sense of sacredness, inducing concealment of the matter from others. The man previously familiar with Scripture, feels as if he had never before known its meaning, and is silent as to the newness of knowledge which has broken over his spirit as light at the dawn of day. The man who has before been indifferent to Bible teaching, perhaps even manifesting some antagonism to it, feels now a strange delight, of which at first he scarce dares to speak, mistakenly fearing lest it should suddenly vanish, and he should feel as one awaking from a dream. Whatever inducement there may be to hide this inner experience from men, its nature is such that it must be told to God. Prayer is the necessity of the hour. He who would make the treasure his own, must go to the owner to ask the rights of proprietorship. If these be once acquired, the fact will soon become known.

Yet how can we speak of *acquiring* eternal life *by purchase?* How can we buy from God the pardon of our sins, and a restored life of holiness? Is not eternal life the gift of God? Is not the prevailing tenor of Bible teaching even this, "By grace are ye saved through faith; and that not of yourselves: it is the gift of God"? What, then, is the meaning of these closing words of this parable as to the treasure: "The which when a man hath found, he hideth, *and for joy thereof goeth and selleth all that he hath, and buyeth that field"?* What mean the selling and the buying? They point to an essential feature in the system of grace. There is an important sense in which the acquisition of property by purchase may represent the acquisition of eternal life. Eternal life is the gift of God, freely offered in the Scriptures; and these Scriptures are open to the searching of all. But that which is of grace is not given irrespective of man's effort. Participation is made dependent on some condition required of those who desire to have the blessing. In a sense, this is the price to be paid for the treasure. The gift of God is purchased by men. All that is surrendered by a man for the sake of newness of life, may be said to be sold for this end: all that is given to God may be said to be paid as purchase-money. A man surrenders for the sake of spiritual life in Jesus everything inconsistent with righteousness, and which would hinder its attainment. The apostle Paul gives prominence to this in his own case. "What things were gain to me, those I counted loss for Christ" (Phil. iii. 7). By this surrender the finder does not lose, but gains. It seems as if it were a mere casting out of that which he would not keep, and which God would not have.[1] Yet these same dispositions and indulgences were the riches of the man before. In parting with them, he gives up things which formerly were greatly valued. Still, he is not thereby impoverished, but made richer, obtaining in exchange the riches of God's kingdom. He who parts with self-confidence, receives instead confidence in a Saviour mighty to save to the uttermost; he who parts with sinful passions, receives holy desires. There is thus a giving up of former possessions, represented by the *selling*. He who comes with faith and holy desire to God, gives these to Him, which is represented by the *buying*. Yet he who thus gives to God, does not part with that he has, and so he buys "without money and without price."

One point more needs to be pondered, that is, the fact that the purchaser is here said to *sell all that he hath* in order to secure the treasure. His judgment of the inherent value of the treasure appears in the complete surrender he makes. Willingness to make this sacrifice is the proof of absorbing earnestness in him who has made the discovery, and now desires to become possessor of the treasure. He will part with everything else rather than want this. If he only have this he will account himself richer than he should, if, by some unexampled turn of events, he had become lord of the world itself. In his eyes no gain would compensate for the loss of this matchless

[1] The property is not sold to the owner of the field.

treasure; no price would be too high to pay that it might be his own. In this connection the Bible reader will recall our Saviour's words to the young man who had great riches: "Sell all that thou hast, and give to the poor, and thou shalt have treasure in heaven." And though men generally are not called upon to part with money, any more than with health, or with life itself, in order to obtain spiritual life, there must be willingness to part with any possession which would prove an obstacle to the love and service of God.

To interpret aright the selling of all that a man has, we must consider what a man is required to part with in order to obtain everlasting life. As the kingdom established by grace is altogether spiritual in character, externals in themselves considered are of no account. They are neither required nor are they discarded. Worldly substance in greatest store could not purchase the kingdom. "Without money and without price" this purchase must be effected. To obtain the spiritual life which God gives, man must part with *all* that has previously obscured God's claim to the homage of his heart. Something to trust in man must have, and if it be not God's grace, it must be personal goodness which he regards as his own. Such goodness is a precarious ground of confidence. It has enough of worth to keep up the delusive trust in it, as if it were enduring and sufficient. With this there ever is a disturbing consciousness of imperfection and inconsistency. The righteousness which a man possesses has no such value as that which God has laid up in store. So convinced of this is the man who has discovered the treasure hid in God's Word, that he will part with all he has in order to secure the other. So needful is this that he at once resolves upon his course, and carries it into execution. Surrender of self-righteousness is indeed a spiritual necessity in the case. Self-righteousness cannot be retained where the righteousness of grace is received. An alloy cannot be found in the heavenly treasury. In human life, evil is so fused with the good as to destroy the value of what in itself could have acceptance. Therefore must men cease from confidence in themselves, and have confidence in God alone. "By grace are ye saved through faith; and that not of yourselves: it is the gift of God."

CHAPTER XVIII.

WISDOM IN SEEKING AND DISTRIBUTING SPIRITUAL GOOD.

THE MERCHANTMAN.

Matt. xiii. 45, 46.

The similarity between this parable and that concerning the hid treasure is apt at first to hinder our appreciation of this. We are ready to suppose that this second parable is only a repetition of the first under a slight variation of figure. The pearl of great price has taken the place of the hid treasure; and this seems the end of the distinction. Comparison of the two parables, however, may satisfy us that the resemblance is not so close as such a view implies.

The marked diversity of commencement for the two parables affords a key to the difference of meaning: "The kingdom of heaven is like unto treasure;" and "*The kingdom of heaven is like unto a merchantman.*" In the one, the treasure is prominent; in the other, the seeker. Diversity in the figurative representation of value—in one case a treasure, in the other a pearl—is not the discriminating feature. The circumstance of this parable having been commonly named "The Pearl of Great Price" has been misleading. It has turned attention on the points of similarity, not on the points of diversity, whereas the latter are the more valuable for the purposes of exposition. The treasure and the pearl plainly agree in representing exceeding value. But in the first parable the finder is described merely as a man, without a single distinguishing expression. He may represent any man. In the parable now before us it is quite different. It is a merchantman who is introduced. Any man will not suffice to illustrate our Lord's meaning here. Passing round to another point of view from which to contemplate man's part in obtaining spiritual blessing, He selects for His purpose the merchantman, as distinguished from other men. This distinctive feature of the parable makes it plain that our Lord here treats of merchandise in the blessings of grace. Not only is it true that a man must seek everlasting life for himself if he would become possessor of the treasure, but he who thus seeks may become a merchant, proclaiming the value of the treasure, and offering it in sale to others. In the former case, the finding appears as if it were all for self, and there were no consideration beyond. And, indeed, it is to be observed in both parables that the finder recognises his own interest as completely involved in what he has found. The speciality of this parable is to point out that, both as a seeker and as a finder, the man is a merchantman. Besides, if we consider the relation of both parables to God as the source of everlasting life, the additional light thrown upon the whole subject is very striking. In the one case, it appears that God has hid the treasure in the field, in order that man may find it. In the other, it appears that God hides the treasure in order that he who values such wealth may make merchandise of it among his fellows.

Verse 45.—"*The kingdom of heaven is like unto a merchantman seeking goodly pearls.*" Such a merchantman may often be seen in the East, carrying rare articles and precious stones, and offering them for sale in the towns to which he comes. He is a man skilled in the knowledge of the treasure he sells, and is looked to as an expert. Of various orders of merchants, the pearl-seeker is chosen for illustration. Such a man has the skill of the seeker for the shell-fish, and the skill enabling him to judge of the relative value of the pearls as they are found.

He is a skilled seeker. It is the work of his life to seek for goodly pearls, and to dispose of them when found. He knows where the shell-fish find their most congenial resting-places, and does not waste his energies over unpromising fields. He peers through the waters, with eyes carefully screened, that the glare of light breaking on the surface may not mislead. Every inch of the channel is subjected to scrutiny, and the form of a shell is quickly detected. He is besides a *skilled judge of pearls.* He knows at a glance the goodly pearls, and instantly recognises any one of unusual purity and excellence. His eye is trained for such discrimination. He is a ready buyer as well as a seller, purchasing with eagerness any pearl of extraordinary value, knowing how quickly he can find a remunerative market. With such treasures he starts on his course as a merchantman, that he may dispose of his selection to those who set account upon such possessions. This is the man chosen by our Divine Teacher to illustrate an additional aspect of man's work in acquiring the blessings of salvation.

Here, as formerly, our attention is directed to the finding of treasure ; but in this case the merchant finds not unexpectedly, but *according to expectation.* The merchant presents an illustration of persistent, methodical search, assured of reward. In this second parable we have a greater range of application to the facts of human history. Some do, indeed, find everlasting life when they seek it not. But, like the merchantman, most find the blessing as the result of a careful search. The latter experience happens to those who make it the very business of their life to search for truth. Their daily engagements may vary endlessly ; they may be merchants acquainted with the details of very different fields of production ; but the one characteristic of their lives is found in this, that they are seekers after truth. And that truth hid in Scripture is like to the pearl encased in the shell, and lying at the bottom of still water. Whether the seekers be men of trade, men of commerce, men of science, or men of philosophy, it matters not ; they belong to one great company, they are searchers after such truth as the human spirit needs for the support of its higher life. For such unbiassed searchers after truth, God has in His grace provided the discovery of a great treasure, which shall be to the soul a source of eternal joy. The more closely inquirers press the great problems affecting personal existence, character, and destiny, the nearer do they come to the greatest reward of human research. Finding that, life itself appears a new thing. Renewed spiritual life springs up in the soul, through faith in the Redeemer, and love to "the God and Father of our Lord and Saviour Jesus Christ."

While, however, some find what they never expected, and others find what they have been seeking, yet there is to all *something unexpected,*—so unexpected as to be altogether surprising to the finders. To many who find it as treasure hid in a field, it is a possession the very existence of which was previously unknown, so that the sight of it occasions wonder. To others who have toiled hard amid the dark problems of life, —who have felt longings after the pure and noble, even when their better nature has been crushed under the rude heel of mean passion,—who have at length come to see that purity alone is noble, and sin the only baseness, and who have cried for deliverance from the dread perplexities of contending motives,—the discovery of Divine mercy and love in Christ Jesus has been the cause of amazement unspeakable. To all such the transcendent value of the pearl becomes apparent; seen in the light, it is pronounced with certainty to be "the pearl of great price." Gospel truth seems of such surpassing value that it far exceeds in worth all that had been conjectured. It is "the glorious gospel of the blessed God."

Observing thus the surprise to the merchantman in the discovery of the pearl, we proceed now to consider his subsequent action. Verse 46.—"*Who, when he had found one pearl of great price, went and sold all that he had, and bought it.*" Intensity of personal interest is apparent here. He has sought goodly pearls, and also gain by merchandise in them. The sight of this pearl at once awakens eagerness to secure it; and this specially because of the delight he feels in such a rarity.

To see it is a joy, but to own it would give surpassing delight. Therefore he parts with all that he has in order to buy it. So it is with the eager searcher after truth, when he comes to the first discovery of the real character of gospel truth. Its singular value is even more appreciated by the man who has struggled long with the problems of moral life, than by the man who is merely contented and delighted to find in it satisfaction for his own present want. The eager penetrating inquirer sees in the gospel, with its provision of spiritual life, a value which may kindle to brightness even the dullest eye. He sees the light of a great deliverance breaking over the disorder, the misery, the self-reproach, and the despair of humanity. He sees in this a value for all the world, and with a merchant's appreciation of a common want, he is eager to buy this pearl, at whatever price. He will part with all that he has hitherto counted his valuables in order to secure this treasure. Necessity lies upon him, just as it was seen to lie upon the man who found the treasure hid in the field. There is a common demand for self-abnegation if we would possess everlasting life. Self-confidence and self-righteousness must be surrendered, in order that confidence in Divine mercy may become a possession of the soul. Only thus can there be participation in the righteousness which God has provided for the sinful.

In a right understanding of this *selling of all that he has*, it will be at once apparent that he who purchases and appropriates to himself gospel truth, is not represented as parting with all other forms of truth in order to secure this. At first sight, it might appear that the parable represented the merchantman as selling, along with other things, the pearls already in possession, in order thereby to attain the means of purchasing the one. But such a meaning, alien as it is to Bible teaching, is not involved here. The merchantman is represented as himself a *seeker* of pearls. A large part of the price he pays for his pearls is the toil he expends in finding them; but for this pearl he will besides part with all the money he has. So is it in the search for truth. No one obtains more than he finds by his own toil. Discovery of gospel truth does not lower the value of other forms of truth, and does not stop the search for them. In comparison, this assuredly surpasses all, nevertheless all other truths have a relation to this. The parable guards against the supposition that other forms of truth are to be surrendered as the purchase-money of that which transcends them. Rather, the opposite is distinctly implied, since it is the very life-work of the seeker of goodly pearls to gather from hidden depths, and add to his stores all the treasures that can be found.

By this line of reflection we are brought to what seems the essential feature of the parable—that *the merchantman buys in order to sell*. This view of the merchant's business is not drawn out in detail, but it is set forth as essential. What needs to be observed is, that no account can be given of the merchantman which does not make him a *seller* of pearls as well as a seeker of them. Nay, so prominent is the business of selling, that he does not restrict himself to personal efforts in fishing for pearls, but goes into the market as a buyer, if he can thereby secure a more valuable stock. The typical man is a travelling merchant. He is not one who has in the city a store of pearls, to which buyers may resort, and where the work of selling may be intrusted to another, while he continues the work of seeking. On the contrary, he carries the pearls which constitute his merchandise, and he travels hither and thither in search of those who will buy. There is meaning here, striking and valuable, giving completeness to the instruction. If there is in the kingdom of God a selling and a buying in order that men themselves may become possessors of the blessing provided, there is also a buying and selling in order that others may come into possession of the treasure. This form of merchandise is distinctively characteristic of the kingdom of God. A secluded meditative life does not fitly represent that of the Christian as a searcher after truth and righteousness. The man who first finds everlasting life for himself becomes a merchant, offering the treasure to others, and pressing it on their acceptance. If the merchant presents his pearl to others that they may become purchasers,—if he is wont to enlarge upon its excellence with a view to induce his hearers to desire it,—if among them he finds some who attempt to undervalue it, and others who acknowledge its value, but are unwilling to pay for it the great price demanded, —and if he travel far, carrying his treasure wherever he goes, and repeating his efforts to secure a purchaser, something analogous in all these respects can be found in the history of the spiritual kingdom. An element of difficulty there is in the circumstance that there is *but one pearl*, which, if once sold, becomes the exclusive possession of the buyer. But this difficulty is only such as adheres to all analogy. The reality here symbolised cannot be conveyed by speaking of many pearls. There are goodly pearls of truth in great number and

254 Seeking and Distributing Spiritual Good.

variety to be gathered in the world. But gospel truth is one, and is the same to all. It must therefore be represented as one pearl of great price. Seeing that the spiritual treasure offered to man must be spoken of as a unit, the engagements of the merchant are not recounted in detail. But passing this formal difficulty, the Christian does the part of the merchant in seeking to induce others to accept the salvation which he himself has received with joy. By his eager attempts to find those who will contemplate the gospel; by his enthusiastic descriptions of its value; by his persuasive reasoning with those who lend an ear; by his untiring efforts continued after repeated failures, the Christian answers to the analogy here employed. How fully the Saviour considered all this effort needful every Bible reader knows. He who said, "The kingdom of heaven is like unto a merchantman," gathered together His chosen and devoted followers, and said unto them, "Go ye into all the world and preach the gospel to every creature." These are the merchantmen of God's kingdom. Their merchandise consists in the treasures of grace; their toil, their travelling, their earnest entreaties, tell how eager they are that others should receive the blessing they describe; and they sell "without money and without price."

Here we contemplate efforts which involve great *publicity*. In the former parable there is intended secrecy—hid treasure; in this there is intentional publicity—open merchandise. At the close we are returning upon the remarks made at the outset, when pointing to the fact that the presence and value of the treasure were made known in the world, and its acceptance pressed upon men, even while it was represented as hid treasure. The two parables bring out the harmony of the whole. How truly is the treasure hid, and yet how truly is it pressed on the acceptance of men! When both forms of analogy are before us, both phases of Christian life become apparent. The reality of both is illustrated, and their fundamental harmony proclaimed, though still only partially explained. Salvation is by grace, yet must it be bought; it is hid from the view, yet is it daily offered for sale. The practical result is, that while God is ever offering the blessing, men must seek it for themselves, and must part with all that they have in order to obtain it, and afterwards urge others to seek it as they have done.

CHAPTER XIX.

GATHERING OF GOOD AND BAD WITHIN THE KINGDOM.

THE NET.

Matt. xiii. 47-50.

We here come in sight of the border-land of the eternal world. The parable now to be considered presents the first scene in the great future toward which all the arrangements of the kingdom are pointing. The Redeemer discovers to us, far in the distance, the line where the waters of Time find their boundary on the shores of Eternity. Here and there on the surface of the waters are sundry marks which indicate the vast sweep of a great net which has been set in the ocean; and on the shores of Eternity are the cords running up out of the waters, and the stakes to which these cords have been made sure. Such is the view which our Lord has given of the relation between Time and Eternity. Enigmatical it is, as befits what is still future, making some things plain, but leaving other things obscure and puzzling; vividly picturesque, presenting many attractive features, and yet awe-inspiring, as we think of the meshes which may entangle, and also the strength of the cord which no strain can break asunder. In outline this is the representation :—Time is an ocean, Eternity is its shore : within the waters God has set a net, the result of whose setting will appear on that day when all that has been enclosed is drawn up on the shores of the eternal world.

That a reference to the future state affords the true point of view from which to contemplate this parable, seems plain from these two considerations : *first*, That the net is represented as being *full* before it is drawn ; and *second*, That our Lord expressly begins His brief and partial interpretation of it with these words : " So shall it be at the end of the world."

What, then, is this Net ? "*The kingdom of heaven is like unto a net.*" It is the kingdom of God. This can hardly mean here the visible Church, as so many have taken for granted. From the words (verse 49), "The angels shall come forth and sever the wicked from among the just," it is apparent that " the wicked" *as a class* are spoken of as included in the kingdom. The wicked are deliberately embraced in a way quite inconsistent with the supposition that the visible Church is represented. It is not merely some few wicked persons, nor even a considerable proportion of such, who are found at last among the chosen ones, but *the wicked* are here present, just as the righteous are. "The kingdom of heaven" thus described is the kingdom of grace, in the plenitude of its range. It is that kingdom which God has in this sin-troubled world, where judgment is withheld, vengeance is restrained, and Divine forbearance and compassion are reaching to all men. It is a kingdom whose sovereignty is grace, all whose administration is gracious, within which are all men on earth. The reign of grace is indeed such, that all have some experience of its reality, in restraining influences which move around the souls of men, as well as in the benefits thrown free to them, and towards which much agency is drawing them. True indeed it is, that only some, with spiritual natures renewed, appreciate and enjoy the choicest blessings of grace; but no less true is it that all the wicked, as well as all the just, are meanwhile within a kingdom of grace. The world-encircling influences of Divine favour are too subtle to be readily recognised, and yet too potent to be altogether unfelt. From them men at times swerve eagerly, as fishes from the slightest touch of the net; against them men often struggle, as fishes entangled in the meshes. No man, however, passes from under the reign of God, which is for every man here a reign of grace. There is, indeed, another and more restricted view of the kingdom of heaven. It is a fold within which come only as many as know the voice of Jesus, and follow Him for defence and satisfaction. But under this wider view, it is a net, embracing all without distinction. If it be clear that the latter is here dealt with, we have only to glance forward in the application of the parable to see that completeness of separation between the wicked and just is here foretold as in the parable of the Tares. This parable in like manner gives us first the mingling and then the separation of classes.

If the kingdom of heaven be a net, we are first concerned with its *setting*. "The kingdom of heaven is like unto a net *that was cast into the sea.*" The absence of any statement as to agency in setting the net is to be remarked. There is nothing here after the manner of those other parables, where a woman is seen lighting a candle, or putting leaven among the meal. There is here *intentional omission*. For though the disciples, when first called, were spoken of as fishers of men, and the occupation of seeking to save souls may at all times be represented under this figure, what is here before our notice is something quite distinct from human efforts to save fellow-men. Consequently, the setting of the net is not represented as accomplished by human agency. Such instrumentality is out of sight here. The setting of the net is left to be thought of as the direct result of Divine agency, belonging as it does to the very essence of Divine sovereignty. The net *was* cast into the sea. This is enough to be said, for men were not there to see it done, and could not have done anything to help. It happens to men as to the fishes of the sea: the evidence that the net has been cast into the waters is obtained only by contact with it. God, who " divided the waters which were under the firmament from the waters which were above the firmament," and who appointed boundaries to the ocean, has set His net in these waters beneath, waiting the fulness of time when He shall draw it on the shores of Eternity. Such a representation is suggestive of most solemn thought concerning the ways of God in dealing with man, telling us much of those cords, hid from our dull vision, which nevertheless connect the earth with heaven, encircling every individual in the universe, and gathering all under one sway.

We pass next to *the standing of the net in the midst of the waters*. Its presence there implies *enclosure* and *restriction*. We have seen with what reason we conclude that this enclosure embraces all on earth.

Within the net-work of grace men come into life, within it they pass their whole existence here. Termination of individual life is kept out of view in a parable dealing with the history of the world as a whole. The outspreading influences of Divine love enclose all on the earth within a restraining boundary, guarding them from evils greater than those which now beset their life, and closing them in to advantages which had been lost in a wider ocean where greater severance from God had been possible. More terrible iniquity and consequent misery there would be in the world, but for the fact that the net of grace is set, and the enclosure made sure. Within this enclosure there is, doubtless, great variety of ground, involving conditions of life more or less favourable; but there is a universal gain in the provisions by which infinite love has shut in our race to all the advantages belonging to a state of probation, where it is possible to escape destruction and attain to a higher life.

Enclosure implies *restriction*, set up by Divine sovereignty, but in such a manner as to give scope for human liberty. Enclosure by the net does not involve destruction of life. There is death only for the fishes rushing against it, or exhausting themselves while they struggle in its meshes. There is a complete difference between the net and the fishing-line. The latter implies struggle and death; but the former, while it stands, necessitates none of these. Within the wide enclosure of the net there is natural and easy movement. Still it is of necessity a restricted action by reason of the enclosure, which it is impossible to break through; but this restriction takes a form of irksome constraint only to those struggling to get beyond its boundaries. It is not even recognised as a restriction by those which find their chosen exercise and feeding-ground within it. These features in the figurative representation of the kingdom of grace are rich in illustrative significance. By arrangement of Divine sovereignty the plan of grace is established, without any power on man's part to change it, or pass beyond its range on earth. Yet within its application there is wide scope for personal choice, and full provision for life in all its functions. No doubt, all restraint is apt to seem a hardship. And in the heart of man there is so much that seeks to shun Divine control, so much that resents it, when its uniform continuance is seen to be inevitable, that there are some who rush against the Divine restraints as fishes vainly rush against the net. Others are so unmoved by signs of sovereign grace around them, or so unobservant, that they live in their own sphere as if Divine grace were nothing. But to multitudes such restriction is not a trial. Sovereignty of grace has fixed restraints, and these are joyfully accepted, while the grace which restricts our action multiplies our blessings. The spirit of obedience, though it places checks upon action, also gives direction and impulse to action, guiding life into spheres of richest experience. Everywhere there is freedom, yet chiefly for the highest type of life.

But here we come upon the difficulty,—How are some bad and others good? *The net gathered of every kind.* The *gathering* is consequent upon the exercise of a power which comes into the waters. But the *kinds* being already within these waters, are not determined by the net which encloses them. Such as they are, the net takes them, and their respective value is determined by the nature they have. The gathering of *every kind*, implies the presence of great varieties. There are not merely two classes, good and bad, but great diversity of kind in each class. Men of all shades of character are to be found within the present dispensation of grace. How, then, is their goodness or badness to be accounted for? The parable offers only a negative reply. As the net does not determine the quality of the fishes enclosed, so neither does the merely restraining power of grace explain the distinction between good and bad. Analogy here, as elsewhere, fails to meet all that is required. Each parabolic story is capable of telling only part of the truth. How it happens, that where all are sinful, some are reckoned in one class as good, and some in another class as bad, the present parable contains nothing to explain. For answer to such inquiry, we are referred to what has been already told at an earlier period, as to seeking those who are lost. Such explanation having been already given, we are here, according to the requirement of the parable, restricted to a description of two classes of men, as good and bad.

The Saviour next points to a period when, the net being full, there shall be commotion in the midst of the waters: "*Which, when it was full, they drew to shore.*" The *fulness* of the net is said to determine the time for its drawing. Its manner of use is not such that it is cast successively in different waters, taking at one point fewer, and at another more. But it stands permanently in the same waters, and is not drawn until it is full. It is cast but once; and only once, at the end of time, is it drawn. This feature in the parable makes a wide distinction between what is here referred to and the work of those who are themselves made fishers of men. Theirs is a toilsome work of continued casting and drawing. But with the majesty of Divine sovereignty it is otherwise. Silently the net of grace is set, unmoved it stands, until grace has had full exercise, according to God's sovereign pleasure, and then the whole design of its continuance is accomplished. In this respect there is no failure.

We are thus carried forward in thought to the drawing of the net. Verse 48.—" *Which, when it was full, they drew to shore.*" The casting of the net supposes the work of fishermen, and so also the drawing of it. But as there were no references to the fishermen in the setting of the net, there is indefiniteness here as to the drawing of it. By a freedom of grammatical structure it is said *they* drew it to shore, without previous reference to persons. Placed in this form, the expression is equivalent merely to the indefinite statement, it was drawn ashore. The question,—How was it drawn?—is really left unanswered. And if we glance to the interpretation supplied by our Lord, we shall see that the reference to the angels does not convey information on the point. In the parable it is explicitly said, " They drew it to shore, *and sat down, and gathered the good into vessels, and cast the bad away;*" while in the explanatory addition it is merely said, " The angels shall come forth, and *sever* the wicked from among the just." This latter statement contains nothing which applies to the drawing of the net —the *gathering together* of the righteous and wicked to the eternal world. It seems almost to suggest that the angels have nothing to do with this preliminary exercise of power. It appears to convey the impression that the angels will be seen coming forth at the command of their Sovereign, just as all men are gathered together under sovereign power. The angels do not bring men before God—do not take part in the work of judgment—but merely sever from each other the two classes whom God pronounces good and bad. It is thus implied that the constraining hand of God Himself brings all men to His feet, as the unerring wisdom and justice of God pronounce the sentence; while the angels as His ministers separate the condemned from those who are divinely accepted. The sovereignty which first set up the restraining influence, in due time applies the constraining power, which brings all to His presence, there discovering their real character.

Around the throne of God stand the ministers who execute His bidding. Instrumentality is employed in the *severance* of the evil from the good. The angels have a part to perform on the great day of adjudication. "He maketh His ministers a flame of fire." "His angels excel in strength that do His commandments, hearkening unto the voice of His word." The judgment is the Lord's; the execution of it is intrusted to ministers "that do His pleasure."

But here there is something worthy of special attention. In the interpretation there is a divergence from the full meaning of the parable, by dropping the reference to the good. The close points only to the wicked. Does this omission not imply in the mind of the Great Teacher a sympathetic feeling as to the parabolic use of the fisher's work, which is essentially a destroying work? Whether the fish taken in the fisher's net be good or bad, there is death for both; for the good, which are gathered into vessels; and for the bad, which are cast away. When, therefore, in reading our Lord's explanation of the parable, we mark the absence of any allusion to the future of the righteous, He is neither uninterested in that future, nor unwilling to dwell upon it; but, recognising the inadequacy of earthly imagery, He will not in this connection even suggest what that future shall be, but leaves for succeeding parables special and and ample description of the blessed state of the righteous. Here He points, in language highly figurative, with imagery of "the furnace of fire," to doleful lamentation, and distressed gnashing of teeth, fruit of the awful condemnation of those who are evil in heart. Severed from the good and from their God, they shall be separated from blessedness; under the ban of the Judge, their bitterness of soul shall be aggravated by deep and lasting self-condemnation. "There is no peace, saith my God, to the wicked."

If we would give completeness to the circle of illustration, avoiding irksome detail, we must somehow keep up the figurative allusion. The God who "divided the waters which were under the firmament from the waters which were above the firmament," transfers vigorous, healthy life from these lower waters to the wider expanse of waters in a more genial sphere above, where development can be more rapid and more certain. The net as set in the waters of Time thus gathers its multitudes for transference to the boundless ocean of Eternity. Not for death, but for life eternal, are these "good" enclosed within the vast net.

CHAPTER XX.

WISE USE OF THIS WORLD'S POSSESSIONS.

THE UNFAITHFUL STEWARD.

LUKE XVI. 1-10.

AFTER illustrating the value the believer sets on the grace provided by God, the Saviour in the parable of the Unfaithful Steward proceeds to instruct His disciples as to their relationship to subordinate possessions.

Our Lord's use of the conduct of bad men for purposes of instruction is one of the perplexities of His parabolic teaching. One example of this has already passed under review, in the parable of the Importunate Widow, in which the unjust judge is made to supply material for elucidation of the mystery of delayed answers to earnest supplication. It is a marvel of condescension that the Divine Saviour is willing, even for encouragement to the suppliant, to take the case of an unjust minister of justice, as if it might contribute something instructive concerning God's dealings with His people. The lessons are, indeed, clear enough, and greatly needed by us,—that justice may be done, though there be long delay; and that the suppliant has reason for perseverance, and has personal gain in it. But it nevertheless remains matter of surprise that

Christ condescends to accept such a misrepresentation of just rule, as affording some help for correct interpretation of God's delay in answering prayer.

We have now before us a second illustration of spiritual truth by reference to the conduct of a bad man. The perplexity here is in one sense less than in the former; in another sense, it is greater. That an upright man may learn some lessons from selfish and dishonest men, does not involve any moral perplexity. Prudence, forethought, and sagacity are qualities which belong to intelligent self-guidance, and may find place even when the line of conduct must be condemned, the motive being utterly wrong. We may therefore learn not only by way of warning, but even by way of direction, from what is observed in the life of the dishonest. Besides, there is really less to occasion difficulty, when we with all our imperfections are set to gain instruction from those who give themselves to evil, than when the Holy God is for a moment compared in His action with an unjust judge. But, on the other hand, there is really more of moral perplexity when we are counselled, even in a modified form, to learn from an example of what is glaringly sinful. It is the unjust act which is used here as in some way a model to us, whereas in the previous parable the unjust procedure of the judge is in no sense an example of the manner in which God rules. Under His government there is never neglect of justice, whatever delay there may be in its execution. There must, then, be some revulsion of feeling, when, for instruction, we are first directed upon the plottings of a dishonest servant. Such revulsion is the natural fruit of the teaching of the Saviour Himself. It is a feeling which He anticipates and appreciates. Accordingly we find that this parable does not break off suddenly at the close of the narrative, but is followed by explanation of its meaning, the presence of which indicates a deliberate intention to guard against misinterpretation. And when we there learn that our Lord's purpose is to inculcate *faithfulness* even in that which is least—faithfulness "*in that which is another man's*"—we are delivered, on purely moral grounds, from the revulsion of feeling which is naturally our first experience under contemplation of the conduct of the steward as narrated in the parable. The Saviour points our observation through dark and drifting clouds of evils disturbing our eyes, to a sight which has instruction, if we can but detect it. He guides us behind a screen which artifice has set up, to blind from passing observation a piece of deliberate dishonesty; He shows us the doings which go on there; and shows us more, the calculating thoughts of the active agent directing the whole, even though there be trouble of conscience and sense of self-debasement, as well as debasement of all who participate in the course pursued. He points out that behind all this pitiful screening of evil deeds, and under all this sinful bartering for gains, there is an illustration of what belongs to the strength of an intelligent nature. If, seeing all this, and recognising its importance, we continue to feel a degree of surprise that Jesus employs the illustration,—and such surprise we may still experience,—it needs to be remembered that there is a fitness in the fact that "the Friend of sinners," "the Saviour of the lost," calling men everywhere to "repent," has an eye which detects anything good underneath all the evil, specially the working of intelligence when facing the deserts of evil-doing. He who accounts the lost soul itself as *silver* under all the pollution of sin, accounts a genuine exercise of rational nature as of real worth, even though the perverse use of it serves to make clear the moral corruption in which that nature is involved. This dishonest man would be received by the Saviour, if, on later reflection, he would abandon his claims upon his master's creditors, so dishonestly established, and submit to the poverty he had brought upon himself by his unfaithfulness, taking the place of a true penitent. For the poor man, as for the rich, there is the test of parting with what is wrongfully obtained. "Sell that thou hast," and give it away, is a demand of wide application. If, then, there is a surprise when the eyes of those whose aspirations and efforts are towards righteousness are directed to the conduct of one who is a mean deceiver, we must mark that our Saviour is training us to a deeper sympathy with His own spirit, and thereby to some genuine sympathy with wicked men yielding to temptation under pressure of unexpected adversity. The wrongness of the conduct is distressing to contemplate, yet a regard to self-interest in the future is a motive not unworthy, but one which may find an appropriate place in a noble life. Dishonesty must be condemned; yet a judicious regard to future need is compatible with the strictest integrity. So does our Lord insist that there is a wise use of substance in making provision for the future.

This lesson is set in a striking light by the connection in which this parable is placed by Luke, by whom alone it is recorded. It comes in immediate relation with the parable of *The Prodigal Son*. The importance of this parable is thus made plain; its secondary place is also conspicuous when brought into contrast with penitence, faith, and love. Prudence is a law of rational life. Looking at the prodigal, we see *its value* demonstrated by the disastrous consequences which flow from its neglect. Waste of substance, and wreck of prospects, tell the value of prudence in the guidance of life. Looking at the elder brother, we see *its secondary place* in the circle of virtues, as we mark that the son who can claim as his own all that remains of his father's possessions, is unhappy in the midst of abundance. Stores of substance, with a fretful heart, scorning a penitent prodigal, show how insufficient is the government of prudence as a rule of life. So far is it from being a sufficient guide, that the reckless prodigal, taught by his imprudence, rises to a higher prudence. Thus in the hard discipline of life, loss leads to higher gain, bringing the self-condemned and newly-awakened soul to the understanding of the great law of the kingdom—"*He that loseth his life for my sake shall find it*" (Matt. x. 39).

Thus, through a somewhat lengthened avenue, we at last reach the structure of a parable, so unusual in its character as to have occasioned much remark.

"*And he said also unto his disciples.*" This mode of introduction, as if it were the continuance of the same discourse, implies that in view of the sacred writer, the parable now to be given is in its significance closely connected with that of *The Prodigal Son*, given just before. We cannot with certainty conclude that this was spoken by our Lord in direct connection with that. The language does not warrant this inference. But it is not left open to doubt that the Evangelist sees in this parable intimate relation with that which precedes it, and a distinct advance along the line of instruction pursued in the earlier parable.

The express statement that Jesus spoke this parable *to His disciples* must be noted. Though there is continuity of thought, there is such advance that the Divine Teacher has openly turned away from the murmurers who complained of His receiving sinners and eating with them (chap. xv. 2). Now, He addresses Himself directly to His *disciples*. Earthly substance is easily lost; it may accomplish little when carefully preserved; let the disciples of Jesus learn a lesson as to its wise use. The dishonesty practised by the steward must meet the condemnation of an upright judge of the conduct of others; but a wise use of property, if it only be our own to use without stint, is rightly recognised by the steward in his extremity.

"*There was a certain rich man which had a steward.*" Whether the "rich man" is intended to represent a particular individual or class of persons is not an inquiry of any importance for interpretation of the parable. The purpose to be served lies clearly apart from any necessity for giving a representative place either to the rich man or his steward. The *relationship* existing between them is all that our Lord needs in order to serve the end contemplated. To suppose, as has been done, that the Roman emperor was the rich man, and the publicans his stewards, or that the rich man represents the Evil One, or it may be Mammon, is to illustrate how fruitless is the attempt to assign a representative character to either. The relationship of a *steward* to his employer is that which our Lord seeks to utilise, and He is so far from helping us to identify a certain person as if He were aimed at, that His purpose is served by speaking of the lord of this steward as "*a certain rich man.*" He appears before us with no greater definiteness than this, a man of wealth, absorbed in earthly things, inquiring into his own interests, in so far as they have been intrusted to an unfaithful steward, and yet having the world's admiration of a cleverly devised piece of dishonesty, while defeating it. Of this rich man our Lord means to make nothing further than that his proprietorship gives him the right of dismissal, introducing occasion for his steward's reckoning as to his own future necessities, on which our Lord would concentrate our reflections.

The man of wealth is described only as "*a certain rich man which had a steward.*" The employment of a steward is the essential fact for the purpose. Stewardship gives to the dependant opportunity for making use of his lord's property in the manner about to be described. The parable being addressed to the disciples, attention is to be concentrated on the relative position of the man who proceeds to dispose of a considerable amount of property. He is a *steward*.[1] To him the rich man has intrusted general superintendence over all sowing and reaping, household expenditure, and sale of produce. The name suggests a place of highest trust. The management of affairs, both in respect of receipts and expenditure, is committed to him, and that implicitly, so that the owner does not maintain any direct supervision of transactions. Such is the authority and responsibility of the man selected as conveying to the

---

[1] οἰκονόμος, not a farm-steward, or out-of-doors overseer, as might be supposed from references to oil and wheat, but a steward who has authority over the household.

disciples some indication of their relation to God, to whom all belongs, and who, in giving to men, makes them stewards for Him. They live and are nourished on God's property,—they buy and sell of His possessions,—their life is in His service,—they hold all things in trust, to secure increase within His household, —and they are ever liable to be called to account for their transactions, though long years may pass on without a demand for such reckoning. Every man is a steward unto God. It is the wisdom and joy of the Christian disciple to own that this is the true view of his position in the world, and to find in this fact stimulus to activity and forethought. Taking this view, the Christian will consider the use he makes of temporal possessions as having a bearing on after experience, both in this life and in the future state. To these considerations it is the purpose of our Lord to direct the thoughts of His disciples.

A crisis comes in the history of this unfaithful steward, when the loss of his stewardship threatens him as a sudden calamity. "*And the same was accused unto him, that he had wasted his goods.*" From some quarter unnamed there comes to his lord a charge against him of unfaithfulness to his trust. The accusation was that of a careless scattering, instead of a careful husbanding, of his master's property. "He had *wasted* his goods."[1] What is alleged against him is not wilful dishonesty in appropriating to his own advantage what belonged to his master. It is a loose-handed indifference, like that of the prodigal, which

---

[1] διασκορπίζων,—scattering loosely about. It is the same word employed to describe the result of the prodigal's riotous living,— "he wasted his substance."

squandered valuable possessions to the advantage of no one, thus allowing his master's property to go to waste. The charge is verified as soon as inquiry is instituted, and the inevitable end is dismissal from office.

Here we touch a point of analogy which in part accounts for the use of such a case. *We all are unfaithful* in our stewardship. Different phases and degrees of transgression must be recognised, but unfaithfulness is the universal sin. There is not an intelligent appreciation of the reality of stewardship in reference to all we possess, and consequently no approach to faithfulness in the discharge of our trust, by full consecration of our powers to God's service. It is the aim of our Lord to bring man to the acknowledgment of stewardship, in the penitential confession of unfaithfulness, as it is His purpose here to lead His disciples to strive above all things to be found faithful. He calls to repentance and faith; but this in order that there may be new life,—a life which shall prove a real self-consecration, dedicating efforts and possessions equally to the service of God. Here also we have a hint as to the measure of responsibility. Wastefulness is unfaithfulness. There must be no loose-handed scattering of property regardless of return. It is of the essence of well-doing to "*economise.*"

Verse 2.—"*And he called him, and said unto him, How is it that I hear this of thee? give an account of thy stewardship; for thou mayest be no longer steward.*" The natural result of unfaithfulness in a steward is set forth in these three statements: 1. Testimony of this kind is condemning; 2. An account of the responsibilities is rightfully required, and is in itself the proper test of fidelity; 3. The loss of position is the just penalty of faithlessness to trust. The unfaithful steward hears the threefold utterance, and has nothing to reply. By his silence he owns the inevitable, and straightway occupies himself with thought concerning the future. The past is branded with condemnation; the future has its necessities, how may it also contain its supplies? The narrative leads forward to this last inquiry as the main feature. But some passing light is falling on various phases of personal responsibility, and quickness of eye may contribute to the ingathering of many lessons. The relation of the steward to his lord illustrates the relation of man to God. The disciples of Jesus are required to be conspicuous among their fellow-men for intelligent and reverential acknowledgment of this analogy. Unfaithfulness in any form stands as its own witness against us. "All things are naked and opened to the eyes of him with whom we have to do." He needs not that any bear witness to Him, yet is it an additional consideration that unfaithfulness readily finds witnesses, and is convicted even in human judgment by the observation it attracts. But further, all stewardship points forward to a time of reckoning. It is the right of the lord of the steward to require account. The time of reckoning depends on the will of the master; his sovereignty appears in its appointment. Our God is, indeed, long-suffering. The fact of unfaithfulness does not at once bring the summons to His bar. He can afford to wait as the man of wealth cannot. Divine government in its far-reaching control does not experience the restraints which belong to earthly proprietorship. Yet is the reckoning sure;

the summons to His presence will come: "Give an account of thy stewardship;" and even though there has been no glaring, wilful dishonesty, want of faithfulness will lead to loss of stewardship. Great force is given to the expression of the inevitable in this last case,—"Thou mayest be no longer steward," or, as it may be rendered,—"It is not *possible* to thee henceforth to superintend." It is not merely the master's right so to decide, but the determination is righteousness itself. A continuance in the oversight may not be.

Verses 3, 4.—"*Then the steward said within himself, What shall I do? for my lord taketh away from me the stewardship: I cannot dig; to beg I am ashamed. I am resolved what to do, that when I am put out of the stewardship, they may receive me into their houses.*" The worst features of the man's character are here disclosed. What he resolves upon must be held in contrast with other possibilities, which are passed over without any sign of their having had a moment's reflection. To attempt a defence is abandoned as hopeless. The facts are as represented, and the culpability cannot be disputed. On the other hand, confession of his fault and an admission of concern and grief are not to be thought of. There is not enough manliness in the character of the steward to suggest the adoption of such a course. There is the falseness of the man who tries to carry his head well, even when his own intelligence bears witness to the wrong he has done. His carelessness in the position of trust has had underneath it actual badness of heart, which now becomes more clearly apparent than formerly. The challenge of his lord finds him ready for unscrupulous dishonesty. He has been content to see his lord suffering untold loss; he himself will not suffer if dishonesty can lay its hand on any of the stored treasure, which for a day or two longer must remain at his command. The moral aspect of the crisis does not move him. He does not live amongst those who talk much of "sin;" nor does he mean to seek his dwelling amongst people of that class. An honest trader would be an intolerable trouble to him as he is now placed. He is dishonest, and his hope now is that others are dishonest likewise, and will co-operate under conditions of self-interest. Unfaithful stewardship encourages dishonest trading. The longer such a stewardship is continued the wider the man's responsibilities become. There is a secret history of growing dishonesty which finds an unexpected measure of its progress when an opportunity offers for unusual gain. What obliqueness of vision descries as "a good chance," a clear-sighted man will perceive to lie on a pathway sloping into a pitfall. "I am resolved what to do, that . . . they may receive me into their houses." There is nothing here to learn save warning—no healthy result save by nourishing our disgust. Helplessness in face of the demand for work—horror of poverty—contentment with the meanest form of dependence on others—are fit companions in a dishonest mind.

Verses 5-7.—"*So he called every one of his lord's debtors unto him, and said unto the first, How much owest thou unto my lord? And he said, An hundred measures of oil. And he said unto him, Take thy bill, and sit down quickly, and write fifty. Then said he to another, And how much owest thou? And he said, An hundred measures of wheat. And he said unto him, Take thy bill, and write fourscore.*" In his case resolution was promptly followed by action. Circumstances were pressing him, and thoughts of honesty were not hampering him. Something may be learned of the Saviour's observations concerning human conduct, when in drawing such a picture as this He represents the steward as calling "every one" of the debtors,[1] and does not suggest that any one was found to reject the offer of a dishonourable escape from a share of his debts by a fraud upon a rich creditor. His plan is unfolded, and it works well, probably all the better because he takes each man apart, and leaves him to keep his secret as to the real condition of affairs. Dispensing present gains to others at no cost to himself, he hopes to make provision for the future. This last item he meanwhile keeps guardedly to himself. Partners in deception easily practise on each other.

By a few rapid strokes the steward has put things as well for himself as pen and ink can do, making a bargain in dishonesty. For a hundred write fifty; and, that things may not appear too exactly even, in a second case write eighty for a hundred. So the thing is managed, and there is little risk that "my lord" will be able to detect what has been so quietly and quickly arranged. There is indeed some betrayal of concern in that word "*quickly:*" "Sit down quickly and write." Dishonesty occasions fear. The more protracted the course, the greater the risk of detection. The blessedness of well-doing appears in this, that there is no need for agitating haste. Where motive and act are right, privacy of personal life may be preserved unhesitatingly as cir-

---

[1] ἕνα ἕκαστον,—each one *separately*, in which phrase may lie some confession of a dread of encountering a man making conscience his guide.

cumstances require, but there is no place for hurried concealment. "He that believeth shall not make haste" (Isaiah xxviii. 16). Faith in justice and the God of justice, faith in Divine providence, which cares even for temporal need, specially upholding man in integrity, will deliver from the tremor which moves around the heart where is the abode of untruthfulness.

Verse 8.—"*And the lord commended the unjust steward, because he had done wisely.*" The connection in which this clause stands places it beyond question that the lord of the steward is the person here intended. It is clearly the same of whom the steward has spoken (verse 3), "My lord taketh away from me the stewardship," and (verse 5) "he called every one of his lord's debtors." He it is who is now mentioned as commending the steward. The concealment which was so needful, and which had occasioned all the haste during the interviews, had not secured its end. A general reckoning of all things had to be submitted to the lord; his suspicions had been awakened by what had been told him; his inquiries proved more searching than had been expected; and this last act of unfaithfulness was detected. Yet when the discovery was made, the displeasure felt at the preparation for further injury was kept in subjection, while a first utterance expressed admiration of a scheme so comprehensive as that which had been promptly executed. The thing was well done, though it had to be ranked among things dishonest; but it altogether confirmed his lord in the wisdom and justice of his decision that this man could be no longer steward. His lord was "a man of the world," accustomed to the world's ways, and he commended his now discredited steward for the dexterous attempt he had made.[1] The ground of commendation is the quick forethought of the man, and the sagacity shown in his scheme. His lord easily read its aim, though the false-hearted debtors, blinded by self-interest, may not have fully considered his purpose. His lord saw that "*he had done wisely.*"[2] This is "wisely" in a worldly sense, according to the current phraseology of those who do not concern themselves with right actions. It is ready foresight, taking advantage of an opportunity which is for a day within reach. It is such prudence as can live in company with sin. Still, as prudence, it can have a share of commendation, while the sin is condemned. Nevertheless, prudence of this inferior order can live estranged from true wisdom, and may have, as in this case, share in the condemnation of sin, being entangled amidst the moral evil with which it is associated. All was done by the steward that dishonesty could accomplish to escape the direct consequences of past unfaithfulness; but the blot of dishonesty lies darkly upon the whole. In consequence, there is reckoning to be made in the future. There is the risk of dispute among these fraudulent debtors when the equivalent comes to be exacted. The dismissed steward will have lost his vantage ground when that dispute arises. Beyond all this is the prospect of being called to reckoning before God's tribunal, where "every man must render account of the

[1] ἐπῄνεσε, *commended*, as an intensifying of the root word αἰνέω, implies considerable laudation, and may carry the sense of a somewhat boisterous applause, such as may be indulged in by admirers of the tricks of dishonesty.

[2] φρονίμως, *prudently*,—not σοφῶς,—not with an exercise of true wisdom, resulting from a rational self-guidance, but purely from self-interest,—a prudence which provides for an emergency by means within reach.

deeds done in the body." But such a man as this does not run so far forward in thought. He has a perverse rendering of the maxim, "Sufficient unto the day is the evil thereof." Neither the steward nor his lord is troubled with thoughts which include death and judgment among human anticipations ; the leaving behind of what we cannot carry hence, and the carrying with us what cannot be left behind.

"*For the children of this world are in their generation wiser than the children of light.*" At this point the parable itself is closed. We pass into a region of general instruction and warning. We pass the limits of commendation, and come upon the sharp edges of censure. Jesus gives the explanation of praise from the lips of a man who had run the risk of heavier loss by the treachery of one whom he had made guardian over his goods. His lord had commended his steward, because the children of this world are stricter in their calculations of personal gain than are the children of God's kingdom. To worldly men, worldly things are all in all ; to Christian men, worldly things have worth, but only a passing worth ; to them, spiritual things are all in all, yet even in these Christian men are not equal to the worldly in calculations of gain.

The manner in which this is stated involves striking contrasts. "The children of this world" are set in contrast with "the children of light ;" and the prudential regard to self-interest in the one class, is set over against that of the other, concern for this present time, standing in contrast with the concern of Christians for the things of the world to come. 1. "*The children of this world*" *are distinguished from* "*the children of light.*" Those who stand in contrast to the disciples of the Redeemer are children of this world, having their interests concentrated on its property, and their efforts directed towards its rewards. Material substance they see clearly, and value at its full worth. But to them spiritual things are invisible and unvalued. They exist in an unseen region,—a region of darkness,—and these are counted as of no value, or, more properly, fail to be taken into account. In this respect the children of this world are by implication children of darkness. By contrast, the spiritually discerned are "children of light," seeing things which are invisible, valuing them as realities; not only including them in all their calculations, but assigning to them the chief place in their regard. Range of vision marks an immense contrast between the two classes of men. This is made conspicuous by the phrase employed.[1] Their vision and efforts, their prospects and rewards, are circumscribed by this period of duration. The children of light embrace the period beyond as the more important and enduring. This contrast presents Christ's condemnation of the worldly. 2. *The men of this world are quicker and more penetrating in their reckoning of personal interest within their single sphere, than are the children of light in reckoning their interests as included within both present and future.* Regard to personal good hereafter is a legitimate and important motive for life. It has in it no selfishness, but rightly used, will carry with it the good of others as a natural complement. And it has within it an impelling power to be carefully utilised, as contributing at once towards the activity and influence of Christian life. Worldly

---

[1] οἱ υἱοὶ τοῦ αἰῶνος τούτου,—the children *of this age*, or *of this present time*, rather than this present world.

men see this as concerning worldly things more clearly than spiritual men do as concerning the spiritual uses of temporal things. The defect of the latter appears in overlooking too readily the bearing upon interests awaiting them in a future age of *material things* which belong only to this age. Though they are children of light, seeing the things both of the present and of the time to come, they are apt to separate the two orders of things. They fall into the mistake of regarding the things of this life as if they were for this life only, too much, overlooking the continuity of life, the unity of the present and the future, and the certainty that the use made of the things of this world will affect individual experience in the next. This is Christ's condemnation of "the children of light." To guard them against this risk the present parable was spoken. For worldly men the calculations of self-interest are kept within narrower compass, while the worldly are commonly stimulated by pressing demands. They narrow down their calculations "to their own generation." The children of light must take eternity with time in their reckonings, dealing with a vastly larger question. In this they have unspeakable advantages. Their reckonings are not hampered by apprehensions such as beset the man whose calculations are disturbed by sense of wrong-doing, as well as the uncertainties of this life. They have, besides, a mind aided by all the training of the Divine Spirit. With all these advantages, however, they have to guard against the risks belonging to them as sojourners in a world of sense, for they are as liable as others to the influence of its allurements, and they have even greater need for discrimination and forethought. Marking their dangers, they may learn a lesson from worldly men in their eager, calculating, and often unscrupulous efforts to make gain. The followers of Jesus are prone to act often as if they did not see the things to which He points their attention; or, seeing them, neglected to assign a due place to them in their calculations. The richness of Divine grace is apt to afford cover to inadequacy of thought even in Christian minds, when not braced for a clear estimate of present duty. Because all spiritual good has been provided by God's grace, they are tempted to overlook the law which assigns future rewards according to present service. Thus with partial and distorted views of the order existing in the Kingdom of Grace, they lay themselves open to the allurements of sense, often using the things of this world as if they concerned this world alone, and as if their use could not affect the experience awaiting the followers of Jesus in the world to come. "The children of this world are in their generation wiser."

Verse 9.—"*And I say unto you, Make to yourselves friends of the mammon of unrighteousness; that, when ye fail, they may receive you into everlasting habitations.*"

"*And I say unto you.*" We now come into the clear light of our Lord's application. For a time detained among the dishonest actions and current expressions of men caring only for the things of this world, we have had a sense of the discomfort of contemplating selfishness and dishonesty, exposed by the hand of the Master drawing aside the thin veil of concealment. We have also seen how, in the midst of the dishonest transactions, there are powers at work capable of being directed to better purpose. Now we see our Saviour moving as judge in the midst of all this, condemning the evil, and calling upon His disciples to seek mastery over it, while they advance in the service of God by a wise use of those powers found working even in the life of ungodly men.

"*Make to yourselves friends of the mammon of unrighteousness.*" There is a making of friends for ourselves, by use of earthly substance, which may be illustrated by the conduct of this steward, but which rises far above all friendships having their source in joint interests of a temporal kind. What our Lord counsels is use of earthly substance with a view to results to be reaped beyond this world—rewards belonging to the certainties of the future state. The relationships of the children of light are not for this life only, they shall continue through the ages beyond; and the manner in which present work interweaves the threads of sympathy will so far determine the manner in which the glorified will regard each other in a world where their work shall be continued under other and more favourable conditions, yet never apart from the *cherished memories* of earthly experience. Riches in the hands of the followers of Jesus should, therefore, find a place as instruments of usefulness, performing a part suitable to a Christian ideal of continuity of life here and hereafter. This so-called "wealth," appropriating to itself the name, as if it were the essence of human weal,—personified as mammon,—is so exclusively a thing of this world, and so much concerned in its evil, that it may be named "the mammon of unrighteousness."[1] It does not need riches to make a

---

[1] Not "the unrighteous mammon," or at least only as personified. For the evil, as our Lord by the parable clearly implies, is not in the riches, but in the mode of their use.

man wicked; but wealth in the hands of the righteous should prove treasure indeed. The source of the evil is so little in wealth itself, that it may be used as the instrument for good, and this is its higher use in the hands of the believer who lives not only for this world, but for the next also, and lives in this world with an intelligent appreciation of what shall go out of this world into the next, bearing marks of what has been achieved here. Under the laws of God's kingdom, personal interest so blends with the interests of others that material substance may construct a pathway for frequent recognition of a community of interests. All worldly possessions Christians are counselled to use not for mere self-interest,—certainly not at all for selfish ends, subverting the interests of others,—but as instruments in the hands of Christian love. This law applies to all forms and measures of earthly substance, to stores of treasure, and to "a cup of cold water" which may refresh the weary; for the maxims of the Christian life are not narrow and one-sided, applying only to great things and not to little,—only to rich men and not to poor. The poor have as large a share in this lofty counsel of their Saviour as the rich. It affords spiritual stimulus alike to master, steward, and labourer. Nor are the workings of Christian love restricted to great occasions, for they are felt in all the manifold meeting times of daily life. Our Lord walks in the midst of the communities of interests within His kingdom, saying to His disciples on the one hand and on the other: "Make friends," mature friendships of eternal duration and worth, remembering that even the mammon of unrighteousness can bear fruit in the next world. Help to the needy, cheer to the weary, support to the failing,—all will be *remembered* after earthly bonds have been snapped asunder. It shall be well with the man who makes many friends among "the household of faith." Such friends may depart from the earth a long time before those who have befriended them, but when their benefactors pass away, finding earthly substance and bodily strength fail together, they shall have a glad welcome into everlasting habitations. "The days of the years of our pilgrimage" on the earth may seem "few and evil," but beyond the boundaries of this visible state the Christian shall be received into habitations for the ages immeasurable.[1] In that region beyond the present he shall find that the streams of friendship which flowed in the lower region have not been lost in the sands of time, but are flowing from perennial fountains in heaven. There is a fellowship of life in the next world as in this; a continuity of influence passes from the one to the other, compacting the bonds of friendship through immeasurable ages. In view of this grand truth, we act wisely if, remembering that our continued occupancy of our stewardship is uncertain, we make good use of our substance, thereby multiplying and strengthening the ties of Christian friendship.

Verse 10.—"*He that is faithful in that which is least, is faithful also in much: and he that is unjust in the least, is unjust also in much.*" If that use of temporal substance here commended to the disciples is the highest wisdom, it is at the same time, in the strictest sense, *faithfulness* to God. Here appears in full the explanation of our Lord's reference to the *steward* as one whose position carries instruction to the Christian;

[1] εἰς τὰς αἰωνίους σκηνάς.

and here also comes into view the reason for selection of an *unfaithful steward*. Our holding of temporal substance is a form of stewardship not for personal ends merely,—not for purposes of self-indulgence has God bestowed substance on His people, but for the furtherance of His own ends in view of our social relations. His people are *stewards to Him*,—holding what they possess for attainment of the great ends contemplated by His love. Stewardship holds true of all temporal substance, whether it be much or little. He gives that they may live, and that they may have to give. The great Giver would have all His people share in the joy of giving, and delight in the promise of future return from what is freely given. Not large givers only, but constant givers, may share in future rewards for use of substance here. But here there must be wisdom. Nothing of careless neglect of opportunities for increase or distribution must there be, if the Christian would be faithful to his Lord; nothing of waste, that there may be nothing of want; nothing of stinting where there is power to bless, but "a liberal heart devising liberal things."

So great, however, is the difference in *the liberty which the Lord of the universe gives to the stewards of His substance*, in comparison with that which an earthly lord allows to his most trusted steward, that it needs the *unfaithfulness* of the earthly steward to illustrate what is essential to *faithfulness* in the steward of the heavenly King. Such proprietary rights does God assign to those whom He makes stewards in His kingdom, that all they hold during His good pleasure is theirs to use according to their own determination. In this lies the sure test of their faithfulness. How far they are *stewards indeed;* how far their whole purpose is set on attaining God's ends in the world, will appear even in the use they make of worldly property. Such property is "the least" among all the possessions which God has bestowed; whether it be much or little, these are but varying quantities among the things which are least in God's kingdom; nevertheless, *the real test* of Christian faithfulness is found in the account to be made of that which is the smallest of all. This will discover how far Christian motive has encompassed the whole activity of life. He that is faithful in those lower levels where earthly substance is gathered and expended, will be faithful in the higher walks of Christian life, where nobler possessions are put to use. The grander conceptions and motives of Christianity must descend for the control of the least things, in order to reveal the essential greatness of a faithful life. But he who is unfaithful to God in temporal substance,—he who allows it to allure him to self-indulgence, and, craving that, becomes unwilling to scatter his possessions for benefit of his fellows and accomplishment of Divine ends,—will prove unfaithful in the higher service of God's kingdom. He will not take full possession of the precious stores of Divine truth, he will not sound the depths of Christian joy, scale the heights of Christian attainment, or approach a fullhearted devotion to God's service on the earth. "He that is unjust in the least is unjust also in much." Only the man who is faithful in his stewardship to God, can change the "mammon of unrighteousness"—money, the miser's god, the spendthrift's curse—into the coin of God's kingdom, and so put it to use, that all around shall be blessed, specially they who are of the house-

T

hold of faith, afterwards receiving to himself a rich reward. From such a steward, God, the Lord of all, shall receive His own,—not in the mammon of unrighteousness, but in the spiritual life and fellowship of those who have been stewards of temporal good, and are now servants together in the glory of the heavenly land.

Finally here, the history of God's kingdom, governed by the laws now described, is continuous on the earth. The possessions from which the steward has been separated are not lost, but *left* in the world to which they belong. There they remain to be intrusted to another steward, to be the test of faithfulness in a younger servant who shall be intrusted with them; and to be the means of ministering help to many more, cherishing fresh Christian affection and preparing for later welcomes into everlasting habitations.

CHAPTER XXI.

WORK AND WAGES IN GOD'S SERVICE.

THE LABOURERS IN THE VINEYARD.

MATTHEW XX. 1-16.

GOD'S service in this world is further illustrated by the parable of the Labourers. His service is continuous, involving daily employment of workers, with all the experience belonging to labour, encouragement and reward for service; and not without its forms of discouragement and discontent. All these are now to find illustration in a parable bringing together within short compass many of the features of God's service in this world.[1]

For interpretation of this parable it is of special importance to study the connection in which it is recorded, and in which obviously it was uttered. A

---

[1] The parable of the Labourers has called forth very varied interpretations. It would occupy too much space to enter upon their criticism. They have been ably discussed by Trench, *Notes on the Parables*, p. 162. To determine the interpretation by arguing the question whether the "penny" can represent eternal life, as Stier has done, is not the best course, yet Alford seems to me still more unfortunate in his criticism of Stier. This parable has in our day been unwisely imported into the discussions of political economy, mainly on account of Mr. Ruskin's use of it under the title, *Unto this Last*.

brief outline will suffice for the whole facts. A young man came publicly to the Saviour with the question, "Good Master, what good thing shall I do, that I may inherit eternal life?" He seems to have been moved by the teaching of Jesus. Under its influence, his imagination had been fired by the thought of performing some prominent work, some outstanding pre-eminently "good thing," on account of which he might receive eternal life. The mistaken fancy came from an enthusiastic nature, favoured by the deluding influence of high position and great wealth. He is first referred to the *common* test of all right conduct for man, the moral law. This seems to him quite commonplace, not meeting the requirements of a lofty spirit. Some one good thing he longs to have indicated which will distinguish him among men. Jesus at once puts to proof his capacity for lofty deeds, by testing his readiness for sacrifice. "Go and sell that thou hast, and give to the poor, and thou shalt have treasure in heaven." Here is something rising quite above common requirements, and which will prove his heroic spirit. The result shows how wide is the difference between ambition to do some "good thing," and complete devotion of heart to God. "He went away sorrowful: for he had great possessions." Sight of his sudden departure led to the solemn utterance, "Verily I say unto you, That a rich man shall hardly enter into the kingdom of heaven." Into this kingdom of God which Christ is organising in the earth—the kingdom of heaven in the midst of this world—a rich man enters with difficulty. Entrance is effected only by penitence, faith in the Redeemer, and entire self-consecration. The rich man, to whom his wealth is his real distinction in this world, has special difficulties in yielding up to God himself and all that he has. It is a hard thing to account giving for God's sake the very joy of his life. The line of Divine grace does not, however, exclude rich men, but running its course amongst the rich, includes many of them, that which is hard to man being easy with God.

The apostle Peter hearing this text applied to the young man, and meditating on the promise of treasure in heaven, refers to the surrender and devotion of his fellow-apostles and himself. They had surrendered work and wages to follow Jesus, and had left their families behind for His sake. What should they have? To this the Saviour answers distinctly, with assurance of honour and influence in the world to come, a hundredfold for all that they had sacrificed, and everlasting life. Reward for all that they have done and endured; and, what is more than all rewards, everlasting life in perfect harmony with God, which is the gift of His grace. "But," adds our Lord, "many that are first shall be last, and the last shall be first." The first in their opportunities shall not be found in the front rank for achievements. Many that were last in their advantages shall stand first in actual deeds, and, accordingly, first in Divine favour. When comparisons can be truly made, it will often appear that the wealth of this world and the treasure of heaven have fallen into different hands.

These are the lines of thought which, in accordance with the introductory particle "for," are leading into the representation of God's kingdom in this world as a vineyard with its day labourers. "Many first shall be last, and last first;" for the kingdom of heaven is like a vineyard whose owner is engaging labourers at all hours of the day.

Verse 1.—"*For the kingdom of heaven is like unto a man that is an housholder, which went out early in the morning to hire labourers into his vineyard.*"

The description of the owner is in keeping with that given of the Lord of the unjust steward—"a certain rich man." What, however, in that parable had only incidental reference, in this receives distinct mention. He is *an housholder*. And yet this fact is not made conspicuous. The family circle does not come into view, nor even the family interests, save as these are connected with the vineyard and its fruitfulness. The householder is one concerned as to the fruitfulness of his vineyard, and *in need of labourers*. Ownership of the vineyard thus gives a position of influence over others, but there is also in some sense dependence for the work to be done in order that the productiveness of the vineyard may be utilised. Accordingly, the owner *goes out to the market-place early in the morning*—just before six o'clock, when such work was commonly begun for the day, and when the labourers of the district were gathering to offer themselves for engagement.

Such is in this case our Lord's representation of His Father's relation to the spiritual kingdom. He is owner of all, and to Him all the fruit of the vineyard must belong; but He is in a sense *dependent* on the instrumentality of His servants for the results. He has ordered things so that it is largely by human agency the prosperity of the kingdom is to be attained. The primary requisites are vines of a good stock, productiveness of soil, and the favouring influences of heaven—the sunshine and the rain. But planting the young vines, cultivating the soil, tending the fruit-bearing trees, and wisely using the pruning-knife, are all needful, that the clusters may be gathered in due season. God appears in His universe as an owner hiring labourers for His vineyard.

Verse 2.—"*And when he had agreed with the labourers for a penny a day, he sent them into his vineyard.*"

The householder described, immediately when he came to the market-place, found a band of labourers waiting to be employed, and with them he quickly concluded a bargain. In view of what follows as to successive engagements of different bands of workers, it is essential to the understanding of the story that we remark the *eagerness of these men* for work. The reference to the time, "early in the morning," implies that the owner was himself a man of energy, seeking a full day's work, and who was therefore in the market-place some time before six o'clock, when work should be starting. These men were also early there, as eager to be engaged as he was to employ labourers. They were beforehand, on the outlook for what might offer, and anxious to make the best bargain they could. They soon agreed as to terms,—*a penny a day*, about 8½d. of our money, which was at the time a liberal wage, according to the price of labour in the market. That sum they promptly agreed to; and forthwith *he sent them into his vineyard*, to enter upon their day's work.

The interpretation of the parable as a whole depends upon full value being given to the representation of this first engagement. The description completely disposes of the supposition, resorted to by some interpreters, that the labourers first engaged were less active than those who entered the vineyard later. There is not in this early portion of the record any key to the equal distribution of wages at the close of the day. The opening statement implies that the men first set to work were men of energy, men who sought good wages, and could obtain them.

The representation of *God's call for service* in His spiritual kingdom is a very striking one. *The marketplace* puts before us the solemn fact, quite readily overlooked by us, that the God of the universe approaches men, seeking to enter into an agreement with them, and offering ample wages for their work. In this, Jesus comes to the basis of moral government, always clearly recognised as underlying the whole conception of the Kingdom of Grace. Everywhere there is individual choice and responsibility. God comes into the labour market with *a general demand*, according to the requirements of His kingdom. The conditions involved are those of *voluntary contract*. Looking next at the matter from the point of view occupied by men, we must recognise that all men, by the necessity of their nature, appear in the labour market. To say that all are seeking reward for their effort, is only in another way to say that by their constitution all men seek satisfaction as the fruit of their labours. In an obvious sense all men bargain for wages. This is a common law of life, having illustration along the whole line of physical, intellectual, and spiritual activities. This is divinely-appointed law. When, therefore, God comes to men with a call for service within His spiritual kingdom—His vineyard in the earth,—He meets men as workers who reasonably, and on the deepest moral grounds, expect reward for their toil, and to whom on these very grounds, and on no other, He offers liberal wages. This offer is here treated as a common illustration of the principle of justice. If God asks spiritual service of those who are spiritually-minded, He promises spiritual reward.

He agreed with the labourers for a penny a day. It is worthy of remark that the word selected by our Lord to indicate the completion of the bargain applies to *verbal agreement*, as is natural in the circumstances. Some moral significance may be found in this. The word employed is that from which our word *symphony* comes—a harmony of sounds; and in this way verbal agreement stands in contrast not merely with written agreement, but also with a full and hearty understanding. They agreed in words, but there was not enough to show that these labourers were thoroughly in harmony with the master into whose service they were entering. They were eager to be engaged, and satisfied with the promised reward. The language of the Saviour, however, leaves room for the possibility of misunderstanding, which actually appeared at the close of the day. Thus He indicates His expectation of discontent and murmuring as inevitable tokens of the imperfect phase of religious life in the vineyard of the Lord in this world.

This brings us to consider *the promised reward*. Daily work with daily pay affords the chosen illustration. The spiritual significance will appear by careful combination of the different aspects of the illustrative case. That the work referred to is that done in this life, in the interests of God's kingdom as existing in this sinful world, admits of no doubt. The work brought under notice is a day's work, and the pay is that given for such service. There is nothing to represent a life-long service. There is deliberate selection of the very narrowest engagement common among men. By implication the work done in course of the day for which the wages are paid at its close, must be resumed on the morrow, and by the same necessity these labourers will be in the market next morning to seek work and pay as before. The analogy suggests a limited portion of the Christian's work in the service of God, and a measure of reward proportioned to what has been accomplished. That which has been done is only a little of what is to be undertaken. Daily work for God brings with it daily rewards. The reward does not tarry. It is not accumulated, to be handed over on some distant day in one sum. Daily wages present the best illustration of the law of rewards uniformly acted upon in God's kingdom. The man who has been in God's vineyard doing God's work, does not close a single day's work without being able to reckon up the gain which he has earned, and which God has paid. We must not be misled here by the personal interview between employer and labourer, so as to suggest man's appearance before God for rendering account of the deeds done in the body. The personal interview means no more at the close of the day than at the beginning of it. The engagement is in the market-place, and the payment is in the vineyard. The allusions as to place are against any transference to another scene for receiving the promised pay. Every man who works in God's service not only accomplishes appreciable results in the vineyard, doing much which provides for a richer harvest of fruit to be gathered from it, but there is a clear gain in personal attainment as the result.

This is the daily divinely-given reward, appearing in the increase of Christian strength, the sense of the Divine favour, and the growing influence obtained amongst those with whom we are associated in the service. In view of this last, introducing human relations and rivalries, we can foresee the risk, and even the certainty of murmuring, such as our Lord hereafter describes.

That the day's wage cannot be taken to represent *everlasting life* seems clear on many accounts. The department of instruction is distinct from this. Neither is the beginning of spiritual life brought before us, nor its transference to a higher sphere, nor the accumulated results of the service rendered in the lower. All these seem excluded by the nature of the statements, and by the relation in which they stand. The context, so far as it guides interpretation, does not suggest it. The young man whose inquiry had turned the discourse in the present direction had departed very sorrowfully, but with opportunity for returning in a better frame of mind on some later day. There is, indeed, reference in his case to reward in heaven, reappearing also in our Lord's reply to Peter's inquiry. There is a glance forward to the time "when the Son of man shall sit on the throne of his glory." But in both cases this reference comes in as an adjunct, reminding the true servant of God that he is more than a day labourer receiving only daily reward for his toil. He stands in such relation to God that he shall be present when computation is made of the fruit gathered from the vineyard, and each one shall then have acknowledgment according to the accumulated result of his labours. In connection with these references to a future state, two things must be considered—*First*, Our Lord distinguishes between the rewards for self-denying service and the gift of everlasting life as a common inheritance for believers: "Every one shall *receive* an hundred-fold, and shall *inherit* everlasting life."[1] It is not Scriptural doctrine that everlasting life is a reward for labour. By faith in the Saviour we inherit everlasting life. But the man who surrenders much for the sake of Jesus, and toils unweariedly in His service, will not enter into the heavenly life empty-handed, but will receive an hundred-fold. All this is definitely taught in later parables. *Second*, Our Lord here concentrates attention on the thought that it is not always those who enter earliest on service, and have the best opportunities, who will stand first in the distribution. From this thought He proceeds in the parable to show that this may be recognised even by observation of the service of earth as it proceeds.

The structure of the parable itself is also adverse to the view that the penny represents everlasting life. The selection of the vineyard as the scene of labour suggests divinely-implanted life in the vines, yielding fruit unto God. A day's wage may fitly illustrate present reward among Christians, but it would feebly represent the value of everlasting life. When, besides, we consider the jealousy and complaint occasioned by the distribution of the wages at the close of the day, it becomes obvious how impossible it would be to find any interpretation for such occurrences before the judgment-seat of God. On all these grounds, the double conclusion is warranted

---

[1] The words employed indicate a marked contrast,—λαμβάνω signifying not only to receive, but to claim, as of a thing acquired by toil; κληρονομέω, to acquire by lot, or inherit, a form of acquisition which is not brought about by personal effort.

that Jesus is not here speaking of the gift of everlasting life, and is not referring to the distribution of rewards in the Heavenly State.

Verses 3, 4.—"*And he went out about the third hour, and saw others standing idle in the market-place, and said unto them, Go ye also into the vineyard; and whatsoever is right I will give you. And they went their way.*"

Successive engagements of large bands of labourers in course of a day suggest vast size of the vineyard, and large resources in possession of the owner. In this way there is indicated the wide range of the spiritual kingdom, and the continual demand for labour which God makes. All disciples who are disposed for work can readily find engagement. The call is ever being repeated, and fresh relays of workers are constantly joining those who are already engaged. There is not at each stage an explicit statement as to amount of wages. The law of reward applies uniformly—the Lord of the kingdom may be trusted for bestowing that which is just—and in the hearts of true servants going into the vineyard at His call there is willingness to trust in the simple assurance of His word. The calculating spirit is not characteristic of those who offer themselves for service at Christ's call. The absence of this is conspicuous, making the want of a definite pledge quite suitable for meeting the peculiarities of spiritual life. Nevertheless, in common with all work, spiritual service has its appropriate reward, which the servant of God rightly anticipates, and which God freely promises. " Whatsoever is right I will give you." This is the promise of the owner. And under such promise it is that our Lord gives encouragement to His disciples. Whatsoever is just that will He give, and in this assurance

His people gladly rest, daily finding in it stimulus for their work.

Verses 5-7.—"*Again he went out about the sixth and ninth hour, and did likewise. And about the eleventh hour he went out, and found others standing idle, and saith unto them, Why stand ye here all the day idle? They say unto him, Because no man hath hired us. He saith unto them, Go ye also into the vineyard; and whatsoever is right, that shall ye receive.*"

This return time after time to the market-place is our Saviour's representation of the continual demand His Father makes for the service of His disciples. He has offered life to men, calling them to Him in faith, that He may bestow upon them this blessing. But He also calls for work, and repeats this call all the day long. Many there are who heed not, and rather labour in the service of another. In whatever way His demand be treated He repeats it continually, and as regularly finds some ready to respond. We have thus before us a view of the ceaseless activity for spiritual good which Divine grace has introduced into the world. The demand which began with our Saviour's call, "Follow me," is repeated not only age by age, but day by day, "Go ye also into the vineyard; and whatsoever is right, that shall ye receive." A willing spirit has appeared throughout the ages which have passed. The vineyard of God has not been left without its labourers; the recurring demand ever secures a number of additional workers. There is a blessing for each believer, and a service also; there is union in the service, for the workers go in bands to their labour; and there is variety of work to do, according to the daily requirements within the vineyard. Individual service is a law within Christ's kingdom, implying divinely-appointed work for each one.

The *diversity of time* at which different bands enter the vineyard needs attention. Repeated engagements throughout a single day afford the illustration under which a large variety of incident and responsibility is included. There is with God continuity of demand, and as a consequence additions are always made to the band of workers. This fact, however, introduces a *contrast between work and idleness*. While some are working, others are standing unemployed. It must, however, be observed that the question, "Why stand ye idle?" is addressed only to those who are found in the market-place towards the close of the day. In their case a response is forthcoming, which, in the circumstances, is accepted, placing their conduct under the description of constrained inaction and not wilful idleness. But nothing of this kind is said at the earlier hours of the day, and in this silence space is allowed for large diversity in personal responsibility connected with response to God's call for work. That call becomes in some measure a test for each Christian, as the call to faith is a test of every unbeliever. Idleness in a Christian is an offence to the Lord of the vineyard. Exculpation there can be only if opportunity for work has not been offered.

The response which is heard from the workers engaged at the eleventh hour, "*Because no man hath hired us,*" is our Lord's acknowledgment of a possible absence of responsibility in the circumstances. There may be men whose entrance on God's service is long delayed because His direct call to such service had not reached them, and they had not known till the day of work was far spent how truly He required their service, and how willing He was to have it. "On some have compassion, making a difference," is one of the maxims given us for our judgment of others; and the Lord Himself finds scope for application of this rule. Some are absent from service because they know not when the Lord of the vineyard is in search of labourers. The Lord will have regard to this in His judgment of inactivity. What here appears under the form of *time*, includes all that may be considered under the name of *opportunity*. Diversity in the measure of service rendered to God may occur without personal responsibility such as would involve Divine condemnation. The essential and uniform test for all is this,—readiness to respond to the call as it reaches them. That call is involved in the very nature of Bible teaching, but there may yet be many without responsibility because they lack a direct call to a special sphere. Opportunity is variously determined for those who are at God's call, and eager to be engaged in His service. In varying circumstances opportunities offer themselves, and according to these is the demand which God makes on His people. The nature and number of such opportunities are according to the position in which the disciples of Jesus are placed, as well as the form of ability they possess; and the Lord, who is judge, will make just reckoning of want of a field for work, as well as of opportunity afforded, and of actual service rendered. On these grounds there is scope under government of the kingdom of grace for great diversity of tests, and for much greater equality of rewards than mere outward aspects of work may enable observers to anticipate.

Verses 8, 9.—"*So when even was come, the lord of the vineyard saith unto his steward, Call the labourers, and give them their hire, beginning from the last unto the first. And when they came which were hired about the eleventh hour, they received every man a penny.*"

According to the structure of the story, the close of the day's work was the time for payment of wages. The work and the pay are actually connected, so that no labourer ceases his work and returns to his home without carrying also the fruit of his toil. The result of the work done may be seen in the vineyard, but the fruit of it will be gathered by the owner only on some distant day when the clusters ripen. The labourer, however, does not thus tarry for his reward. Accordingly the owner issued instructions to his steward that the wages should be paid. Having a purpose in view, he orders that payment begin from the last to the first. Our Lord clearly gives this turn to the story to suit the end He had in view in utterance of the parable. Those who had been at work merely for the closing hour of the day came, and instead of receiving only a fraction of the day's wage, they each received pay as if for a day's work. The lord of the vineyard had said, "Whatsoever is just I will give you." Under that promise they might have received much less. But he exercises generosity in their case, and gives them under name of wages more than they had earned,—a wage as good as if they had toiled all the day long. These labourers had an unexpected reward, and departed with joy, telling their fellow-workers as they went that they had received the full day's pay.

The introduction of *the steward* when pay is made is natural in the case, but specially suggestive in interpretation. God, as possessor of all, ruling in all the affairs of the spiritual kingdom, has His representative among the workers, who receives the labourers under the terms arranged, and distributes the rewards granted to them. There is, indeed, a subordinate sense in which every worker in the vineyard is a steward under God, as has been suggested in the previous parable. But there is one who is God's representative in the world, having authority directly from Him and extending over all the workers. This personal allusion Jesus inserts, and leaves His hearers to interpret.

Those labouring only one hour received full day's wage. This first act of payment, when taken with the succeeding acts of the same kind, clearly turns our thoughts to concurrent rewards in the Christian life, —rewards connected with service, not accumulated rewards bestowed after long and varied service. It is not, indeed, unwarrantable to suggest that the whole Christian life may be represented as a day, its entire labours as the work of a day, and its rewards as those blessings bestowed when the earthly life has ended. But the structure of the parable seems much better to harmonise with a more restricted view, not indeed such as would shut us up to regard the day as a literal day, but any limited portion of time in which a body of Christians are united in a common service. Whenever God in His providence may be described as going forth to call men to a special service in His kingdom, that is a time to which the parable obviously applies. Then also there is special risk of jealousies among His servants; and against such jealousies Jesus here leaves a specially solemn warning.

Frequently under the providence of the God of Grace

there are unexpected rewards for comparatively brief service. The disciples of Christ being often witnesses to such events, are here taught to expect them, and to rejoice with all who rejoice in receiving tokens of the Divine bountifulness. The apostles themselves were to have experience of such things, as when Stephen, the man "full of the Holy Ghost," had special tokens of Divine favour in his service; and Saul of Tarsus, appearing strangely among the disciples of Jesus as "one born out of due time," was at once laden with special honours. Such things are common in the history of God's kingdom, and apt to awaken astonishment. They are not easily explained except by the sovereign disposal and bountifulness of our God, and are always full of testing for those who are startled by them,—not only for such as are surprised in witnessing them, but specially for those feeling themselves placed at a disadvantage by their occurrence. The dangers of pride and jealousy are real dangers within the Christian Church.

Verses 10-12.—"*But when the first came, they supposed that they should have received more; and they likewise received every man a penny. And when they had received it, they murmured against the goodman of the house, saying, These last have wrought but one hour, and thou hast made them equal unto us, which have borne the burden and heat of the day.*"

The day closed in discontent. Those labourers formerly to be commended because of having been early in the market-place on the outlook for employment, and who had readily accepted engagement on the pay named, were now dissatisfied with that pay when it was put into their hands. It was, indeed, strictly in accordance with the bargain made with them; and had they simply done their work and received their pay, they would have been satisfied, going forth contentedly from the vineyard, and taking their course towards their homes and families with a cheerful heart. But they had seen others coming lagging behind to join in their work; the last had not come till the afternoon was well spent; and they who had been toiling from early morning had been gathered around to see the last comers paid the full day's wage. The circumstances were undoubtedly trying, and things had been deliberately arranged in such a way as to make them rather exasperating. Had they been first paid, and allowed to go, there might have been no trial in the case. But to witness the full pay given to the last who had come, and to wait on all the while, thereafter receiving only what the others had got, was an unexpected test. What they had witnessed had afforded quite reasonable ground for hoping that they might have more than the promised wage. This did not indeed amount to a claim in justice. But it was a reasonable expectation they cherished, when "they supposed that they should have received more." If their employer meant to show a spirit of generosity on the occasion, it was at least probable that he would allow it to guide him in his dealings with the whole of the labourers for the day. The result, however, proved that the expectation was not well founded. He gave full day's wage to those who came late, but gave only according to his agreement in the case of those who had been at work from early morning. He was bountiful in the one case, and not niggardly in the other, though viewing it by contrast some might feel disposed so to describe his conduct.

He was in the case of all strictly faithful to the contract. It does not appear that he made any explanations of the reason he had for acting as he did. It was his own good pleasure to give the day's pay to all, and no one could have a right to object. In so far as anything in the previous narrative helps to an explanation, it is found in the expression of disappointment and trial which came from those last engaged : "No man hath hired us." Their want of employment had been occasioned by no fault of theirs ; it had been a cause of sadness of heart,—a trial to them all the day long,—as they thought of the wants of their families, and saw the day passing on, and the hope of a day's wage slowly dying out. Over against the bearing of " the burden and heat of the day" the owner sets the burden of disappointment and the weary vexation of the day. This is the explanation which stands before us as accounting for a course somewhat singular. The owner is one who thinks of the private sorrows as well as joys of his workers ; and wherever he sees a cloud settling, he directs thither some token of generosity, gleaming like a streak of sunshine through the gloom.

Often in God's government such occurrences are found. We must not mix up with such cases the trials of those withdrawn from active service under weakness or disease. The parabolic description before us does not apply to such afflicted ones. In the spiritual kingdom, indeed, these sufferers are in *active service*, as truly as those who are toiling most laboriously. Service differs so that one may lie silently all day long thinning the clusters, or may toil arduously turning up the soil. The lord of the vineyard has regard to such differences. That which is just will He give to all His servants; none will be left to do any work for which reward will not be given. Lines of strict justice do not, however, make limits to His giving; in all reward He transcends the claims of His people; but there is ever with Him a particular and tender regard for those whose circumstances have placed them at a disadvantage; a fine sensibility to differences in the distribution of what is altogether the expression of His good-will.

The manifestation of such tenderness and generosity is not, however, without its test, and even its element of trial, for those having both opportunity and will for constant work. Had they a full appreciation of all that is involved in the doings of their Lord, there would be no such trial and vexation. But it is not always possible to detect the full purpose and meaning of God's doings; and there is so much proneness to allow thoughts of self to rule us as to distribution of rewards, that we readily find grounds for vexation where men that we fancy have done less, have been equally favoured. Hence it becomes an occurrence sadly frequent among the disciples of Christ that "they dispute by the way which of them should be the greatest." Occasion often arises when a little child should be set in the midst, and the Saviour's words heard once more, "Be as little children;" "Let him that would be great among you be servant of *all*," —this is the measure of greatness in the kingdom of love, a kingdom in which the love of the Ruler specially encompasses those who are weary by reason of waiting long, with hope deferred. The weariness of the day's work is little as compared with the weariness of waiting, and the God of Grace makes large account of this fact in human experience.

The Labourers in the Vineyard.

The real difficulty in the way of perceiving the essential justice and attractiveness of God's generosity in dealing with those who have been restricted in opportunity, is the tendency to allow thoughts of self to have undue influence. Those who are most busy in Christ's service most need the warning. Work is the leading feature in their life; calculation of results is their regular exercise; co-operation is a uniform condition of service, easily gliding into competition and rivalry; the conditions of their life predispose to eager calculation of rewards. These things are inevitable and well known, and by means of them the indwelling evil of the heart is apt to be detected and even fostered. To this great danger Christ solemnly directs the attention of His servants. In the service of God there is constant need for guarding against a tendency to compare the varying measures of reward obtained by those co-operating in carrying forward the same definite undertaking. The workers have need to train themselves to rest in the assurance that a full reward will be given them day by day as they continue their service, and to guard against disquieting comparisons unfavourable to faith and love and holy zeal. These practical maxims are continually required for Christian life on earth : Work unweariedly, accept gratefully the reward each day's work brings, and, leaving all in God's hands, have no care over the proportions distributed, as if in the inner heart reward were the end of work. Rivalries and quarrellings about honours amongst fellow-workers in the cause of righteousness and peace betray sinfulness of disposition, and are apt to involve murmurings against God Himself. This warning is set forth distinctly to Christians engrossed in service, and especially to those who have a leading part under the burden and heat of the day.

Verses 13-15.—"*But he answered one of them, and said, Friend, I do thee no wrong: didst not thou agree with me for a penny? Take that thine is, and go thy way: I will give unto this last even as unto thee. Is it not lawful for me to do what I will with mine own? Is thine eye evil, because I am good?*"

The murmuring does not seem to have found open utterance, yet was it clearly observed by the owner. The expression of displeasure mantled the countenance of the workers, and as soon as the pay had been distributed, the band began murmuring among themselves. The reply of the owner, however, did not take the form of a public defence, as if his procedure could be rightfully challenged. It came rather by way of private rebuke. He spoke to *one of the band* who happened to be near, and was most inclined to linger under pressure of his discontent. Him the owner addresses as "Friend," not employing the name expressive of actual friendship cemented by genuine harmony of feeling, but that which marks mere proximity as a neighbour or associate. "Friend, I do not wrong thee: didst not thou agree with me for a penny?" The measure of payment had been matter of contract, to which the complainer had voluntarily agreed. Between morning and evening no change had occurred to alter the terms of service, or warrant any dissatisfaction when the employer's part was being fulfilled. There is accordingly in the language of the owner some sharpness of tone, as if he had reason for displeasure. "Take thine own, and go!" That which the man had was his own; no one would dispute possession of it: but his expression of discontent the owner could not justly be asked to receive. The murmurer was left to depart, feeling that even with money in the hand there is scant joy when discontent dwells in the heart. He went, too, pondering the fact that he had lost favour with the owner, and would not so readily be engaged for another day's work, unless he returned to confess that his complaint had been unwarranted. "I will give [1] unto this last even as unto thee;" it is *my will* so to do: there could be no claim in justice for my doing so, as there could not be a just claim for more pay by any of my workers; but I may pay out of my resources as I will, even as thou mayest spend of thy wages as thou wilt. "Is it not allowed to me to do what I will with the things which are my own?" The claims of justice had been met, and there was room for exercise of generosity, in accordance with the rights of property. "Is thine eye evil, because I am good?" This charge of *an evil eye* brings home the source of the mischief, and fastens the responsibility of the whole trouble on the murmurer. The thing done had no evil in it, but there is evil in the eye. There is not merely defective vision,—a species of colour-blindness in things moral, which would, indeed, be a sad calamity, but the eye is evil, there is a jaundiced tinge from a jealous heart: thus is the whole explanation from within. This disordered condition of the observer is still more marked on this account, that the thing regarded as evil not only has no evil in it, but is morally good, is an exercise of generosity which all would commend save those supposing their own interest overlooked, and having no better test of the

[1] θέλω δοῦναι—I will to give unto this last even as to thee.

conduct of others than the measure in which it contributes to his advantage.

Christ is in the midst of His disciples as one who condemns all quarrelling which can be traced to jealousy, and warns His people to guard resolutely against the comparisons which easily lead to such disputes, and thereby to the fostering of an evil spirit. There is continual danger in Christ's Church from neglect of this condemnation and warning. In every heart lurks the evil, which is quick in throwing its influence over the eye, inclining the observer and critic to see evil where it does not exist, and to take no account of the good. It is part of Christian discipline in this life to keep down thoughts as to distinctions among the workers, comparisons of the honours gathered by ourselves with those received by others, and restlessness of spirit when those who have done less work seem to have equal reward. Such calculations are pernicious, and contrary to the Christian spirit. The servant of Christ who allows himself to be swayed by them, fails in the duty of self-consecration, descending to the position of the mercenary who works only for wages, and cares little for the work and its results, if only he obtain the pay he expects and desires. At the basis of our Lord's warning against the bitterness of jealousy lies this maxim of the Christian life: Find in God's service its own reward, rejoicing with God in the gathering of fresh labourers, and in all the encouragement they have in the work to which they give themselves. Even when men come late into the vineyard, and receive some special encouragement for their work, it belongs to all who have been far in advance of them to rejoice. Anything contrary to this in disposition and action is an injustice, and must incur the Divine displeasure.

Verse 16.—"*So the last shall be first, and the first last: for many be called, but few chosen.*"

Even those who have been foremost in work, if they murmur against special encouragement being given to others less favourably situated than they, will be thrown far back in Divine favour. This parable, giving prominence to a marked feature in Christ's teaching, stands between a double utterance of warning as to a reversal of position often occurring in the history of God's servants on the earth. This verse is almost identical with that preceding the parable. Yet the repetition at the close is so modified as to take its altered form from the displeasure which the murmuring had justly awakened in the lord of the vineyard. In the first instance, the utterance is prophetic, announcing a certain result; at the close, it is condemnatory, applying to an actual illustration of the evil condemned. A warning supplies the introduction: "Many that are first shall be last, and the last shall be first." The need for condemnation appears at the close: "So the last shall be first, and the first last." But here appears a solemn addition: "For many be called, but few chosen." A single day's work in the vineyard has raised the contrast between the call to service and the choice to favour. God calls all men to His service. Many refuse to come, deliberately shutting themselves out from His favour, and even proclaiming publicly in the market that they will not serve God. Others enter His service with all eagerness, and prove themselves possessed of energy and determination. But while their energies are directed on the work, their hearts are turned towards the reward, and this to such a degree that they are ready to fret if those who have been less conspicuous are allowed to equal them in favour. Among the workers for God, those are rejected in distribution of reward whose efforts have been stimulated largely by the gain to be gathered, and who lower in their hearts true devotion to God and His cause. Called they have been, but not chosen. Such may be found as readily among those who are new to the service as among those long engaged in it. In a quite different spirit must such men come again at God's renewed call, bewailing the past, and confessing their unworthiness, if they are to find a place among honoured servants. Even amongst those who are servants indeed, jealousy and eagerness for present reward often find place, tarnishing their honour, hindering their faithfulness to God, and consequently throwing them back from a first place to the rear rank in Divine favour,—still numbered among the chosen by reason of the faith and devotion found within them, but less honoured because of unworthiness of disposition fostered in the heart. He who would rightly serve God in His Church on earth must delight in the service, and must have a clear eye and joyful heart in witnessing large encouragement to others.

CHAPTER XXII.

UNFAITHFUL OFFICE-BEARERS IN GOD'S KINGDOM.

THE WICKED HUSBANDMEN.

MATTHEW XXI. 33-44; MARK XII. 1-12; LUKE XX. 9-18.

IN turning to the parable of the Husbandmen, we obtain a view of the joint responsibilities of office-bearers in God's kingdom. The parable is recorded by three of the Evangelists, and all three represent it as spoken to the rulers of the Temple, demanding of Jesus His authority for appearing there as a teacher. This challenge thus came from the rulers in God's house, and was made in presence of the people. "The chief priests and the elders of the people came unto him as he was teaching, and said, By what authority doest thou these things? and who gave thee this authority?" This demand He met first by questioning the rulers as to the baptism of John, thus pointing public attention on His forerunner, and asking what explanation they gave of his appearance and teaching. They at once saw the risks to their influence from being publicly questioned on this subject, and they openly declared that they could not tell. Finding them refuse to meet Him directly, He passed to parabolic teaching. According to Matthew, He first uttered the parable of *The Two Sons*, to which reference has already been made, as illustrating individual service in God's vineyard. After that, the present parable of *The Wicked Husbandmen* is given, in which we have a wider view of the kingdom as a whole, and, at the same time, the most direct historic references. Neither in Mark's Gospel nor in Luke's does the parable of The Two Sons intervene. Matthew alone acquaints us with the fact that the Great Teacher interposed a parable bearing a lesson to each individual among His hearers before He proceeded to this parable directed against the chief priests. Luke says that the parable was spoken "to the people," but this obviously implies nothing more than the fact that it was uttered as a portion of public discourse, in contrast with direct questioning of the rulers. A study of the three Evangelists makes it clear that the parable was directed to the chief priests and other rulers of God's house, and was uttered in consequence of their demand for Christ's authority for appearing as a teacher in God's name. There is thus no room for doubt as to the interpretation of the parable. "When the chief priests and Pharisees had heard his parables, they perceived that he spake of them" (Matt. xxi. 45). This parable carried condemnation of those office-bearers of God's house in whose hearing it was spoken, as well as prophetic warning of the treatment the speaker should have at their hands. The general bearing of the parable, in view of which it occupies its own distinct place, is, however, the matter of greatest interest in studying the Scriptures, and upon this I concentrate attention. Naturally the parable found utterance towards the close of our Lord's public ministry; and, in harmony with the circumstances in which it was spoken, it is full of most solemn teaching as to the responsibilities of those intrusted with office in the Christian Church. Its chief warning is, that bitter opposition to God's claims may be cherished within God's house, and even by those who have been set in authority there.

In the opening of the parable there is *a double representation of the owner of the vineyard.* Attention is apt to be occupied prematurely with the vineyard itself. The primary and essential feature of the parable is the owner whose authority determines the duty of all concerned. He is a *householder* and *owner of a vineyard.* Mark and Luke are content to say "a certain man," but the term which Matthew has preserved has distinct value in harmony with the usage of the two parables preceding. The fact that proprietorship comes out conspicuously, makes it of consequence to dwell here on the first representation. The proprietor appears in all, and his authority explains all. To the eye of Jesus the householder, being proprietor, appears clearly above every object attracting attention,—above the Temple and all its rulers, and above the people who crowded the courts of the sanctuary. "GOD is over all." This thought fills the mind of the Saviour. When the chief priests and Pharisees are engrossed with thoughts of their own honour and influence, as if everything connected with Temple service were involved in these, the Great Teacher, who has come through hosannas to the Temple, thinks of the glory, the proprietary rights, the authoritative requirements of the Lord of all. He is the great householder providing for all; the proprietor requiring due return from every servant. He is first householder, afterwards proprietor of this vineyard. A householder He is, with His household gathered together in that home of which our Redeemer says, "In my Father's house are many mansions." He further becomes possessor of a vineyard, Himself *planting* each tree, from which He may gather fruit in due season. The direct influence of a gracious God explains this growth of the wide-spreading groups of vines, having a common life, under uniform tending. On this vineyard of the Great Householder attention is now again to be concentrated. The primary question for each one who rules, teaches, or in any way works in God's name, concerns the fruit God is to receive from His vineyard. Our Lord presents conspicuously this thought, impressing it on all,—on rulers in the midst of the temple who set themselves in opposition to Him,—on the people who listened to His teaching,—and on His own disciples solemnly devoted to Him, and anxious to follow His leadership. In dealing with the details of the parable, the form given by the first of the Evangelists may guide in exposition—Matt. xxi. 33-44.

Verse 33.—"*There was a certain householder, which planted a vineyard, and hedged it round about, and digged a wine-press in it, and built a tower.*" Having already remarked that the householder was the planter and not the mere purchaser of the vineyard, we have the proper standpoint for contemplating the representation of God's relation to His Church. This householder went forth to survey a piece of ground suitable for a vineyard. It is not suggested that a purchase was made; it seems rather implied that the ground selected was on his own property, which was greatly more extended than that now brought under notice. Having marked off the ground, he planted it with vines, next he planted a hedge; and when the enclosure was complete, he digged a wine-press for pressing of the clusters which should be gathered. Further, he built a *tower*. This word indicates that the intention was defence.[1] The expression is that used for towers on the walls of a city, implying large size, great height, and special strength. This erection within the vineyard was, therefore, planned for warding off attack, implying an unsettled state of the country, and such want of organised authority as to make it needful for an owner to look to the protection of his possessions.

By a few rapid touches in the introduction to the parable, our Lord has given His view of God's kingdom in the world. This background is comprehensive and distinct enough to give unity of effect to each of the scenes afterwards depicted. The vineyard, with enclosures, preparation both for ingathering of fruit, and for defence, stands clearly before the eye. God's kingdom in this world is as a chosen vineyard in the midst of a large estate. "The earth is the Lord's, and the fulness thereof; the world, and they that dwell therein" (Ps. xxiv. 1). In the midst of the earth, as God's most valued possession, is a spiritual vineyard, of His own special planting. The vines are "Trees of righteousness, the planting of the Lord, that he might be glorified" (Is. lxi. 3). His spiritual kingdom is an *enclosure*, marked off by a conspicuous boundary, within which the work of cultivation constantly proceeds. The

---

[1] καὶ ᾠκοδόμησε πύργον. The word is often used metaphorically of a man, as when a leader is described as a tower of defence.

enclosure also indicates separation in the sense of *exclusion*, and the symbol of the hedge, presenting a prickly surface, suggests that the enclosure is likely to be felt as an offence by some who resent exclusion, or seek to intrude upon it. To others it will be only a visible boundary line, and to many a thing altogether lost to the view, as they dwell afar off. Thus represented, the spiritual kingdom is an enclosure within which *fruit-gathering* is continued from year to year. It is a place of silent growth and slowly ripening fruit, a place of joyous ingathering and pressing of the rich clusters as they are brought to the wine-press. Peaceful as all is within, it is a vineyard in a *hostile land*, where are many moved by evil intent. Its fences are liable to assault, its trees to ruthless injury, and its clusters of promise to be wrenched from the branches before the time of harvest has come. These are our Lord's representations of spiritual dangers threatening to injure spiritual life, to destroy spiritual promise, and to rob God of the fruit which would otherwise be gathered. Against such risks God has taken precaution, providing *defence* for His people. His defence is as a high tower. The Saviour's description is thus exactly after the manner of that given in Isaiah v. 1, 2 : " My beloved hath a vineyard in a very fruitful hill : and he fenced it, and gathered out the stones thereof, and planted it with the choicest vine, and built a tower in the midst of it, and also made a wine-press therein."

Attention is now directed to the history of the vineyard so planted, enclosed, and protected. The householder " *let it out to husbandmen and went into a far country.*" The owner did not continue to reside on his estate, and therefore was unable to maintain personal oversight. As his absence was to be of long continuance, he hired out the vineyard to a company of husbandmen, under a contract pledging them to yield to him a fixed proportion of the produce. In accordance with the bargain, he handed over the vineyard, so that it passed under their management for the time as if they had complete control and were rightful owners of the land. The words "let it out," literally refer to a delivering up or handing over, in such a manner as to imply that the original holder had not for the time control over his property. The rights of ownership were temporarily transferred, the real owner voluntarily restricting his rights to that of annual claim out of the return obtained. When this arrangement had been completed, the owner *went into a far country.* He went abroad, departed for a period of travel to sojourn in foreign lands, residing now in one country, and again in another. His intended course of travel implied absence for a long series of years, and accordingly he had made arrangements by which annual reckoning should be made with the husbandmen, through agents whom he should send at the proper time.

Such is the representation of the relation here subsisting between God and the responsible office-bearers in His kingdom. He is in a sense as an owner who is far off; they have delegated rights of control over the kingdom, with the obligation to make annual return to Him, and with cumulative responsibility in prospect of His coming to reckon with them for the whole period of occupancy. Thus Jesus Christ presents metaphorical illustration of the liberty, joined with responsibility, which is characteristic of human life, all the prominent features of which are set forth with special vividness. Individual work is depicted in different parts of the vineyard, revealing personal responsibility in the midst of common obligations. As the series of pictures is continued, there are clear indications of diversity of result in the gathering of fruit year by year. The measure of responsibility, individual and united, is first reached when reckoning is made of the returns annually obtained from cultivation of the vineyard; and finally, in the remote distance, at the coming of the owner to take possession. Underlying this general introductory passage there is a striking representation of what constitutes faithful government during the period of action allotted to the office-bearers of the Church, before the Lord of all calls them to account. There is wide scope for individual thought, experience, and effort; each year brings opportunity for ingathering of fruits; and these are rightly applied when, along with the direct reward they bring to the husbandmen, they are deliberately presented to God. There is a still deeper truth, which the clusters of the vine cannot represent, involved in the joint exercise of faith, and consequent fellowship in service and in gladness. Jesus had made full account of all these things, and we cannot fail to supplement the present representation by reference to them. The immediate purpose, however, of the Great Teacher in the present case is to set forth the responsibility of office-bearers.

Here we are at once introduced to representations of confusion and unfaithfulness within the kingdom. Man's part discovers so much of this, that the historic references are many which illustrate our Lord's words, besides those more immediately under His own eye at the time. Even where open rebellion against God's authority is regarded with abhorrence, there is frequent failure to render unto Him the fruits of His vineyard. Against peril of this, there is warning to the faithful, while there is unmingled condemnation of the openly unfaithful, who make public avowal of their resistance to Divine authority.

Verse 34.—"*And when the time of the fruit drew near, he sent his servants to the husbandmen, that they might receive the fruits of it.*" Long after the absence of the owner had become familiar to the husbandmen, leaving them free to act according to personal determination, and to consult together as to the probable results of their bargain, they were suddenly brought to consider the proportion of the vintage to be handed over to their superior. The arrival of his agents was the immediate occasion for raising the subject. No place was left for attempting deception, by misleading accounts of disaster, or telling of inferiority of the harvest. These were rendered impossible by arrival of the agents when the time of the fruit *drew near*, while the clusters were yet on the vines, only approaching to ripeness. The owner showed no slackness although he was far removed from the scene of production. The early appearance of his agents made conspicuous his determination to require fulfilment of all that had been undertaken.

There is large spiritual significance in this appearance of the servants "when the time of the fruit drew near." The obligations of office-bearers are according to the opportunities given: faithfulness will be tested by the fruit of personal and united effort. Full allowance will, however, be made for the action of causes beyond control of the workers, as for variations of season affecting the vintage. But, in passing under this test, there will be no place for concealment of any unfaithfulness, whether by neglect or by infliction of positive injury on the cause of God.

The question arises under this clause, Whether a distinct interpretation is to be assigned to the agents sent by the owner from the far country, and named "*his servants*," in contrast with the husbandmen?[1] The word employed designates more properly those *born into the service* of their master, rather than those who enter into his service by contract. The word *servants*, by ordinary usage, implied a relation of subjection, which had in it some mark of inferiority; but, on the other hand, it indicated much closer relation to the master, much more abiding and intimate association with the householder, than existed in the case of those to whom he had let out his vineyard. The feature of bondage must disappear from the interpretation, but the more intimate relationship implied must remain, clearly indicating a distinct reference here. These servants must be regarded as belonging to the household of God, in closer union with Him than those other servants who are designated only by reference to their employment, "husbandmen." These wicked husbandmen are workers in His "vineyard," and for the time have authority over it; but their conduct shows that they are not in heart His servants. They are the real *bondmen*—bound to Him by contract, not devoted to Him in heart. Their obligations are irksome, and would be thrown off if that were compatible with self-interest.

[1] τοὺς δούλους αὐτοῦ, the name applied to slaves, and regularly so used when the contrast is drawn between freedmen and slaves.

These others have been born into the household, and are devoted heart and life to their Lord, accounting His service their honour. That the Saviour directly referred to the *prophets* as a class distinct from the regular office-bearers in the Tabernacle and Temple service, hardly admits of doubt. These prophets appeared more directly as servants coming from the presence of God, bearing His message for the time, giving warning against rebelliousness, and requiring that the fruits of righteousness be rendered to God. Passing beyond the peculiar phases of Jewish history, with the specialities of inspired teaching, we enter the wider arrangements of the Christian dispensation. Within this we cannot speak of a particular class of agents, bearing an inspired message for the age in which they appear. In absence of such, the message preserved in Scripture fulfils the same purpose, pressing home on the consideration of the office-bearers in God's house a sense of responsibility and a test of faithfulness.

Verse 35.—"*And the husbandmen took his servants, and beat one, and killed another, and stoned another.*" The unfaithful character of the husbandmen comes out on the first occasion for asking fulfilment of their obligations. The servants pressed their master's demands, the husbandmen resisted the claims, and the result was an outbreak of violence, which overwhelmed the servants, and did not end without the murder of one of their number. The representation which the Saviour here selects implies an unsettled and lawless state of the country in keeping with earlier touches in the picture, specially the erection of a tower of defence. Where such measures are needed on account of the state of things without, there is apt to be special risk within, when the owner, being far from his property, is unable personally to enforce his claims. Against such risk the tower of defence proves of no avail; the evil has arisen *within* the vineyard, and the servants of the lord are cast out in the most violent and murderous manner. Force can accomplish thus much, gaining temporarily the advantage, and having all the appearance of complete mastery. The hidden influences leading to this outbreak require attention. *Self-seeking* is at the centre of the whole. The proprietor had given the husbandmen a position of authority within the vineyard; they see in that an opportunity for enriching themselves, by setting at nought his claims; and *dishonesty* has such power within, that they eagerly seize the chance. There is at this stage *no evidence of enmity* against the owner. It is not alleged that they hated him, nor is there the least reason to suppose that there was any enmity towards the servants personally, who are introduced as messengers previously unknown to the husbandmen. Self-seeking was the ruling force in their hearts, and under its power considerations of honesty to the owner, and kindness or even fairness to his servants, were swept down. Dishonesty, unkindness, and injustice are all allowed unchecked indulgence, if only the production of the vineyard can be appropriated. The consequences to the servants differ according to the position they occupy in the history of the outbreak. Less violence appearing at first, one is beaten; but when this act is resented and resisted by the other servants, greater violence breaks out, and one of the servants is murdered in the affray; when the rest betake themselves to flight, they are pursued, and one of the number being overtaken, is stoned. The *end* of all this is *enmity* where none previously existed,—enmity against the servants, and enmity also against the lord of the vineyard. Accumulated responsibility is the consequence. Now they have to account not only for fruits kept back, but for grievous wrong-doing besides, and the end is not yet. The intervention of legal authority is not suggested; the owner himself will make reckoning.

Such is our Saviour's representation of unfaithfulness within God's kingdom, and consequent ill-treatment of God's servants. He points to the fact that many of those who had entered upon office by pledging themselves to His service, preparing for a harvest, and gathering in the ripened fruit, prove unfaithful. They occupy a position of special trust in the world, having undertaken large responsibilities. Their position clearly expresses a voluntarily assumed relation to God, and they have fully admitted this when entering upon office. That their fellow-men should uniformly recognise their special position is not needful. It is determined by covenant made between God and themselves. Men who set no value on religious privilege and Church organisation, but shun all thoughts of Divine authority, wishing to live as if there were no God, will make no account of a theory of special obligation resting on office-bearers in Christ's Church. In the eyes of all such, ministers of religion are only men drawing their income in a particular way, holders of a vineyard yielding a good annual return. But within Christ's Church a different account must be made of the position, and this our Lord here solemnly teaches. The husbandmen are indeed to have their own return for service rendered; "the labourer is worthy of his hire," as has already been declared under parabolic teaching; but the direct end to be accomplished is the rendering a due return to God. The work of the office-bearers in the Church is to watch over the spiritual life of others, to promote the development of that life, and to carry out all those arrangements which tend to secure to God the fruits of spiritual life, as "fruit which shall remain" when the vintage of the field has passed away. But our Lord here indicates that the only way in which office-bearers can accomplish this is by regulating their entire life in accordance with the covenant they have made with God, as the God of Salvation seeking the fruits of righteousness in the midst of the creation which has been "made subject to vanity."

Unfaithfulness within the kingdom of grace is here traced to failing religious life, or utter want of it,—*self-seeking* becoming the ruling motive, *instead of devotion* to God's cause. In the case of the husbandmen, gain alone is contemplated as the result of refusing the demand of the owner. This must, however, be laid aside here as not belonging to the interpretation of the parable. It is not suggested that mere gain, in the sense of money reward, inevitably sways the mind of office-bearers who prove unfaithful. This certainly may happen, but more commonly other influences operate, as suggested by the occasion for the parable. Self-seeking takes another form in their case. It is the type of self-seeking incidental to rule over others. Desire of influence, love of power, and habits of rule greatly influence the mind, and are prone to come into competition with the grand motive for all spiritual work, the glory of God in the advancement of righteousness. This temptation is connected with all office, and is not peculiar to the Church of God; within and without the Church the tendencies of human nature are the same; the conflict with self can nowhere be shunned by the man who would fulfil duty and be faithful to his engagements. Yet is it required by God that a man be found faithful. From those who enter upon office in the spiritual kingdom special service is demanded, while special grace is promised, that the highest results in our world's history may be secured.

It is not implied that all office-bearers fail in the manner here described. These husbandmen do, indeed, represent the chief priests and Pharisees who heard this parable; and in this is warning for all who enter upon office, for self-love is a subtle influence, spreading easily through the engagements of devotion, as well as through the activities of industry, commerce, art, or government. What God condemns without, He condemns within. When He has planted His vineyard and appointed His husbandmen, He looks for the fruits of righteousness, and waits to receive them. Failure in the harvest may, indeed, indicate unfruitfulness in the vines, but it may also represent unfaithfulness in the husbandmen; and this it must mean, if office-bearers treat lightly their obligation to God in connection with the spiritual life of those under their care.

Verse 36.—"*Again, he sent other servants more than the first: and they did unto them likewise.*" Immediate expulsion of the husbandmen from the vineyard did not follow upon discovery of their dishonesty and violence. The servants who escaped from their hands did not resort to civil authority in vindication of their master's claims. References already made seem to imply that this would have been of little avail. They travelled back to the distant land of his sojourn, and reported what had taken place. The husbandmen were meanwhile left to rejoice over their success, and to boast of it among their neighbours. When the owner had heard the story, he did not resort to extreme measures, but sent other servants to repeat the demand already made. He had shown determination to claim his own; but he manifested no apprehension as to his property, and whatever the displeasure awakened by what had taken place, he resolved simply to renew the demand for that which is his own. This is done; much time is spent; much expense incurred; but there is no better result.

This verse gives a concise declaration of the principles of God's government of His spiritual kingdom. Under parabolic guise, we have an authoritative interpretation of His procedure. In absence of all visible tokens of God's presence among us, it is apt to appear, as it did at first to these husbandmen, that there is success in unfaithfulness. God's government of His Church is in some respects as that of an owner dwelling in a far country; consequently our thoughts are often shaped as if matters were altogether in our hands. A delusive sense of success may attend neglect or refusal of God's requirements. The power of His arm does not bring sudden judgment on the unfaithful; and it is often easy enough to silence and scatter those who press the Divine claims. God exercises *forbearance and patience*, yet He regularly *repeats His demands*. He does not manifest the haste of a man concerned for his possessions. When some servants are treated with despite, He sends others to press His claim. *He appeals to the sense of right,* leaves men to reflect on their obligations, and bids them consider the consequences of persistent unfaithfulness. Better results may not follow from forbearance, patience, and renewed appeal; but only thus will He deal with those who have deliberately undertaken large obligations.

Verses 37-39.—*" But last of all he sent unto them his son, saying, They will reverence my son. But when the husbandmen saw the son, they said among themselves, This is the heir; come, let us kill him, and let us seize on his inheritance. And they caught him, and cast him out of the vineyard, and slew him."*

The remnant of the second body of servants returned, after a long time, to their master with the tidings of their failure to obtain from the husbandmen the fruits of the vineyard. They had the same account as their predecessors to give of defiance of his authority and lawless violence. His property had been again refused him, and his servants cruelly treated. Why, in these circumstances, he did not himself return to claim his own, does not appear. Either more important interests required his presence where he was, or he did not consider that things had come to such a pass that more was required than the appearance for him of one having higher authority, and more obvious claims to submission. He accordingly despatched his son, with a sufficient body of attendants, to demand fulfilment of the compact, while he himself watched over other interests in the distant land of his sojourn. In due time the son appeared to claim in his father's behalf the fulfilment of the compact on which occupancy of the vineyard had been granted. His appearance, however, discovered a worse disposition among the husbandmen.

They had previously driven out the servants, and in the scuffle had become so violent as to occasion the death of some. This, however, had been the accidental result of unpremeditated outbreak rather than a deliberate plan. Now, however, they enter deliberately into a plot to murder. According to natural progress in evil, they pass from their first intention to refuse payment, to an attempt to rob the owner of his possession. The appearance of his son gives them an unexpected opportunity for attempting this more daring course. If they murder him, they may readily enough be in a position to hold undisputed possession of the vineyard. Previous violence had prepared for the murderous design, and it was speedily executed; previous success had led to greater boldness in rebellion. They seized the son, cast him out of the vineyard, and there murdered him. The band of servants attending him fled in all directions, and when they gathered together they had to return to their master with the terrible tidings of the death of his son.

In view of the closing portion of the gospel history, there is something inexpressibly touching in the structure of this part of the parable. A murderous design against Himself was now apparent to our Lord, and in the treatment of the son He publicly depicts His own fate. Often in the hearing of His *disciples* he had given warning that the Son of Man "must be slain" (Luke ix. 22); but now, under guise of this parable, He openly discovers to *the people* what is awaiting Himself, and declares to the chief priests and scribes that He is familiar with their secrets. The successive statements here are of such illustrative value as to require separate consideration.

God is represented as long-suffering even towards the most rebellious. He acts as an owner of a vineyard, who having twice received tidings of refusal to render Him the fruits of His own ground, yet does not expel the husbandmen, but sends still another message, even making His Son the bearer of it. Thus does Jesus now represent the loving-kindness and forbearance of His Father, as indicated by His own appearance on earth. Still more than this is conveyed in the description. It is not simply patient waiting which is represented, as if time were being allowed for repentance. There is *renewed effort* to induce obedience, and not this only, but special means are adopted to awaken in the husbandmen a sense of their obligation. In addition to the fact that the son is the bearer of the message, we have to remark the ruling thought in the owner's mind as fitly representing the purpose of God: "*They will reverence my son.*" The word signifies a turning round from the former rebellious state of mind, and a turning towards the son with respect, on account of his relationship to the proprietor. It thus appears that God appeals to a distinctly *moral influence.* The thought of enforcing His claim is not here, nor is the strict justice of it pushed into prominence, though this is silently implied. The purpose is to awaken higher disposition, regard for Himself, stirred and strengthened by respect for His Son. Such an appeal to the higher nature of man there is in the appearance of the Son, in the patience and gentleness and loving-kindness He manifests. While thinking of God as the Almighty, men must also think of Him as the long-suffering; yet while they ponder the fact that He is all-enduring, they must still remember that He is absolute, " Lord over all."

The Son is set forth as the representative of the Father. Jesus has come as the Son of the owner of the vineyard, *not to use force*, but to renew the appeal which had been reiterated by many messengers. "I came not to judge the world, but to save the world" (John xii. 47). So Jesus said, and this consideration was never absent from His mind. His appeal always was to moral considerations. But He came as a Son representing the owner, *to claim for God the true fruits of righteousness*. He appeared to press this claim on the office-bearers of the Church, and through them upon all. He came not to abate the claim by a single iota, but to require that the whole be rendered to God. His gentleness and His atoning work also point to this as the real end. Whatever there may be of forgiveness of sin and hope for the penitent, there must be righteousness for God,—a perfect righteousness. "Herein is my Father glorified, that ye may bear much fruit,"— "fruit which shall remain." But the mystery all gathers into His own suffering, here quite clearly anticipated, though only partially explained. In coming to press God's claim on men, *He came risking His life— He came to sacrifice it*. This result is unhesitatingly anticipated. Still, the Saviour cannot enlarge upon it. The dread reality can be made known to the world only in its occurrence; and only after that can it begin to be dimly understood by those who reverently own Him the Son of the Highest, and gaze into the exceeding mystery of the death of Him who is the representative of God seeking to bring men back to righteousness. Here we touch the deeper mystery of the atonement, which lies greatly beyond the suffering of death by the wrath of man. "The Son of man came not to be ministered unto, but to minister, and to give his life a ransom for many" (Matt. xx. 28).

Unfaithful office-bearers are condemned as self-seekers. That the spring of action in the husbandmen was self-seeking had been apparent from the first; but the depth of their baseness becomes more manifest, and the violence of their antagonism more terrible. They seized the son, cast him out of the vineyard as if he had no title to be within the fruitful enclosure, and there put him to death. Thus they fancied all could be appropriated to themselves, forgetting that the lord of the vineyard had unceasingly pressed his claim, and that he might come not only to require his own, but to inflict penalty on account of persistent iniquity. The Saviour is an offence to the selfish heart, conspicuously so in the history of unfaithful office-bearers in His own Church. Nevertheless, there is fruitfulness in the vineyard. He who cheered the outcast may himself be cast out. He who appeared claiming for God the increase of fruitful life, may himself be deprived of life. God indeed suffered that it should be so. But selfishness ends at last in emptiness; wilful wickedness fills up the cup of wrath; behind the Saviour is the Judge, and behind the faithless husbandmen God secures His fruitful vineyard.

Verse 40.—" *When the lord therefore of the vineyard cometh, what will he do unto those husbandmen?*" Jesus can no longer defer reference to judgment. The form of His question implies the certainty of its approach. That the lord of the vineyard will come admits of no doubt. The outstanding feature at this critical point is the fact that *Jesus propounds the question to the people,* What will he do? He does not Himself pronounce sentence on the unfaithful, or even suggest what shall be their doom. He calls forth from the people themselves what must be the judgment in such a case. To those who have been hearing him, absorbed by the narrative, undisturbed by thought of its application, not even anticipating a violent end as the possible doom of the Great Teacher to whom they were listening, the answer seemed clear as noon-day, and their response was prompt.

Verse 41.—"*They say unto him, He will miserably destroy those wicked men, and will let out his vineyard unto other husbandmen, which shall render him the fruits in their seasons.*" The people declare such husbandmen to be altogether wicked, regard destruction as their inevitable doom, and contemplate as the sure arrangement of the lord the letting out of the vineyard to other husbandmen who will render to him the fruits of the soil. This is the voice of conscience, a voice the husbandmen might easily have heard but for the constant clamour of selfish desire, and the tumultuous outbursts of passion. The fruitfulness of the separate vines, and the faithfulness or unfaithfulness of individual husbandmen, are not here referred to, and may be classed among uncertainties under human calculation; but that the Lord shall require account is sure. There cannot anywhere be ultimate success in unfaithfulness. Fruit shall be required of a man according to his opportunity for production. Those who are found faithful shall have praise of God and rich reward; but destruction must come upon those who have been faithless and rebellious. The Saviour accepts the verdict of the people; in words of awful solemnity immediately following, He confirms and enforces it; he opens a little the gate which leads into the great Future, discovering to the disturbed gaze of the people the once rejected Son ruling in the vineyard, and the rebellious husbandmen outcasts, miserable in their self-condemnation. "The kingdom of God shall be taken from you, and given to a nation bringing forth the fruits thereof."

The future of the vineyard, beyond this period of tumult and retribution, is brighter and full of promise. Its detailed history in the world cannot be forecast by men, with its varying degrees of faithfulness on the part of the husbandmen and varying fruitfulness of the vines. But the Lord gives the assurance that the vineyard shall yield to its owner its annual return. God shall claim, and there will be willingly presented, "the fruits in their season," year by year continually.

Division IV.

RELATIONS OF GOD'S KINGDOM TO THE FUTURE STATE OF EXISTENCE.

INTRODUCTORY.

THE CONNECTING LINES OF TWO WORLDS.

The three divisions of parables already considered illustrate how fully the teaching of our Lord dealt with the requirements of the present life. He gave detailed instruction as to all that man needs in order to live the life of faith, and to travel upwards on the way of righteousness, teaching that what is grandest in life is within reach of all men. He clearly proclaimed what society everywhere wants, what the world as a whole requires, in order that there may be a progression of the race towards a lofty ideal of individual and social life. While His aim was to save every one who would give ear to His call and follow Him, this aim was embraced in the still wider purpose of making the history of succeeding generations something better than a repetition of the history of those which had gone before. His plan embraced all nations, extending to the ends of the earth, and to every creature in it.

At the same time, the whole tenor of our Lord's teaching gives prominence to the connecting lines between two worlds,—the one world destined to pass away, the other to be permanent; the one the field of conflict and discipline, the other the sphere of order and perfect service. In His view death is a mere point of transition. The underlying truth giving unity to our view of the two worlds is the continuity of moral life. Death does not touch the sphere in which the real life of man exists. Notwithstanding decay of the body there is persistence of the life. A sinful career may hurry bodily decay; earnest devotion to holiness cannot prevent dissolution. But decay of the outward man does not mean destruction of the inner life. There is persistence in a bad life, the source of its evil being deeper than physical energy; and there is persistence in a godly life, advancing in spiritual strength while bodily vigour is declining. Though there must be severance from the present sphere of action, there is continuity of moral life under conditions voluntarily established by the agent in this state of existence.

There now comes into view a closing division of parabolic teaching, bearing on the future state, and indicating that the test of personal life will be reached when transition is made into the other world. An intense solemnity pervades the whole utterances of the Redeemer as He speaks of the realities of the world to come, all visible to Him while invisible to us. This drawing aside of the veil which hides from view a future state of existence,—the life continued into another world,— discovers much that human imagination and reasoning had been feebly attempting to anticipate, though always with much uncertainty and misgiving, so that accents of doubt had always fallen upon the words even of the wisest.[1]

In course of the parabolic teaching applicable mainly to existence in this world, our Lord has frequently given references to a state of experience beyond the

---

[1] Intensely interesting to all students of the Bible are the forecasts of thinkers beyond the range of Jewish privilege, and preceding the revelation of God's Son. The words of Socrates after he had been condemned to death ran thus :—"There is great reason to hope that death is a good; ... that no evil can happen to a good man, either in life or after death."—*Apology*, 40, 41. "I have good hope that there is yet something remaining for the dead, and as has been said of old, some far better thing for the good than for the evil."—*Phaedo*, 63. The thought of Plato is unfolded as the dialogue advances, and the expression put into the mouth of Socrates becomes more decided. "Are we to suppose that the soul which is invisible, in passing to the true Hades, which like her is invisible, and pure, and noble, and on her way to the good and wise God, whither, if God will, my soul is soon to go, ... perishes immediately on quitting the body? That can never be."—*Phaedo*, 80. After the argument has been far advanced, Plato describes the nature of the other world, saying, that after death "men have sentence passed upon them, as they have lived piously or not" (113). He then describes four different states into which men pass according to the diversity of moral character apparent on the earth, separating those who have led but indifferent lives; those who by their crimes seem hopelessly bad; those whose evil deeds resulted from sudden temptation rather than delight in wickedness; and those "who are remarkable for having led holy lives." Having described these four distinct states of experience, Plato says,—"I do not mean to affirm that the description which I have given of the soul and her mansions is exactly true; a man of sense ought hardly to say that. But I do say that, inasmuch as the soul is immortal, we may venture to think, not improperly or unworthily, that something of the kind is true" (114). Specially distinct is he as to those who strive after a holy life: "Wherefore I say, let a man be of good cheer about his soul, who has cast away the pleasures and ornaments of the body as alien to him, and rather hurtful in their effects, and has followed after the pleasures of knowledge in this life; who has adorned the soul in her own proper jewels, which are temperance, and justice, and courage, and nobility, and truth" (114). See Jowett's *Plato*, vol. i., or Cary's translation of the *Phaedo* in Bohn's Library, vol. i. of Plato's Works. The quotations as here given are from the former.

present. These it is desirable to recall now, as they are the true scriptural preparation for study of the group of parables still to be considered. They reveal the connecting lines of our Lord's instruction, running parallel with human action here, and pointing forward to human experience hereafter. A brief summary will show how frequent and important the references have been.

In the opening group of parables, representing the soul's deliverance from condemnation and a life of sin by the merciful and loving interposition of God, we have reference to "citizens of a far country" separated from the Father, and an older brother left unreconciled after the prodigal's return. The returning prodigal is received into the light of a joyful home, but others remain in the outer darkness. When confession of sin receives illustration, with assurance of justification following, there is one in the attitude of devotion who is deceived in self-righteousness, and does not go to his house justified. A man justifying himself, yet not justified of God, disappears from our view a victim of self-deception. In the parable of the Great Feast there are those who refuse to come, of whom it is said "none of those men shall taste of my supper" (Luke xiv. 24). In that of the Royal Marriage Feast, destroying armies are sent out against those who despise the invitation, and slay the servants of the king; and of the man who appears without a wedding-garment it is said, "Bind him hand and foot, and take him away, and cast him into outer darkness; there shall be weeping and gnashing of teeth" (Matt. xxii. 13).

When transition occurs to the privileges of God's people in prayer, references are made in the parable of the Importunate Widow to the wrongs inflicted on God's people by those who oppress them, and Jesus leaves before us the question, "Shall not God avenge his own elect, which cry day and night unto him, though he bear long with them? I tell you that he will avenge them speedily" (Luke xviii. 7, 8).

When we are introduced to the duty of working in the service of God, with the son who repents and enters the vineyard we have associated the son who said, "I go, sir," and went not, and who has his account to render to his Father for wilful disobedience (Matt. xxi. 30).

Attention is largely directed to the mixed state of things within God's kingdom here. We are introduced to the wilful wickedness of sowing tares among the wheat. To the question, What shall be done? there is the answer, "Let both grow together until the harvest: and in the time of harvest I will say to the reapers, Gather ye together first the tares, and bind them in bundles to burn them: but gather the wheat into my barn" (Matt. xiii. 30). "The harvest is the end of the world; and the reapers are the angels. As therefore the tares are gathered and burned in the fire, so shall it be in the end of the world. The Son of man shall send forth his angels, and they shall gather out of his kingdom all things that offend (all scandalous things, all things which cause stumbling), and them which do iniquity (them doing what is unlawful, continuing this as a practice), and shall cast them into a furnace of fire: there shall be wailing and gnashing of teeth. Then shall the righteous shine forth as the sun in the kingdom of their Father. Who hath ears to hear, let him hear" (Matt. xiii. 39-43). There are thus two phases of moral life, marking contrasts of experience, which all men have reason carefully to distinguish, as manifestly tending with continuity of life to wider severance. Of the things which men see and hear none deserve more serious consideration than this.

Finally here, the parables bearing on the varied aspects of God's service in the earth carry similar references. Even in the use made of temporal blessings, Christians are trained to have regard to heavenly rewards. To them it is said, "Make to yourselves friends of the mammon of unrighteousness ; that, when ye fail, they may receive you into *everlasting habitations*" (Luke xvi. 9). The rewards distributed in this world to those labouring in God's vineyard are represented as affording glimpses of the principles of the Divine government in the kingdom of grace, which is appointed to pass into a kingdom of glory. They tell of reward provided for all service, and Divine favour for those least privileged, the value of which will hereafter appear to the satisfaction of all who delight in righteousness. Again, the history of Christ's kingdom here makes us familiar with the sufferings of His faithful servants, and the successes of unfaithful husbandmen. The parable which depicts these things leaves undescribed, but most certain in the future, the coming again of the lord of the vineyard to take possession of his own, and to call to account those who have held possession in wickedness, having proved selfish, cruel, and dishonest. The issue Jesus barely suggests by presenting the question, which we are left to answer, "When the lord of the vineyard cometh, what will he do unto these husbandmen?" (Matt. xxi. 40.) The people who first heard this question, answered, "He will miserably destroy those wicked men." The Saviour heard, but did not enlarge, save that he quoted that Scripture, "The stone which the builders rejected the same is become the head of the corner: this is the Lord's doing, and it is marvellous in our eyes."

From this summary it appears that throughout His whole public teaching our Lord had been continually pointing towards a future state. Sometimes He did so by the unfinished portions of a parable, indicating that there was still to come an adjustment of things left in confusion. What was remarked upon as visible was the deliverance of individuals from their lost condition; what was suggested as always invisible, yet certain to come, was God's reckoning with those who rejected His authority here. At other times, in language quite direct, He pointed the thought of His hearers towards the time when Divine authority would be manifest to all in the condemnation and punishment of unrighteousness, in the approval of righteousness, and full reward of all patient longsuffering and faithful service. Life was thus shown to be converging on a future state, all moral life having continuity beyond the present. By lines of teaching concerning the future constantly running parallel with others concerned with the present, those guided by Jesus were led to a life of holiness destined to stretch away beyond the range of present vision and experience. Thus are we prepared for the series of parables referring directly to the great realities of a future state of existence.

CHAPTER XXIII.

CONTRASTS OF EXPERIENCE IN THE PRESENT AND FUTURE STATES.

THE RICH MAN AND LAZARUS.

LUKE XVI. 19-31.

EXTREMES running parallel in this world and in the next are presented to view in this parable. In one line is seen all that earthly substance can give, and unmingled misery thereafter; in the other line, all that privation and suffering can entail, and unmixed happiness beyond. Absolute extremes are, indeed, unknown in the history of men here. Things are too much mixed in this world to admit of undisturbed satisfaction on the one hand, or unmingled misery on the other. Our Lord utters a parable, in which the extremes of experience find embodiment, in order that there may be vivid representation of the true contrasts here and hereafter. The modifying circumstances are kept out from the background of the picture. There never was such a rich man as this, and there never was such a poor man. When our Lord constructs a parable He does not write history. He encloses within parabolic story delineation of selected portions of truth. The vividness of the picture admits of no doubt as to its symbolic purpose: the height of wealth here, the depth of privation beyond; the extreme of misery here, the fulness of riches hereafter. Our Saviour is illustrating the best that can be gathered out of worldly possessions, and the worst that can come by their loss. Over against these two representations He places other two: the utter loss of the good enjoyed in the next world; the exceeding gain of having blessedness as an everlasting portion.

The relation of the parable to the context is somewhat difficult to trace. The immediately preceding reference to divorce and remarriage occasions this. The condemnation of the breach of marriage vows, in order to enter anew into marriage relations, seems to stand as a thing apart, almost as if it had been a side utterance called forth by some circumstance unmentioned.[1] This parable stands in direct relation with that of the Unfaithful Steward. The lesson of that parable is continued in this. The truth there enforced is here further illustrated. The unfaithful steward there is a representation of the rich man here. The main lesson of that parable concerned the dutiful and wise use of earthly substance. This shows the self-regarding life in the midst of profusion, disregarding alike the misery of others and personal stewardship to the Giver of all. This is the enforcement of the lesson (ver. 13), "Ye cannot serve God and mammon." It is a vivid representation of the warning (ver. 15), "That which is highly esteemed among men is *abomination* in

---

[1] One commentator, quoted by Stier (*Words of the Lord Jesus*, vol. iv. p. 200), has even spoken of the "*disjecta membra* of the discourse;" a good illustration of the risks to which internal criticism is exposed.

the sight of God." This word "abomination" occurs five times in the New Testament besides this example: "The abomination of desolation" (Matt. xxiv. 15, and Mark xiii. 14); three times in the book of Revelation, twice in chapter xvii. (verses 4, 5), "The woman was arrayed in purple and scarlet colour, and decked with gold, and precious stones, and pearls, having a golden cup in her hand full of abominations and filthiness, . . . Babylon, the mother of abominations;" and in chapter xxi. (verse 27), "There shall in no wise enter into it anything that defileth and worketh abomination and a lie." These examples of Scriptural usage give force to the Saviour's words, "That which is highly esteemed among men is abomination in the sight of God;" self-indulgence in midst of earthly splendour, glorying singly in personal magnificence, which multitudes admire and praise, God, the Giver of all, utterly hates. The whole passage is thus by direct line of discourse a warning against absorption in earthly splendour, as idolatrous and selfish in its whole tendency and history. The picture is vivid because the warning is greatly needed, and is easily disregarded in midst of the snares of earthly glory. When such snares are allowed to fascinate and carry away the mind, the life becomes godless,—it is impossible "to serve God and mammon;" and by speedy consequence it becomes immoral, the most sacred of the social ties are broken, —divorce is treated as a ready avenue towards another alliance promising higher wealth and rank, and the name of adultery is treated as one of the words which worldly fashion does not allow to be used. This is the explanation, not formally stated, but clearly implied, of the reference to divorce and adulterous marriage in the verse which makes the transition to the parable of the Rich Man and Lazarus. The whole discourse is a warning of the most solemn kind, drawn from all the relations of this life and of the next, to the Money-Lovers (φιλάργυροι), who lose their life in the lavish profusion of the *things* which belong only to this short part of their history.

Verse 19.—"*There was a certain rich man, which was clothed in purple and fine linen, and fared sumptuously every day.*"

The parable opens exactly as did that of the Unjust Steward at the beginning of this chapter,—" a certain rich man;" and here, as well as there, appears an absence of distinguishing references, as if it were no part of our Saviour's purpose to represent a special individual. He is here constructing a parable, which does not record an individual's history, but will be found applicable to a class of cases. A view is therefore given of a rich man, whose sole distinction lies in his wealth, with the lavish grandeur and gratification it affords. All that unlimited expenditure can provide appears in gorgeous clothing, in accordance with Eastern custom, allowing for flowing robes and varied colouring. The costly Tyrian dye and the finest linen manufactures are brought into requisition, to meet the demands of daily adornment. And he *fared sumptuously every day*. An occasional feast, where many guests were gathered, was as nothing in the arrangements of this household, where was continual feasting. The phrase implies that the rich man daily made merry in the midst of all the accompaniments of grandeur. His house constantly bore witness to the vast wealth of the lordly owner; his halls were filled with guests; the wide-spreading chambers were continually in requisition; there was a perpetual coming and going; retinues of servants attending to arrivals and departures, keeping luxurious apartments in order, providing for or arranging the festive board with all accessories which could add to the splendour. Wealth was in profusion, ever doing its best to display itself, to the admiration of guests and the astonishment of the passers-by, and even of citizens familiar with the common tokens of worldly rank. The general effect of this description is such that the man himself appears even less than the abundance of the things he possesses; he is "a great man," but only by reason of the surroundings which his wealth procures. He is the owner and provider of all that is constantly under his eyes, and he finds his enjoyment in it. The description applies to his wealth, and omits all else. What he was as a man does not appear; that he had brethren, and some tenderness of heart towards them, are facts afterwards discovered; but everything that would give us any clear distinguishing view of the man himself is deliberately omitted. This intentional omission must be pondered if the parable is to be exactly interpreted. The purposes of the parable are best served by silence as to individual qualities and peculiarities, thereby becoming more effectively a representation of the state of wealth, showing what wealth does for its possessor, and what an impression it makes in the world. The man is before us in this aspect alone, the man to whom earthly grandeur is all in all. He is an outstanding man in "society," but only as the arid hill is outstanding from the plain,—glaring in the sunlight yet fruitless, attracting the attention of those around, whether they will or not, but accomplishing nothing more, except that it affords a shelter to groups of wayfarers who find a temporary settlement around its base. Some service such a luxurious life renders in the world by its circulation of money; but even this it does, not because it designs it, or delights in it, or expressly seeks the good of any, but simply because it cannot otherwise find needful ministry to personal gratification. Such is mere earthly grandeur, money-produced splendour, showing through its magnificence how poor it is. Such luxurious life is full of danger to the soul, having too little of mystery in it, leading even to the pernicious fancy that circumstances are sufficient for all life's requirements.

Verses 20, 21.—"*And there was a certain beggar named Lazarus, which was laid at his gate, full of sores, and desiring to be fed with the crumbs which fell from the rich man's table: moreover, the dogs came and licked his sores.*"

Our eyes rest now on a contrast earthly life often presents to view. Extremes of experience are enclosed within human history; some having so much, that there is no end to their luxury; others so little, that they never have enough. The extremes are often found in close proximity; want lies near the gates of wealth. The contrast attracts attention, awakening sad regrets, even leading to reproachful taunts against the providence which guides the world, and giving occasion for ineffective theories, in which bad thought and bitter feeling often commingle. Jesus simply puts the contrasts as they exist, and are seen by us; He offers no explanations, and expresses no feeling, save as sympathy flows in upon the description of suffering.

The Rich Man and Lazarus.   353

He simply says, "Blessed are the poor," in which brief utterance lies a philosophy of human life deeper than the world has yet discovered, or is even willing to study. Dangers beset wealth; blessings lie near to poverty. Eternity will supply the true measure of the contrast between wealth and want.

"*A certain poor man.*" Here, as in the other case, there is absence of personal characteristics. The state is described rather than the person.[1] Sheer contrast of situation is before us; a state of extreme privation is seen in the neighbourhood of all this wealth, just outside the gate, and is laid there, not by the wish of the rich man, but under pressure of the poor man's want. This poor man occupies a beggar's place. Save the worn-out garments which hardly give covering to his body, he has nothing he can call his own. He has no strength to earn his livelihood. Besides enduring poverty, he is a constant sufferer, covered with sores, his body wasting and his heart weary, under the dominion of loathsome disease. How to get a morsel of meat to satisfy the cravings of hunger is a perplexity. As he lies suffering and thinking, there is for him enough of trying mystery in life. But that he may not, besides his other troubles, suffer pangs of starvation, he is carried daily to the gate of the rich man, hoping to have some share of the fragments many times a day swept from the table. His life thus depends on supply coming somehow from the rich man's stores. As the splendid equipages pass through the gate, he need not lift his voice to ask alms; nor can he rise and go towards the house to beg;

---

[1] "Ἄνθρωπός τις πλούσιος· Πτωχός τις—"A certain rich man:" "A certain poor man."

nor would he, with such disease upon him, be suffered to approach if he could. He can but lie there, sorrowful, weary, and waiting, in the hope that some one among them who serve may bring him a piece of bread, or some more fortunate beggar leave with him a little share of the fragments carried away. Through long hours he must lie in neglect, with all the signs of wealth before his eyes; even the dogs of the city, while they pass, seem to have some sympathy, as they turn aside to lick his sores, their coming and going at the same time telling how utterly stricken and helpless he is. Human want and woe are here depicted at their worst.

There are, however, two bright gleams of sunshine falling on this otherwise dark picture of wretchedness. Poor as he is, and loathsome as are his sores, there is some friendly one, unnamed and undescribed, who cares for him; some one who does not forget, does not allow natural shrinking to vanquish feelings of compassion; some one who bears him on his shoulders morning by morning, to lay him down on his familiar spot for weary waiting, and who returns at nightfall to bear him back to the place where some poor shelter is found during the darkness and cold of the night. That heart of sympathy is an oasis in the desert of privation and woe. But there is much more, lying covered from passing observation, in the name which Jesus assigns to this representative of human woe,—Lazarus. The loathsome disease wasting the frame has taken fast hold on the imagination of men, making this name a symbol for consuming disease. This secondary and derivative use has obscured the actual meaning of the name. We have "lazar" to describe a sufferer from wasting disease; and "lazar-house," or "lazaretto," to designate a public hospital for such sufferers, or hospital for quarantine. Spreading through many of the languages of Europe, evidences appear of the deep impression made by the description given in this parable. But this sensitive shrinking from wasting maladies, though it has done much to remove their loathsomeness from the abodes of others, has also hindered the true appreciation of the parable by obscuring the original meaning of the word. The name Lazarus is a modified form of the Old Testament Eleazar, and signifies, "God my help."[1] The selection of this name is significant. Our Lord gives no explicit statement as to the faith, or character, or hope of the poor sufferer. All this is deliberately kept out of the description, showing that it was His purpose to describe a state, not a particular person. But He does not paint in dark colours this picture of human woe, without placing in the name of the representative figure the reminder that trust in God is the key to patience and comfort under trials here, and the security for blessedness hereafter.

Verses 22, 23.—"*And it came to pass, that the beggar died, and was carried by the angels into Abraham's bosom: the rich man also died, and was buried; and in hell he lifted up his eyes, being in torments, and seeth Abraham afar off, and Lazarus in his bosom.*"

The visible contrast ends in the common lot of death. The body of the rich man and of the poor find together a resting-place in the dust of the ground. The poor man has precedence in time. He has disappeared from the place where he has long been seen lying near

---

[1] Robinson's *Lexicon;* Smith's *Dictionary of the Bible;* Alford, *in loco.*

the gate, before the owner of the wealth is taken by death. No allusion is made to the pauper's burial as a last trace of the lot of penury, from which passers-by are apt to turn away. Then the pauper's body may even be treated with disrespect, burial being so conducted as to tell to the stray onlooker that affection has small share in what is being done. Nothing is erected in such a case to mark the spot; yet had it been here, however simple the structure, upon it could have been set the poor man's memorial, "Lazarus,"— "God my help." Our Lord, however, does not introduce to our thoughts a pauper's funeral, does not even refer to it, but omits it as a thing which need not have attention. That which passers cannot witness, yet which would fill them with wonder and admiration, could it only be seen, is depicted in this case as if it were the only occurrence, almost as if the body had been carried upwards as well as the spirit, as if translation had been granted to Lazarus as to Elijah, and even in a manner more glorious, with angels as bearers and attendants, instead of the chariot of fire and horses of fire. "The beggar died, and was carried by the angels into Abraham's bosom." From the side of human observation, it could only be said, "It came to pass that the beggar died;" from a higher standpoint a greater event could be seen, "It came to pass that the beggar was carried by the angels into Abraham's bosom." Thus is represented a great reality beyond vision of men, and we, thinking of it as illustrated in the history of a life, may say, "It came to pass;" but seeking a general interpretation, we find in the words a revelation of Divine government, subsisting in a spiritual sphere beyond the confines of this material world. We who marvel at the strange contrasts in worldly things, may here adjust our thoughts with greater sense of certainty, as with large deliverance from our perplexity. The destination towards which the angels conduct this poor one is described by reference to *relations of persons* rather than to *place*. In this way Jesus suggests a continuity in the moral relations of men,—a spiritual unity much greater than that of an epoch or generation of men in the history of time. Trust in God is support enough through the worst tribulations of earth; fellowship with the best who have sojourned on the earth is the destiny of those who have trusted in God through life's trials. It is not here said that the beggar was carried to Heaven, or to Paradise, or to the Father's house of many mansions, but to Abraham's bosom. Thus is the instruction of the parable best given. The solitariness of the pauper is set in contrast with the fellowship of believers. The man named Lazarus, "God my help," finds his home in the midst of the family of Abraham, "the father of a multitude,"—"father of the faithful." By connecting these two names, Lazarus and Abraham, by uniting these three points in history,—a believing life in patriarchal times, the death of a poor sufferer in far later times, and his welcome into the family of believers with the patriarch at its head,—our Lord indicates the spiritual relationship which, under God's government, unites all who believe. One difficulty may be felt in making Abraham the centre, but it is removed by the fact that Christ is on the earth as the speaker. The Saviour Himself is still a sojourner in the world from which Lazarus disappears; He has still the great salvation work to accomplish;

but when this is done, He shall ascend to the throne on high, and wielding all power in heaven and in earth, shall be the centre of all, and Lord over all, specially the centre of attraction and influence for that great family of the faithful, of which Abraham is the father. But as to the abiding relationship of those who believe, it is here indicated that their life beyond the present is in a fellowship of faith and love, within a wide family circle, and fellowship with God, who hath begotten them.

"*The rich man also died, and was buried.*" In contrast with blessed fellowship with the ransomed throng, there is here placed exclusion in solitude and misery. The man of wealth has suddenly lost all. This result is visible to all onlookers. When under stroke of death he disappears, all his substance remains for reckoning. His funeral may have a word of reference. As it passes along the streets with all marks of ceremony and pomp, it will seem as the trailing fringe of the robe of wealth, which was that day to be appropriated by another. But as to the Beyond,—the Real for the man,—in contrast with ceremony over his dead body, Jesus speaks with definiteness. Yet He speaks in a manner so restricted, designedly exclusive of necessary particulars, and so aided by accessories drawn from earthly experience, as to harmonise only with parabolic teaching. The far-reaching import of our Saviour's words appears only by recognising what is essential to the parabolic form, enclosing combinations otherwise incapable of being brought into close relation. Two states of being, far apart from each other, are temporarily united, as if they were in contact, just as in this world, yet with express warning that they are not intermingled as in our order of things, but completely severed.

"*And in hell he lifted up his eyes, being in torments.*" There is here what wears more the aspect of a reference to place than appeared in the account of the experience of Lazarus, yet here also it is the state rather than the place which is described. The word "hell," when, as in this case, the name " Hades " is used, though often associated with condemnation, applies generally to the state of the dead. Accordingly, there is no reference here to flame or fire, generally connected with the darker description of the place of woe, when the name " Gehenna" is used,[1] though afterwards the sufferer speaks of his

[1] New Testament usage may be seen from the following account, embracing all the passages in which " Hades " is rendered by " hell " in our version. There is the reference to Capernaum (Matt. xi. 23, Luke x. 15) exalted to heaven : " Thou shalt be thrust down to hell," involving destruction for the city, and condemnation for its inhabitants. As to the Church's security : " I will build my church, and the gates of hell shall not prevail against it" (Matt. xvi. 18), which may include a reference to the counsels of hell, or "the powers of darkness," and also the Church's continual loss by departure of its members through the gates of death. The passage before us in this parable comes next in order. After this, we have two references in one chapter (Acts ii. 27, 31), where we have Peter's address at Pentecost, in which he quotes from the Psalms, "Thou wilt not leave my soul in hell, neither wilt thou suffer thine Holy One to see corruption." These words the apostle interprets thus : He " spake of the resurrection of Christ, that his soul was not left in hell, neither his flesh did see corruption," showing that "Hades" here is rather the state of the dead—the separate state—than a place. Next we have Paul's use of the word (1 Cor. xv. 55), " O death, where is thy sting? O hell, where is thy victory ?" rendered in our version, " O grave." The reference here is to the Christian's triumph over the state of death. Lastly, there are four passages in the book of Revelation. One in which Christ says, I " have the keys of hell and of death" (i. 18), control over both soul and body in their separate state. Next, there is the description of the "pale horse " and his rider, when death and hell are personified : " His name that sat on him was Death, and hell followed with him" (vi. 8), where the allusion seems to be to death of the body, and separation of the soul. There are only two more examples, both found in the twentieth chapter (xx. 13, 14) : " Death and hell delivered up the dead which were in them,"

torment as like the burning of a flame. There is, besides, a deliberate omission of external circumstances or accompaniments of his state. There is even a complete absence of all that would account for his misery. On the other hand, there is no allusion to companionship, as if others were sharing in his lot, though by implication all who pass from the earth as he has done must have a similar destiny. We have thus a parabolic contrast, implying that there is a worth in companionship among the believing, which has no counterpart in the case of those who have left their all

clearly meaning the grave and the separate state; and, "Death and hell were cast into the lake of fire," that is, the corruption of the body and the separation of the soul were ended; "no more death," no longer continuance of a disembodied state. These are the whole of the New Testament passages in which the word "Hades" occurs. In view of them unitedly we may warrantably interpret the words in the parable as meaning, "In the separate state he lifted up his eyes." The darker representation of a place of condemnation and woe, also named "hell" in our Bibles, are those in which the name "Gehenna" is used. The complete list is appended for contrast. There are three references in the Sermon on the Mount. To the warning against wronging a brother, as a breach of the sixth commandment, Jesus adds, "Whosoever shall say, Thou fool, shall be in danger of hell fire" (Matt. v. 22). To the warnings against breach of the seventh commandment, He adds twice the solemn words, as to parting with an eye or a hand: "It is profitable for thee that one of thy members should perish, and not that thy whole body should be cast into hell" (Matt. v. 29, 30). When counselling His disciples to face boldly the danger of death, Jesus says, "Fear not them which kill the body, but are not able to kill the soul: but rather fear him which is able to destroy both soul and body in hell" (Matt. x. 28). This warning is given in Luke's Gospel thus: "Be not afraid of them that kill the body, and after that have no more that they can do. But I will forewarn you whom ye shall fear: Fear him, which after he hath killed, hath power to cast into hell; yea, I say unto you, Fear him" (Luke xii. 4, 5). Connected with foreshadowing of offences, and consequent condemnation in the future, is placed the risk of being "cast into everlasting fire" ($\epsilon\iota\varsigma$ $\tau\grave{o}$ $\pi\hat{v}\rho$ $\tau\grave{o}$ $a\grave{\iota}\acute{\omega}\nu\iota o\nu$), which in repetition, under reference to the eye, reads, "Into hell fire," or behind them, and are overwhelmed with the sense of desolation in absence of everything which could sustain and cheer, with the presence of everything to embitter thought and feeling. To share in faith gives power to companionship; to be involved in a common disaster destroys the help of companionship, and awakens a drearier sense of hopelessness.

"*In hell he lifted up his eyes, being in torments.*" The lifting up of the eyes is introduced in harmony with the language of earth, though the eyes once familiar with earthly splendour lie glazed in death, the body the hell of fire (εἰς τὴν γέενναν τοῦ πυρός) (Matt. xviii. 8, 9). Parallel with these are three examples in Mark's Gospel (Mark ix. 43, 45, 47). Following a warning against inflicting wilful wrong "on one of these little ones," there is separate mention of the hand, foot, and eye, and a threefold utterance of nearly the same words: "It is better for thee to enter into life maimed," than having two hands, feet, and eyes, "to be cast into hell, into the fire that never shall be quenched (unquenchable); where their worm dieth not, and the fire is not quenched." In these passages the references to duration are conspicuous. They are three in number: fire unquenchable, *their* worm dieth not, the fire is not quenched. These seem to imply these three things: That the fire is persistent; that experience of misery is continuous; that there is no interposition of a higher power to destroy the burning. There is thus double reference to the fact that the fire is not quenched. The significance of "not quenched" may be judged from Christ's use of the positive, as in the next parable: "Give us of your oil, for our lamps are gone out"—are quenched (Matt. xxv. 8). Further aid in interpretation is found by an example of the use of the negative in a different relation: "A bruised reed shall he not break, and smoking flax shall he not quench" (Matt. xii. 20). There remain two more references in Matthew's Gospel, connected with our Lord's denunciations of the scribes and Pharisees as hypocrites, provoking others. When a proselyte is made, "ye make him twofold more the child of hell (υἱὸν γεέννης) than yourselves" (Matt. xxiii. 15). At close of the lengthened passage of condemnation are the words: "Ye serpents, ye generation of vipers, how can ye escape the damnation of hell?" (Matt. xxiii. 33.) The last passage in which the name appears is James iii. 6: "The tongue is a fire, a world of iniquity: . . . and it is set on fire of hell."

having found a resting-place in the tomb. The words imply clear observation of the altered position, preliminary to the reflection which such a change as his is fitted to awaken. The body with its special senses and all its sensibilities had been left behind, so that the suffering endured was not of a physical nature. But as he lifts up the eyes of the soul he takes account of his change of destiny, feels his great loss, ponders his foolish and utterly reckless disregard of his duty to God, and of all the higher requirements of human life. Reflecting on these things he is in misery; he is unable to stop his bitter regrets, and equally unable to find any comfort under his sense of self-condemnation: he is "in torments." It is not suggested that this torment came from any external source, least of all that God inflicted torture upon him as one now brought under His power. There is nothing to suggest such thought. The structure of the parable implies the reverse, making almost conspicuous the absence of external causes of trouble, representing even a strange solitariness. The key to the torment is within the man, along with absence of all that he had been wont to regard as of value. His own history, with the full sense of all that it has involved, and the quickened action of his reflective powers, presents all that the parable supplies in explanation of a suffering so full of agony that it is described as the state of one who is in torments.

The purely parabolic nature of the story now comes prominently into view with the reference to the seeing of Abraham and Lazarus; and a narrative of conversation between the three, as if they three had been the sole occupants of neighbouring regions, separated only by a narrow, though deep and impassable, ravine. He lifted up his eyes, and "*seeth Abraham afar off, and Lazarus in his bosom.*" This combination of incident, aided by contiguity of place, is essential for our Lord's purpose in putting the contrasts of the future state as vividly before the mind as the contrasts of wealth and poverty in the present state. Sight and speech supply the necessary conditions for bringing out these contrasts; and they are employed specially to meet the requirements of those still dwelling in the present state. Previously, our Lord had described the *state* of the rich man and Lazarus, rather than the *place* in which they were; but now the accessories of place are introduced according to the requirements of our senses, under those conditions familiar to us. This is so essential for the structure of a parabolic story, that we should misunderstand the whole plan of our Saviour's teaching here, did we allow ourselves to take it as suggesting sojourn in the same place, or even in the same neighbourhood, as if within a distance so small as to be compatible with sight and speech as those are exercised by us in this world. That they were all three in the separate state, in Hades, regarded as a state of existence, is true; but it is a fact which contributes nothing in favour of actual proximity of place. The lines of contrast in personal history which crossed each other at the point of death must be regarded as diverging lines, separating from each other as they are continued. Contiguity here means nothing more than parabolic combination of distinct and widely separated realities, in accordance with conditions of life on earth which must be quite inapplicable beyond death. These

realities are: The complete contrast of torment and
blessedness; recognition of this contrast as involving
wide separation of individuals according to life and
character under the moral government of God; perception of the terrible truth that these contrasts in
state and thought are inevitable by mere continuity of
life, and because of personal choice deliberately maintained throughout the earthly life. To the view of
the rich man, as he lifts up his eyes now, the contrast
between a life of faith in God, patient waiting on Him,
with devotion to His will, and a life of unceasing self-
indulgence, allowing no place to thoughts of God and
of the grand end of human life, appears a contrast so
great, that he is overwhelmed with a sense of the
wickedness and madness of his own career. The sight
of Abraham far away from him, and the poor man
Lazarus resting and rejoicing in closest fellowship with
the great father of their people, gave intensity to his
otherwise disturbing reflections. There is no sight of
God, no light from His presence, but only sight of
Abraham. The ready recognition of Abraham, however, and that in the separate state, a recognition as
ready as that of Lazarus, is our Lord's suggestion of
the strong and ensnaring tendency of the people to
trust to their descent from Abraham as sufficient
warrant for acceptance with God. The thought of
" father Abraham" had gone deeply into his mind;
the current congratulation, " We be Abraham's children," had often found expression in midst of the
circles within his reception rooms; and a continuous
influence from this source had been kept up by regular
appearances at the Temple service. The result is
before us here in the quick recognition of Abraham,

and the prompt appeal to him under sense of overwhelming misery.

Verse 24.—"*And he cried and said, Father Abraham, have mercy on me, and send Lazarus, that he may dip the tip of his finger in water, and cool my tongue; for I am tormented in this flame.*"

In harmony with the remoteness of the sight of blessed companionship "*afar off*" from the place where he was, the rich man is represented, not merely as speaking, but as crying aloud. Attention to him he felt to be the pressing need; he was fully in earnest with utterance of this prayer addressed to the great father of the faithful. His sense of actual relationship and consequent claim appears first in the address, "Father Abraham." The name comes naturally to his lips as a recollection of a familiar phrase, a survival of a form of faith, which had been powerful enough to mislead, though not to wean and awaken, far less to elevate. "Have mercy on me!" Have compassion; show some regard to *me*, whilst thy chief regard is given to Lazarus. Have pity on me, whose case is pitiable indeed. This prayer is in complete contrast with that of the publican in the parable (Luke xviii. 13), not only as it is offered to Abraham, while the other is offered to God; but as it is a cry for pity, whereas the other was a pleading for pardon. Reading our English Bible, we are apt to miss the contrast, as both prayers seem to involve a cry for *mercy;* yet are we saved from misunderstanding by the difference of the quarter to which the cry is directed in the two cases. The words employed, however, are quite different, having a perfectly distinct meaning, though the similarity of rendering is natural in accordance with our own usage, which takes "mercy to pardon" as one meaning of the word, while compassion, disposition to mitigate anguish, or deliver from it, is even more common. The contrast is marked.[1] The rich man pleads for pity, begging even for that as a thing to which he has no more claim than Lazarus had during his life on earth to the fragments swept from the festive board. In this world beyond he is utterly destitute, and endures misery far greater than the penury of earth, and the wasting disease which afflicted Lazarus during his sojourn in the earth.

"*Send Lazarus, that he may dip the tip of his finger in water, and cool my tongue; for I am tormented in this flame.*" This entreaty shows how little he now feels warranted to expect even from the compassion of Abraham, yet how intense is his wretchedness. Our Lord puts these things together as the revelation at once of his experience and desire, while by omission of all reference of prayer to God, He indicates how hopeless is the condition of the man's soul. There is no gleam of light here, no trace of hope, save this little spark struck by the thought that Abraham might have some power and inclination to help a son of Israel; but that spark almost instantly disappears in the gloom. In accordance with the general features of the story, his suffering is described in language commonly applied to bodily experience. The intensity of his distress is such that he feels as if he were tormented in flame. There is nothing in the description of the situation to suggest

---

[1] The publican's prayer is, 'Ο Θεὸς, ἱλάσθητί μοι τῷ ἁμαρτωλῷ— "God be merciful to me a sinner;" the rich man's prayer is, Πάτερ 'Αβραάμ, ἐλέησόν με—"Father Abraham, have compassion on me." His misery is the chief concern of the latter, not his sin.

such a representation, but the intensity of his feeling could find expression in no other way. Willingly, most willingly, would he accept aid from Lazarus, if the beggar who once lay at his gate would now dip even the tip of his finger in water, and for an instant touch the tip of his tongue. The language is still that of earth, as if bodily experience determined the whole state. Thus Jesus describes the whole man, mind and heart, as disturbed and tormented at thought of the awful calamity of being separated at once from wealth and all wellbeing; having once been a great man among the children of Israel, but now far off from Abraham's circle; having gained and lost the world, and with it lost his soul; having pleased himself, but lost the good pleasure of God. One drop of consolation would mitigate his torment, but even that cannot be had. Yet will he cry aloud, if peradventure comfort might be brought from afar. He does not ask to be taken out of the flame, nor that the flame itself be put out; these seem to him things not to be thought of or named; but even the least mitigation would be inexpressible gain.

Verses 25, 26.—"*But Abraham said, Son, remember that thou in thy lifetime receivedst thy good things, and likewise Lazarus evil things: but now he is comforted, and thou art tormented. And besides all this, between us and you there is a great gulf fixed: so that they which would pass from hence to you cannot; neither can they pass to us, that would come from thence.*"

As the rich man's prayer points to the dreadful contrast between the state into which he has come and that upon which Lazarus had entered, Abraham's reply declares that the contrast is the natural result of that

which had existed in the preceding life. This is the
solemn warning from a loving Saviour against the
blinding tendency of worldly allurements, aided by
groundless hope that in the world to come the destinies
of men will not be found greatly to differ. Jesus
would destroy false peace, by casting light upon
contrasts existing in the invisible state. This purpose
becomes increasingly clear from study of the answer
put into the mouth of Abraham. The suppliant's
appeal is not disregarded, but the answer tells how
impossible it is to have the desire of the heart fulfilled.
The claim of kinship involved in the appeal, "Father
Abraham!" is not disallowed, for Abraham, responding
to him as one who had been numbered among his
children, addresses him as "son," or rather as his
"child." But the reply is a call to remember the
great contrast between himself and Lazarus, as it existed
during their earthly life. Such recollections only add
fuel to the flame; yet must the sufferer remember and
reflect. These memories have already caused to him
intensity of suffering, but they cannot be stayed; the
thought even of appealing to Abraham only gives
increased force to distressing recollections. Memory is
a helping power for those advancing to higher things,
—a tormenting power for men taking a downward
course. Even for those travelling in the way of
righteousness, it carries much to humble, as well as
much to cheer; but for those who empty their life of
godliness, there is a filling of the memory with such
stores as self-seeking and self-indulgence accumulate,
the counting up of which will cause heaviness of heart.
In the final reckonings of a godless life, gain counts as
loss. This certainty stands out the more impressively

in the parable, because the structure of it does not suggest a life blackened by vice and crime. The memory is not filled with bitter recollections of those who had been lured to ruin along a maddening course of licentiousness, whose reproaches sting like vipers, because their testimony is true and their condemnation just. From fear of such recollections men may well shrink as from scorching flame. Dreaded memories there must be when the hand of wealth has offered the bribe which tempted to wickedness; dreaded memories for those who have stooped to accept the price of iniquity, with need for afterwards hearing the reminder, "Thou hadst thy reward." To have escaped such memories by having shunned the wickedness which places the recollections within, is unspeakable deliverance. Even with memories less dreadful, however, the misery is as the torment of a flame. This man had all that wealth could give; he had spent his days in luxurious ease and indulgence, eating, drinking, and making merry; he welcomed others to share liberally in the pleasures his resources could so amply provide; he was esteemed and honoured by multitudes; and it does not appear that he did more by way of evil influence than encourage the hundreds of welcome guests to spend their days as he did, in a constant round of self-indulgence, caring nothing for those beyond their gay circle, nothing for their own life beyond the present state, and nothing for God the Giver of all who speaks from above, saying, "Be ye holy, for I am holy." After all this thoughtless, godless gaiety, and because of it all, there is torment, in the midst of which the sufferers have only to recollect the past to see that they had chosen their portion, making light of the consequences. "Remember that thou in thy lifetime receivedst *thy* good things, and likewise Lazarus evil things." The form of reference to the abundance of the things previously possessed—"*thy* good things"—indicates personal choice, and the use made of them. It is not said of the very different lot which had fallen to Lazarus, that the want and suffering were *his* evil things; his they were most truly, being the source of trial all his life through, but not his by choice; and they did not extend beyond the earthly life. The evil had been patiently endured, and had been so used as to make it minister to good,—good of that higher kind, extending itself into the world beyond, there showing its real and abiding worth. The two states are the natural and inevitable sequence of two states which preceded them: "Now he is comforted, and thou art tormented."

The impossibility of transference or change involved in the continuity of life in both cases, is next set forth under impressive parabolic forms. Contiguity of place, introduced first to meet the requirements of speech, is now employed to give greater vividness to the reality of complete separation of state. The purely parabolic nature of the representation is obvious, a spiritual impossibility being translated into a physical. Verse 26.— "*And besides all this, between us and you there is a great gulf fixed.*" During the earthly life each had made his choice, the one to trust in riches, and that trust had failed; the other to trust in God, and that had proved all-sufficient. But beyond what lay purely in the choice of the individuals, there is a righteous sovereignty which suddenly becomes more apparent than it had been in the earthly state. Hitherto it had proved easy to shut the eyes to this reality; now it had become impossible. A sovereignty there is in distribution of wealth, and a sovereign appointment of want. But we find it easy to speak of the one as good fortune, and the other as sad misfortune. Divine sovereignty does not here force itself upon our notice, however apparent its reality may be to those who reflect. But when wealth passes away from the grasp, the moral results remain, abiding in the heart; when poverty and disease end, losing their power by destruction of the body, God's favour abides, its rest and gladness filling the soul. The new state of existence makes the moral government of God appear as the one certainty. The life of self-seeking and self-indulgence, which treats lightly of godliness and regards religious earnestness in others as an offensive profession, has its hollowness and wickedness exposed in God's presence. The life of lowly trust, confessing personal sin and longing after righteousness, is commended of God, finding its recompence in His favour. These two states are far apart, severed by a vast chasm. As the life of worldliness and the life of godliness are at variance, even when they dwell in closest neighbourhood, tending by their continuance to a wider severance, so by the sovereign decree of Him who rules in righteousness, and by the necessity of His unchangeable nature, the chasm which separates them is fixed. In the world beyond, a great gulf separates godlessness from godliness. It is a gulf wider than the vastest ocean of this world, "fixed" more immovably than "the everlasting hills." The separation is clear even here, had we only eyes to see it; there it is unmistakable, for nothing obscures it, everything forces it on attention. Even in the present state of existence, each one may ascertain the severance between the self-seeking and the God-fearing life; even with our imperfect appliances for measurement, we may satisfy ourselves of the widening separation of these two, and, continuing our reckoning onward, may be impressed with the conviction that it must be an awful chasm which ultimately separates these two lives. Extremes of human history are, indeed, placed before our view in this parable; between these extremes are endless diversities under the hurry and eagerness, the glitter and sadness of life; the God who rules above will take account of all these diversities, and have careful regard to all disadvantages; but He is holy, ruling in righteousness and for righteousness, and He has set a vast chasm of severance between holiness and unholiness.

"*They which would pass from hence to you cannot; neither can they pass to us, that would come from thence.*" In view of the account he gives of his torment, the rich man's request is a small one, that Lazarus might bring him some little mitigation of his anguish; but even this much cannot be granted,—the chasm lying between is impassable. The exclusively parabolic nature of this conversation being recognised, we cannot interpret it as suggesting an intermingling of feeling, any more than interchange of communication, on the part of those completely separated. The parable does not here warrant the inference that there is among the ransomed an unfulfilled desire to go as ministering angels to those in the place of woe, nor that there is among the condemned the expectation of such coming. The impossibility of coming and going is set forth; and with this, the still more solemn truth, the impossibility of altering the misery of the self-condemned by the best efforts of those whose joy and hope are in the Divine favour. We cannot go; thou canst not come. The impossibility here does not spring from any want of longing for deliverance on the part of the suffering, nor from any want of willingness on the part of the ransomed. Both states of feeling may be represented as natural to both in their circumstances. Yet such feeling is powerless for alteration of the state of torment, as for alteration of the conditions of blessedness. The life of worldliness which has led into the present misery cannot be changed now; the recollections of a past life cannot be altered, any more than the events which have registered themselves on the tablets of memory, and they cannot be obliterated by power of the purest and deepest sympathy; the sensibility of the mind under presence of such recollections, and the self-reproach they occasion, cannot be deadened. All these are fixed results, as fixed as the results of a life of patient trust in God; as persistent as the recollections dwelling in the soul of the escaped sufferer, or the sense of rest and thankfulness flowing steadily in upon his spirit. The inevitable fixedness of result flowing from the life we are now living is what a gracious loving Saviour would have us ponder while we live. We are living, and we must hereafter continue to live, under the government of fixed law.

Verses 27, 28.—" *Then he said, I pray thee therefore, father, that thou wouldest send him to my father's house: for I have five brethren; that he may testify unto them, lest they also come into this place of torment.*"

The death of hope for himself is the rise of fear for his brethren. If Lazarus could not help him, he might help them. If there was no path between the two states beyond death, there might yet be return from the state of the blessed back through the gate of death into the earthly state, where shines the light of hope; and fresh work might yet in this way be assigned to one who had escaped from life's troubles and conflicts, by passing into peace. The words of Abraham had directed his attention to a terrible reality, of which he in his eager desire for mitigation of suffering had been oblivious. He had, indeed, recognised the inevitable in his torment, but he had not considered the impossibility of relief. When the impassable chasm became apparent, his prayer fell back into his own heart not only as a useless thing, but as an additional source of trouble. Even thus dismayed, however, he thought of his brethren. Awakened thought takes in the realities of earthly life, directing affection for kindred into a form of concern which had been crushed down while its influence might have done good. A man who had felt no care for his own soul could not seek salvation for others; and this is now fresh evidence of the wickedness of the life he had spent on the earth, and a reason for anxiously desiring to avert the dreaded consequences. To stay his own responsibilities, to stop the action of influences he had set in motion, to turn the course of all his five brothers in a different direction from that which he had taken,—from a life of self-indulgence to trust in God and earnest striving after righteousness. These things were now ardently desired. How impossible of accomplishment they now seemed to him. He is now learning in a bitter experience how slender are the links between desire and fulfilment, if thoughts of God are banished from the life and Divine love is not esteemed the true source of blessing. He is discovering how fruitless is the attempt to arise in agitating fear, seeking to stay by his single effort the stream of influence which took its rise from his own life. Might, then, the thing impossible for him be done by Lazarus, with consent of the father of the faithful, under sanction of God? This is now his single desire. But here also hope must die out, while he learns what a dreadful penalty of sin lies in power of thought. Affection for his kindred had not died out of his heart; what had been good in his character remained, as well as what had been evil in it; and the good awoke as a flickering light, to show dimly to his eye how sinful in itself, and how cruel to others, a life of worldliness had been. Now, he would avert the consequences if he could; he would save his brothers from the doom to which he had come. This seemed to him now matter of greatest urgency. For its attainment he would even have Lazarus return from the state of the dead. But in this also he must endure disappointment. For them, as for himself, the earnest desire of his heart is directed upon what cannot be granted.

Verse 29.—"*Abraham saith unto him, They have Moses and the prophets; let them hear them.*"

Neither is want of knowledge, nor lack of warning, the explanation of men living a godless life. In his eagerness to avert the consequences of such life, he forgets the inducements to it, and the allurements which had dazzled his own eyes and had carried his own choice. The Scriptures set forth with clearness and fulness God's call to the life of faith and holiness; the great lesson is kept before the mind daily, and is supported by reflection and conscience, if men only give heed to the voice within. There is the plainest instruction as to man's most pressing need. The need for pardon of his sins, cleansing from its pollution, and acceptance with God, were all set forth in the Temple service then, as they are to-day in the preached Gospel of our Lord Jesus Christ. The altar of sacrifice, the laver of washing, the altar of incense in the holy place, and the Most Holy Place within the veil, have a harmonious course of instruction, of which each contributes its own part. So in Gospel teaching, the cross of Christ, the influence of the Holy Spirit, the fellowship of prayer, the prospect of perfect life, are clear beyond mistake, if men will only give heed. God has not left any house to make its choice for life, guided only by the warning of a solitary messenger returning from the abodes of the dead. All the lessons of providence, and all the teaching of conscience, converge on the same point; the Scriptures abound in the repetitions of God's call to men, and in renewed assurances of His willingness to bless all who come. True it is, nevertheless, that many disregard the instruction, and defer considering the invitations, giving themselves no concern. To little purpose do they possess God's Word; more tolerable it must be for the heathen in the judgment, than for them who have the Scriptures and profit so little by the possession. Those to whom the name of Abraham is familiar as a household word are also familiar with the lesson of faith. They have Moses and the prophets, let them hear them. Let them give heed, ponder, and apply revealed truth. Such exercise constitutes true hearing, and in such hearing there is sure reward.

Verse 30.—"*And he said, Nay, father Abraham: but if one went unto them from the dead, they will repent.*"

The words of Abraham seemed familiar in his ear. They sounded as the echo of familiar accents from the earthly state, which had daily fallen on his own ears and produced no effect. Reference to the Scriptures sounded even as something powerless; for the sake of his brothers he longed for a surprise. If Lazarus would return again to the earth; if, as men dwelling on the earth think of it, he should *arise from the dead;* if his spirit were to reanimate the body now resting in the dust; if Lazarus were to appear in the midst of his father's house with words of warning from a brother in anguish, the effect would be startling and immediate. So this poor sufferer thinks, so accordingly he reasons even with Abraham, pressing his petition on this ground. All this is parabolic; the conversation is constructed to represent what does not readily find expression among men, yet greatly needs pondering. The utterance is not altogether mistaken, yet is it effectually misleading. The man who has slight sense of sin, has great confidence in the power of fear. He reckons it the *strongest motive* in life, and does not reflect long enough to settle for what end it is efficient. There is an awe of death, a power of superstition, a dread of hopeless anguish. He knows these things by experience; he trusts in their power; to his view, fear, superstition, and shrinking are the most efficient agents for working a change on human life. So little does he trust intelligence, so slightly does he value truth, so imperfectly does he understand the attractiveness of God's love, so poorly does he even yet estimate what repentance really means. Yet the insertion of that word "*repent*" is the Saviour's warning of what is needful, while the answer following indicates that repentance is something more than a wiser bargain,—something else than a surrender of earthly indulgence, on consideration of escaping future woe. It is more than a change of outward plan, under which thought and disposition continue as before. Calculating prudence might, indeed, change the course of life so far as to lead to a degree of self-denial, and appropriation of funds to "benevolent objects," in prospect of future reward. Such a change would be a great gain to these rich men themselves in the exercise of self-restraint, and to others in a wider distribution of benefits; it would besides have its value as bearing on the life beyond, involving escape from some of the tormenting recollections now embittering the experience of the brother who had died first. But this would involve repentance only according to the influence of fear. Self-denial and benevolence would exist only in semblance; the result of a wiser reckoning would be escape from a measure of torment which had otherwise been inevitable; but such a change would be powerless to secure the suppliant's end, who dreads "lest they also come into this place of torment." True repentance is that which changes the centre of interest from self to God, vexation on account of miscalculation and loss into humiliation because of sin, self-interest into love of God, and makes the grand end a life of holiness instead of self-gratification. But even under dread of future suffering men are slow to believe in the value of such a thorough-going change. Even a semblance of refuge suffices to avert deliberate reflection under the most solemn warning. That present interests are pressing, that most men around are absorbed in worldly good, that the interests of the future may be considered afterwards, and that God who has placed us here under pressure of our circumstances will be merciful,—these are common resorts under the most earnest appeals. Something more heart-stirring than apprehension for the future is required to secure a genuine change of mind. The suppliant is mistaken in his expectation that a temporary surprise would result in a complete change of life, and consequent escape from the misery flowing like a desolating torrent after a misspent life. This man's thinking is still on the low level to which his earthly life had brought him. Poverty does not lead to Abraham's bosom, neither does a generous use of wealth. This would be insufficient to guide a man to the family of God, or provide escape from the mingled miseries of self-seeking and self-reproach. Thus there is a repenting which needs to be repented of, a change which calls for still further change, in order that a man may truly love God and live in His favour. This the Temple service had been daily testifying to this sufferer during the days of his sojourn on the earth, yet he had not learnt it; this the living and dying of Jesus as the Son of Man and the Saviour of man has made manifest to the ends of the earth.

Verse 31.—"*And he said unto him, If they hear not Moses and the prophets, neither will they be persuaded though one rose from the dead.*"

Abraham is represented as answering with all condescension and patience, as well as with all firmness. The answer is utterly disappointing to the suppliant, but it is not a mere blank refusal. Neither is it, " I will not send," nor is it, "Lazarus will not go;" but, Even if I send, and Lazarus goes, they will not be persuaded. The *manner* of this final reply shows how far the Saviour is from suggesting that in the punishment of the unbelieving a hard, repellent, or defiant attitude is assumed. It implies that the deepest element in punishment is the conviction that the government of rebellious men is ever maintained with strict justice and tender compassion. The *matter* of the reply is that the unwillingness of men to repent and be persuaded is the true explanation of their condemnation. They live in carelessness as to God and His will, and in death they awake to self-condemnation in sight of what they have done in despising the message of Divine love. The self-reproach which now torments the suppliant is, alas! the contradiction of his own expectations. His plea for his brothers affords no excuse for himself. Unwillingness to repent, which is the source of continued evil in the life, and this would not be affected by some days of surprise because of the reappearance of Lazarus. Another Lazarus did come again from the dead into the midst of the sorrowing circle of Bethany; and while his coming was hailed with joy by the believing, and even aroused the wonder and curiosity of multitudes, it did nothing to convince, far less convert, the Pharisees, and did not turn them even from their murderous designs against Jesus, whose word had brought him back from the dead. So completely do facts in the life of Jesus go to confirm the truth and moral power of His teaching. God does not seek the conversion of men by a succession of resurrections. The dealing of God with man is wiser than the excited longing of the self-condemned heart. The wisdom becomes apparent, if only we consider the source of the evil. The words of Abraham are designed to make this conspicuous. Our English version partially conceals their force. The answer literally is : " If they *will not hear* Moses and the prophets, neither will they be persuaded though one rose from the dead." The cause of their living as they did was the same as had been the cause in his own life—deep-seated reluctance to hear, unwillingness to be persuaded, leading even to the deliberate shunning of those influences which might impress on them their duty to God. This is the key to the irreligion which exists. There is no lack of compassion on God's part if He do not send men from the state of the dead to bear witness to the unbelieving. If true compassion could be manifested in such a course, there would need to be a continual coming and going between the two states of existence. Surprise would then fail to accomplish the desired result. Under a series of surprises, surprise itself would die. The instrument would be destroyed by use. It is vain to regard excitement from external causes as a reliable agency for inward renewal. If men will not hear the teaching, warning, and encouragements of God's Word, neither will they be persuaded to repent, turn to God, and walk with Him by any warnings coming from the state of the dead. Thus the parable closes with a word for the living, for whom, indeed, the entire parable has been designed, giving explicit teaching concerning continued life beyond this state according to its direction here. Our Lord thus supplies in the best form that which the despairing suppliant longs for in behalf of those to whom opportunity of repentance is still granted. He presents the contrasts between life with God and life without God ; He carries the lines of contrast through the portals of death, where we lose sight of our fellow-men ; and He shows the completeness of the contrast as the lines are still further continued into states of existence separated by a great chasm. There are two states in the invisible world, which are as complete contrasts as the extremes of poverty and of wealth in this world. On the higher level, removed from all experience of trouble, is fellowship with Abraham and all who are of his family,—fellowship in a faith working by love in a holy and unceasing service of the Most High God. On the lower level there is separation from all this, in the midst of unceasing experience of self-reproach, whence there is no pathway to the state of the blessed, to which comes no provision for mitigation of its woe, and in which the reigning desire is that of escape, which is ever seen to be impossible.

CHAPTER XXIV.

CHRIST'S COMING, THE TEST OF CHRISTIAN PROFESSION.

THE TEN VIRGINS.

Matthew xxv. 1-13.

After the extremes of contrast, both in this world and in the next, have been set before us, we have a representation of the Messianic kingdom as it will appear on the day of our Lord's coming in glory. He shall appear as a bridegroom coming to receive his bride. The direct purpose, however, is to set forth a truth which lies nearer to us than the marriage itself, full of practical value for the present life. The parable, therefore, does not contain special descriptions of the bride and of the marriage ceremonial. The imagery of marriage union cannot well be maintained, along with a representation of judgment and separation, which it is the purpose of our Lord here to set forth. On this account direct allusion to the bride and the marriage is withheld; and the story is concerned with the distinctions which Christ's coming reveals among those who are professed disciples. That the representation should be that of a marriage ceremony and not of a royal progress, is in marked harmony with our Lord's teaching concerning His relation to His Church; and it has the special value of obvious continuity in the line of analogy presented in the parable of The Royal Marriage Feast.

This parable of the Ten Virgins is one spoken by our Lord toward the close of his public ministry, when, with the cross only a little in advance, He gave utterance to the most solemn warnings concerning His coming again in glory and might. In this connection we must interpret the reference to *time* with which the parable opens. "*Then,*" when the Son of man cometh, "*shall the kingdom of heaven be likened unto ten virgins.*" He had begun His ministry by preaching that the kingdom of heaven was at hand; He is closing His public teaching by revealing the appearance of His kingdom when He comes again in glory. His coming then shall be in joy, as in the midst of "marriage rejoicings;" but even then there shall be painfulness of separations, as well as joyfulness of reunions. One thing stands out clearly in the opening words of the parable, and must be regarded as regulating its interpretation, that it applies to the kingdom as a whole. In that previously considered individuals are placed in contrast; in this, the kingdom as a unity is contemplated. What is true on an immeasurably wide scale, when all nations, including multitudes innumerable, are reckoned together, is here brought within narrow limits, easily embraced by the eye, a group of ten maidens representing the whole Messianic kingdom.

Verse 1.—"*Then shall the kingdom of heaven be likened unto ten virgins, which took their lamps, and went forth to meet the bridegroom.*"

The Saviour thus speaks of Himself as the bridegroom; but He has still to go away; much lies before Him connected with this going, and a long interval thereafter must elapse before His coming in glory. The bridegroom is therefore spoken of only as one expected. There is no appearance of his coming, not even any sound of his approach, not the slightest certainty as to the probable time of his coming.

Attention meanwhile concentrates on a group of virgins, fully occupied with their own preparations for expected marriage rejoicings. In order to give vividness to the parable, the preparations are assigned to the night for which the arrival of the bridegroom had been fixed. This belongs to the structure of the story, and at the same time has a manifest fitness in view of the direct spiritual result desired by our Lord, in counselling present and earnest watchfulness. These ten maidens collectively symbolise the kingdom of God on the earth. The state of all men is not here indicated, for there are many unrepresented who fade from the view in the darkness of the night. The virgins represent all who with gladness look for the coming of the Son of God; the entire Church of Christ, those whom He has gathered together in the bonds of common faith, interest, and joyful activity. They expect the coming of the bridegroom, and prepare themselves for it. They light their lamps, and go forth into the darkness of the night, advancing on the road along which he is to come, until they reach the appointed meeting-place, where they may watch for the signs of his approach. This little band so equipped, interested, and active, represents the Christian Church on the earth.

The general significance of this opening description

is so plain as hardly to admit of diversity of opinion. The characteristics of those belonging to Christ's Church on earth are *expectation* of Christ's coming in glory, *dedication* to the duty of giving Him a joyous welcome, and *preparation* for such a welcome. The Church in the earth is a testimony concerning a great Future, a witness to the promise of Christ's reappearance, with throngs of attendants, as a bridegroom in the midst of his marriage rejoicings. This expectation is professed by all who declare themselves disciples of the Lord Jesus. They do not profess merely to cherish the hope that at death they shall be privileged to enter into the heavenly kingdom; but keeping their eye along the plane of this world's history, they see a bright period far in advance, when they shall arise from sleep and exult in the coming of the Lord of Glory. When this anticipation is realised, when Christ's glorious appearance is at hand, "then shall the kingdom of heaven be likened unto ten virgins, which took their lamps, and went forth to meet the bridegroom."

In view of what follows, dividing the group into two, the wise and the foolish, it seems impossible to regard the whole as representing genuine disciples, though this view has been largely taken. There is nothing in the structure of the parable to warrant the suggestion that the five foolish maidens represent only a less devoted and less watchful portion of the true servants of Christ. The circumstance that virginity is often symbolically employed to represent purity such as must belong to the people of God, cannot be regarded as deciding our interpretation here. The group of virgins is a usual accompaniment of marriage festivities selected by our Lord as best representing His coming again. And the circumstance, that of the gathering some prove wanting in forethought, thereby utterly failing in fulfilment of their purpose, is taken to represent a dark and sad reality in the history of the spiritual kingdom on earth, which shall be made glaringly conspicuous when He comes in glory, testing the preparedness of all who appear before Him. The solemn warning of this phase of the parable is specially desired by the merciful Saviour, who has in all things a regard to the practical effect of His words in this present state. There is nothing adverse to this view of the parable, but much in harmony with the realities of Christian profession, in all the group bearing *lighted lamps*. This fact must be remarked as going far to determine the significance of the *light* in the parable. That the lighted lamp does not mean spiritual life in the soul seems clearly proved by many considerations. The use of these lighted lamps is restricted to a special season, and has its significance determined by this fact. The lamps are naturally accompaniments on account of the need for going out in the darkness of night. They were to add to the expected effect of the welcome only on account of the darkness. Again, the lamp is a merely external accessory to be used for a time, and then laid aside. Its effect is to be felt only on the way. When the joyous company enter the festive halls, the lamp is to be put out and laid aside. Expectation comes to an end when the Lord appears. Behind the lamp as it is borne there is conviction and expectation, accounting for its being carried. Further, even in recognising the relationship of lamp-bearing to the inward conviction of the bearer, we must regard the lamp itself as something external. In harmony with this must be our interpretation of the light, whether we consider its source in the *oil* which sustains it, or its influence in the spreading beams which pierce the surrounding gloom. All these things combine in support of the view that the lamp or light is outward profession of personal expectation of the coming of our Lord. This is a profession openly avowed by all who outwardly connect themselves with the Christian Church, equally by the sincere and by the formal. Such a profession, whatever be the real condition of the heart, is carried as the light of a personal testimony. Profession has visibility in the surrounding darkness. The lamp which so shines, however, is not the heart, but the outward testimony; not the life within the man, but the profession made by him. In all cases there is conviction, expectation, and interest in the arrangements for Christ's coming; and these are awakened and sustained by the clear declarations of God's Word, as a storehouse of oil, from which the lamps of Christian profession are replenished. From this store scant supply may be drawn, only sufficing to kindle the lamp of a temporary profession; or a deeper draft may be taken sufficient to provide for the continuance of the profession even in the presence of the Master. The test of true Christianity, therefore, is not found in the light of mere profession, but in its endurance because of real devotion to the Saviour, whose coming is anticipated as the bringing of completed "salvation ready to be revealed in the last time." All professing Christians are, however, included as sharing in the expectation of Christ's coming, and even in the general preparations for the event. As Trench has said, though hardly in keeping with his reasoning as to the significance of the light, "All are included who would desire to include themselves in the number of His believing people."[1]

Verses 2-4.—"*And five of them were wise, and five were foolish. They that were foolish took their lamps, and took no oil with them: but the wise took oil in their vessels with their lamps.*"

As the virgins came forth they appeared a united band, sharing in the same expectations, interested in the same great event. But there were marked differences in their preparations. There was folly as well as wisdom apparent,—a true preparedness on the part of some, but partial preparation in the case of others, really preparing for disappointment and failure. There was a clear shining lamp in the right hand of each one; but only some among them carried a store of oil sufficient to replenish the lamp, and maintain its light throughout the night watches. Quick they all were in their movements, united and hearty in their concerted action, but not all equally ready. Wisdom appearing in provision according to the expectations cherished; folly manifested itself in want of prudent forethought as to what the fulfilment of their expectations might require.

The Christian Church is by reason of its profession a unity. All joining its ranks profess personal interest in the coming of Jesus. But there is a serious division destined to appear at His coming, arising from want of preparation on the part of many for the great event which all agree in anticipating. There is reality in the agreement, but unity in this respect carries condemnation of defective preparation, branding it as *folly*.

[1] *Notes on the Parables*, p. 244.

Some have drawn but slightly from God's Word in accepting the expectation of the Saviour's coming, not pondering the question whether they regarded Him as Saviour for them. Others, acting more wisely, draw deeply from the teaching of God's Word concerning the Saviour, His first coming and His second, His suffering and His triumphs, His invitation and His coming to receive His disciples. These are prepared for all that may be required; they will be found ready whensoever their Lord may come.

Verse 5.—"*While the bridegroom tarried, they all slumbered and slept.*" After the band of maidens had advanced a considerable distance along the road by which the bridegroom was to come, they reach the appointed gathering place, where it had been arranged they were to await the warning of his approach. There, ample accommodation had been provided for their comfort; and they went in to await the moment for which all their preparations had been made. For a season their conversation was sprightly, giving all the tokens of the joy of a festive occasion. But as the night advanced, and the ordinary season for repose had been considerably past, conversation began to flag, quietness set in, drowsiness became general, and soon they had all sunk into profound slumber. Their appearance betokened the object of their gathering, their lamps lit up the room as they burned in the stillness of the night, vigilant watchers were on the outlook for signs in the distance of an approaching company, all things were in readiness, and they might fairly rest while the bridegroom tarried. Sleep in the circumstances was natural and refreshing, preparing for the engagements in which they were shortly to take a conspicuous share.

This part of the story is not necessary to the occasion, not contributing anything to the preparations and rejoicings of the time; but it is necessary for the instruction to be communicated in the parable. The general period of sleep does not appear unnatural, and the introduction of it is quite needful to meet our Lord's purpose. He is going from the world as one who shall be able to say of His great atoning work, "Father, I have finished the work which thou gavest me to do." He shall come again as a bridegroom in the season of general rejoicing, receiving a glorious welcome; but before His coming there shall be long tarrying, and they all shall slumber and sleep. This is the universal sleep, the sleep of death. It is represented for us here by the midnight hour, when not only those who had prepared to meet the coming bridegroom had fallen asleep, but when, besides, the city from which they came was wrapped in the darkness, and its inhabitants generally were sunk in deep sleep. Thus our Lord introduces the suggestion of an intervening period of universal sleep while He tarries, deliberately delaying His promised coming. The event will not be hastened. All shall fall asleep and wait a time of waking, when the trumpet call shall be heard rousing them from the slumbers of the tomb. For them who "sleep in Jesus" a blessed experience is in store, when they shall awake and arise to give exulting welcome to their glorified Redeemer. Our Lord does not here pass beyond the sleep to speak of experience in the unseen. This He has done in the parable of the Rich Man and Lazarus; the structure of the present story does not admit of transition to what is beyond, having been constructed to serve a quite different purpose. Attention is restricted to that which belongs to this world. Reference is to the profession made during the earthly life, to the sleep of death, which brings to a close this life's preparations for the coming of the Lord, to resurrection from the slumbers of the grave at warning of His approach, and to the testing of their preparation for this great event. Our Saviour places before our view a threefold representation of human history as connected with His mission of mercy and love. *First* there is the period of busy preparation in prospect of His coming, in which profession is made of acceptance of His teaching, devotion to His service, while fellowship is enjoyed with His professed disciples, and expectation is cherished of His joyous coming again, with His welcome to life in glory. *Second* there is the sleep of death, traces of previous profession and activity lying around the resting-place, when nothing further can be accomplished by way of preparation, but all await the summons which shall bring unerring test of the previous activity. *Third* there is the coming of our Lord in glory, surrounded by heavenly attendants, at whose approach men awake from the dead and come forth to meet Him.

Verse 6.—"*And at midnight there was a cry made, Behold, the bridegroom cometh; go ye out to meet him.*"

For a season the quiet rest of the assembled group of maidens was undisturbed. They slept on, while their lamps continued to burn, reducing the oil supply which each contained. The bridegroom tarried beyond expectation, allowing their rest to be prolonged. At length, however, the rousing call was sounding through all the house, Behold! he cometh, he cometh! go ye out to meet him. The signs of his approach had been seen in the distance, and the signal was immediately given; his advance was rapid, and there was need for promptitude in order that all might be in readiness.

It is thus the Lord sketches that crisis, which He anticipates with certainty, and of which He has always spoken with utmost solemnity. The midnight may best represent the time, for men shall be as those sunk in profoundest sleep; the sudden summons of those watching may symbolise the trumpet call which shall sound in the abodes of the dead; the scene of busy preparation may represent the rising from the tomb to meet the Lord in His glory. "The Son of man cometh at an hour when ye think not." Preparation there may be in the life that now is, when there are no signs of His appearing; but when the event itself comes upon us, there can be no alternative but taking previous preparation according to its worth.

Verses 7-9.—"*Then all those virgins arose, and trimmed their lamps. And the foolish said unto the wise, Give us of your oil; for our lamps are gone out. But the wise answered, saying, Not so; lest there be not enough for us and you: but go ye rather to them that sell, and buy for yourselves.*"

Dismay, because of unpreparedness, mingles with the joyous eagerness of those who trim their lamps, expecting now the welcome, the festive halls, and the marriage rejoicings. The folly which had been unheeded as the band came out from their homes was now obvious, painfully obvious, in the little light, ready to die, which was seen flickering in no fewer than five of the ten lamps. Yet could not the five whose folly was now becoming matter of painful self-consciousness, at once admit that their case was desperate. "They all arose and trimmed their lamps." Such trimming only made more clear their unpreparedness for the welcome, to join in which had been the entire purpose of their setting out. As Stier has well expressed it, "The cleaning of the wick will not avail, if at the decisive hour there begins to be a want of oil." The needlessness of such lamps being trimmed was manifest; the need for oil was the one thing plain; what could they do; whither could they go? They appeal to their companions; what they themselves recognise with a sinking heart must be confessed to others, as indeed it is visible to all. Their nearest, and seemingly their only hope, is that their companions' may have so far exceeded their own requirements as to be able to transfer a sufficient supply of oil. To them they appeal; but the appeal is vain; and they are filled with dismay. The supply carried by the others is ample for their own need, but insufficient to allow of deduction. To the request, "Give us of your oil," there can be but one answer, "Not so, lest there be not enough for us and you." That some of the lamps were actually going out was disaster enough for such an occasion; they must not risk an utter failure, dishonouring the bridegroom by tarnishing the welcome.

This is the dark and affecting picture which a Saviour's hand has painted of the woful dismay of resurrection in unpreparedness. The preparation of the lifetime is the measure of preparedness at the resurrection. A profession of discipleship, even though it rest on the teaching of God's Word, foretelling Christ's coming, if it does not draw more deeply from the Word opening to us the sufficiency of a Divine Saviour's work, is inadequate for the requirements of spiritual life. It is a profession deceptive in its semblance of the reality, self-condemning because containing enough to expose its own manifest lack, and is in truth preparation for inevitable dismay. Various parts of the picture vividly suggest that disaster is *inevitable*. The tarrying of the bridegroom, the deepening of the darkness even till midnight had come, the suddenness of the call to awake, the quickness of the approach, these are the things which tell that the bitterness of dismay is certain in the case of those who have fallen asleep with no greater preparation than is implied in professed expectation of Christ's coming, and desire to share in His welcome. There is a mistaken suggestion, because unwarranted by the parable, in the introduction by Stier of the wish that "the Lord would but come while the lamp burns brightly." This tends to cover misleading profession, fostering false expectations. This assigns a meritorious value to the light, and nevertheless implies that it is to be estimated according to haphazard affecting the time when it is tested. The suggestion is at variance with the whole parable. It is not the lateness of the bridegroom's coming which is to be deplored, but the folly of unpreparedness for the great event. At whatever time the Lord may come, mere profession cannot endure. This will first be recognised by the men themselves who have made the profession, and on that ground alone have cherished the hope of sharing in the rejoicing. It will be recognised by themselves even before it is condemned by the Lord; arising from the dead, they shall find their profession itself ready to expire.

The same truth as to their state is reflected from the contrast set over against their case, in the eager, joyful preparations of those who awake to find that they have all things in readiness. The coming bridegroom is their Saviour. They have in the years of their earthly life drawn daily comfort and prospect of eternal good from the saving work of the Lord Jesus; they have enjoyed closest fellowship of spirit with Him, and now they are ready to meet Him, full of the gladness which inclines the heart to exclaim, "Blessed is he that cometh in the name of the Lord." This overflowing joy depends upon fulness of preparation; it comes from possession of Divine truth drawn from the rich supply of the Word, giving full assurance of blessing in this grand crisis, enabling those ready to exclaim, "When he shall appear, we shall be like him, for we shall see him as he is." But the preparation of each can prove nothing more than preparation for himself; it cannot involve provision for another. The truth which fills the heart, giving preparation for the day of the Lord's coming, must be drawn from God's Word, and cannot be obtained by mere appeal for aid from a fellow-disciple. This prayer addressed to companions, "Give us of your oil," can be no more effectual than the cry of the rich man in the season of torment that he might have help from Lazarus. Those possessing the truth, and finding in it true preparation for the coming of Jesus, can but advise others to go to the same store from which they have drawn, and obtain for themselves. Well it is when the counsel so given is taken and acted upon in the days of the earthly life, when opportunity is at hand, and the stores are freely bestowed by the Spirit of God on all who seek supply for their own need, in view of Christ's coming.

The words, "*Go ye rather to them that sell, and buy for yourselves,*" have occasioned much discussion. It has been suggested that they express well-meant but misleading advice, given in the excitement of the hurried preparation ; that they were uttered in derision, those exulting in their own supply yielding to mockery of others unprovided for the occasion, and that they were words of deliberate condemnation of the folly of which they had been guilty who were so poorly supplied. All these lines of interpretation seem at fault from mixing parabolic form with spiritual significance. These two must be kept strictly apart, and if this be done, the significance of the words becomes apparent.

In the midst of a group of virgins so situated, there could be nothing more natural than that those who found themselves in unexpected difficulty should apply to their companions. When this appeal made it obvious that the others had not a supply which could meet the demand, there could be no other reasonable suggestion than that which finds expression. The only course in order to escape utter disappointment was to hurry back to the city, rousing the nearest seller of oil, and obtaining hastily a supply. The bridegroom's party was advancing towards the city ; if they hurried forward, they might still be able to meet the company before the house was reached, and so join in part of the rejoicings over the bridegroom's arrival. This was their only hope, and the urgent advice to go at once and quickly was the expressed desire that by running in advance they might yet be able to return before the scene of the marriage rejoicings had been reached. The parabolic story would have been unnatural without this. Our Saviour does not sketch incidents in social life without expressing sympathetic feeling towards those in trouble. Suggestions of intention to mislead, of wilful mockery, and of bitter reproach on the part of the wise, are entirely misplaced. The words, "Go ye and buy," are words of urgency from those who would say, "Haste ye, and be ready."

That these words can be taken as implying a possible mode of preparation even at the resurrection, it is impossible to maintain in view of the closing part of the parable. The attempt of the foolish virgins proved fruitless, and it is the distinct purpose of the parable to warn of the inevitable result of neglected preparation. The words, "Go ye and buy," do, however, harmonise with the spiritual significance of the story, as well as with the circumstances of the marriage company. In accordance with earlier parabolic teaching, it is suggested that there is buying and selling of the things of the kingdom, that there are "merchants" who trade in the truth, offering it to those who are eager to secure personal possession. Whosoever goes to them will find great readiness to sell, and gladness according to the greatness of demand. There is thus present practical instruction in these words, entirely agreeing with the direct purpose for which the parable is spoken. The parable is obviously uttered for solemn warning as to present duty, rather than with deliberate intention to afford a revelation of all that shall be hereafter. The warning could not be given without revelation of that which shall be; but the revelation is granted mainly to secure that which should be done here. To draw from the stores which exist is present duty; if hereafter men awaken to a distressing sense of their unpreparedness, companions of former days can do nothing but refer to the stores from which they have drawn their own supplies. As the wise could not suggest to the foolish virgins to go forward with their darkened lamps, and ask from the bridegroom supplies of oil wherewith to light them, men shall not on the great day of the Son of Man be able to meet Him with entreaty that He should supply their want. To advance is to encounter condemnation; to retreat on the long neglected store may be thought of when it is too late. Such is the lesson coming from this point in the parable. Severance from the company prepared for going out to meet the bridegroom, disappearance in the opposite direction, vanishing from the view in the shadow of the night bearing darkened lamps, sounds heard somewhere of excited knocking at barred doors, and eager entreaty, "Give us of your oil,"—these are the suggestions lending vividness to the warning to beware of the wretchedness of self-reproach, even before the judgment of the Lord is pronounced.

Verse 10.—"*And while they went to buy, the bridegroom came; and they that were ready went in with him to the marriage: and the door was shut.*" From the door of the bridegroom's house, the bright lights of the approaching company are seen, and the shouts of those rejoicing in his advance are distinctly heard there, while there are no signs in the opposite direction of the coming again of those who had gone swiftly by on their way to the places of merchandise. The five virgins with lighted lamps, and all the other friends who had gathered for the joyful occasion, had joined the marriage company, and, swelling the ranks, had added to the volume of sound as the crowd came towards the house.

This crowd constituted the company ready for the marriage celebrations; they entered together in attendance on the bridegroom; the door was shut; there was brilliance and feasting within; darkness and silence reigned without.

This description of the progress of the marriage rejoicings distinctly bears evidence of being drawn with a special regard to the absent five. There is no account of the circumstances attending the welcome of the bridegroom; no sketch of the appearance and advance of the company; not even a single mention of the marriage ceremonial, the central event of the occasion; and no detail of the festivities held within. Our Lord has given us a general representation of His coming, but He is not guiding us by positive and minute statements into a discovery of the great realities which shall belong to the grand period of rejoicing appointed to usher in the triumph of the spiritual kingdom, opening upon an eternity of joyous service. With the reigning disposition of one whose very work it is to warn and rally those in danger of being shut out, the Saviour in His parable gives greater prominence to what concerns them than to the experience of those who are joining in the celebrations. He is content to pass quickly all that concerns His own glorious appearance, and the fulness of joy which gladdens the hearts of all who gather together in the sunshine of His presence. He will say no more than this by way of revelation of the coming glory: The Saviour shall appear in joy as a bridegroom, and His people, hailing His coming, shall enter with Him into His glorious home. As He teaches the people at this time, He thinks mainly of the closed door and the darkness without, and the dismay of those who seek but cannot find entrance. His reigning desire is this, that all would give heed and make ready while opportunity is given. Towards still more solemn warning the parable is here unfolding.

Verses 11, 12.—*"Afterward came also the other virgins, saying, Lord, Lord, open to us. But he answered and said, Verily I say unto you, I know you not."*

After the shutting of the door is the arrival of those who had been unprepared for joining in the welcome. They had been thrown into dismay, but this had not destroyed the desire they felt to have a place in the festive gathering. They were covered with shame, and were open in their expressions of lamentation, but they had not abandoned the hope that they might yet have some part in the rejoicings; they had not determined to disperse as those frustrated in their plans. Whether they obtained the oil they sought, or failed in the attempt, is not said; even if supply had been got, it was now useless, for the welcome was over, the darkness of the night has been left behind; the company had assembled in the brightness of the festive halls—their lamps had all been laid aside. Whether the lamps carried by these five are still dark, or have been lighted up, does not signify for the special occasion. However appearing, they press onwards to the house of the bridegroom, and knocking at the door, lift up their voices in entreaty, "Lord, Lord, open to us." The bridegroom refused admission, though he did not withhold reply. Whether he opened the door is not stated. It is rather suggested that he did, to look upon the group, after having heard their knocking and entreaty. He could not recognise them as of the circle of his friends. They had not any claim in friendship. They seemed a company moved only by the spirit of self-seeking; and as he uttered the words, "I know you not," the conversation was closed. Their opportunity was gone.

Interpretation here requires that due weight be given to what is unsaid as well as to what is spoken. On their part there is the absence of confession while there is the utterance of entreaty. On the bridegroom's part there is no expression of his own will or determination, but a declaration of fact as to the relation of the suppliants to himself. These features in the parable are full of meaning. Receiving such instruction as we have here, we are standing beyond the region where confession of sin is made, beyond the sphere where profession of friendship is of value, whether sincere or insincere; we are on the threshold of the scene of rejoicing where friendship is tested by previous intercourse, where the gladness is that of reunion, and the festal company are united to their Lord by a thousand ties of cherished associations. To have been known unto the Lord and have had the relationship of friends in earlier times, is security for admission here: to have been a stranger to Him, with no prior fellowship, is to make admission impossible. That they should seek admission is natural, for there is a desire which is unquenchable. That they should enter is impossible. For the joys of friendship, friendship itself is needful. The bare statement of the relations of the persons is made, without expressed reference to judgment; but this is the reality of judgment itself. The formalities of judgment are not before us; but the solemn issues of judgment are manifest.

Verse 13.—"*Watch therefore, for ye know neither the day nor the hour wherein the Son of man cometh.*"

There is uncertainty as to the time, certainty as to the fact. The lesson is clear. Let each one be ready! With foreknowledge of the coming of the Lord, we have opportunity for preparation. The truth placed within our reach concerns more than assurance as to the future event; it presents the fulness of a Saviour's merit, and explains how friendship with Him can be enjoyed now. In such friendship we find the true preparation for His appearing whensoever it may happen. His coming shall be with the joyfulness of the bridegroom; to receive His people's welcome; to witness their gladness as they share in His joy. The duty for all may, therefore, be concentrated in a single word, Watch! They who share not His friendship have need to beware, lest He come and they find themselves unprepared for meeting Him, and yet longing to share in the joy to which He introduces. They who are friends of the Lord join in wisest preparations and joyful expectations. In their fellowship it can be said, "Beloved, now are we sons of God; and it doth not yet appear what we shall be: but we know that, when he shall appear, we shall be like him; for we shall see him as he is."

CHAPTER XXV.

DIFFERENT TALENTS YIELDING EQUAL REWARDS.

THE TALENTS.

MATTHEW xxv. 14-30.

WE now reach the closing portion of our Lord's teaching as to the Future State. This bears distinctively on the rewards provided for His own people. Two companion pictures, representing the distribution of rewards hereafter, close the series of parabolic views of God's kingdom. In one picture, we see diversity in the distribution of gifts, followed by distribution of equal rewards. In the other, there are equal gifts; but when the division of rewards comes, there is marked diversity in the value of what is bestowed.

In the first of these two parables, as we look at the aspect of things in the earthly state, we see marked differences in the talents granted to men, in their opportunity for service, and in the results being achieved. From these intricate and perplexing contrasts, which confuse us in our attempts to obtain a comprehensive view of the picture as a whole, inducing us to return to it continually for fresh study, our attention is next directed to the aspect of things away beyond this state. In that brighter scene the complexity is escaped; simplicity of arrangement becomes apparent. All faithful workers are seen equally happy in the presence of their Lord, equally cheered by His words of encouragement, and by His introduction to reward. Yet even here a shadow is found along the horizon. In the darkening background, towards one side, is seen a group of servants driving an unfaithful one into the outer darkness.

Verse 14.—"*For the kingdom of heaven is as a man travelling into a far country, who called his own servants, and delivered unto them his goods.*"

Here once more, as in the parable of The Husbandmen, Jesus suggests His severance from His servants. They receive their talents, have their opportunities afforded, and are left to carry out their work while their Master is at a distance. He is "as a man travelling into a far country." Absence from the disciples, distance of separation between their sphere of direct personal activity and His own, and lapse of a long period of time between the bestowal of the property and the season of reckoning, are all suggested by this introductory statement. The bearing of all these considerations on the history of the spiritual kingdom is manifest. The passage has its earliest application from the time when Jesus in person was in the world intrusting to His servants their individual share in the work which He required to be done; it finds continual application in the Church's history through all subsequent ages; and it has its complete realisation in the great meeting-time appointed for the testing of all things, when Jesus shall come in His glory. The distribution of gifts is preparation for the ultimate distribution of rewards. Discipleship places a distinction between men. There are those whom Christ calls to

Himself as "His own servants,"[1] and in contrast those who cannot be so reckoned. And even amongst these servants there are some who are servants rather in profession than in hearty devotion. But to all who present themselves at His call, ranking themselves with His servants, He gives of His goods; and of all of them, whether devoted to Him in heart and life, or only in outward profession, He shall by and by require account according to that which they have received.

Verse 15.—"*And unto one he gave five talents, to another two, and to another one; to every man according to his several ability; and straightway took his journey.*"

The day of distribution was one of peculiar interest in the household. The servants were summoned to their master's presence in circumstances very unusual. He explained his intentions as to lengthened travel, and intrusted to each one some portion of his substance, with which they might trade in his absence. An equal distribution of his property was not proposed by him. He had come to know pretty exactly the powers of the men in his service; he knew what to expect of them; and accordingly he gave to each one a sum which he thought might be wisely intrusted to him in view of his ability, and the nature of the trade or merchandise in which he was able to engage. Proceeding in this way, a very marked difference appeared in the amount handed over to each servant. To one he gave five talents, to another two, to another one.[2] The

---

[1] See in the Parable of *The Husbandmen*, p. 326.

[2] The value of the talent has been variously estimated, the gold talent being about double the value of that in silver. The latter has been computed at £206 sterling, and as low as £187, 10s. Taking the lower as the least sum bestowed, the next would be £375, and the highest £937, 10s., approaching a thousand pounds.

money thus delivered to them became for the time their own, to be used according to their own judgment, though always with the understanding that the capital would be required of each of them on his return, and also an account of the gain which had been made by its use. Portions of land may also have been left to be farmed, in accordance with the illustration adopted in another parable. Of this no mention is here made, save as it may be implied in the statement of the preceding verse, when it is said that "He delivered unto them his *goods*," which signifies his possessions or property. When the distribution had been made, their master took his departure, leaving them to plan their course of action according to their own judgment.

Such is the view of the distribution of talents among men, and more particularly among the servants of Christ. In interpreting this introductory portion, the word "talents" must be taken as including all that fits a man for God's service, as well what belongs to his own nature as what is external to himself. The "ability" is a gift from God as well as the "goods." When considering what we possess as fitting us for doing the will of God, each one may hear the question, "What hast thou that thou didst not receive?" All that a man is, and has, must be included among God's gifts, to be made account of when the working season here is over. Talents, means, and opportunities must all be reckoned as Divinely supplied. When so regarded, there is seen to be great diversity among the disciples. There are differences as to the power to serve God, as to the means available for the service, and as to the field of occupation providing daily opportunities for accomplishing what the disciple desires to achieve. The form of the parable naturally restricts reference to external possessions; the spiritual significance must have wider range. This being recognised, the *withdrawing* of possessions must be contemplated as well as the withholding. There is no disaster involving loss of substance, no affliction placing restraint upon activity, no change of sphere altering the character of our opportunities, which can be overlooked in computing the diversity of distribution of which our Lord makes account in view of the testing-time which is to come for all.

Verses 16-18.—"*Then he that had received the five talents went and traded with the same, and made them other five talents. And likewise he that had received two, he also gained other two. But he that had received one went and digged in the earth, and hid his lord's money.*"

As soon as the servants were left to themselves, each proceeded to act according to his own choice. Each had his own occupation for which he had been trained, and this led naturally to a different course being taken in each case. Thus there were three distinct lines of life; but in reality the three represent only two distinct classes of servants—the working and the idle, the faithful and the unfaithful. The holders of the five talents and of the two are brethren in service, each doing his appointed part for their master; the holder of the one deliberately refuses to do the work required of him, and concerns himself only with the preservation of that which had been placed in his charge. He has only one talent, yet the sum is a large one, and he has so much regard to the need for rendering account of it that he takes special precaution for its safety. He seeks a place suitable for secrecy, and digging a pit in the ground, he buries it there, and carefully covers it over, none but himself knowing where the treasure is concealed.

The picture which includes these three figures depicts the doings of those who profess themselves servants of Jesus. A short sentence is enough to describe a lifetime of service. And the description is not of a meagre form including each one in a common destiny,—lived, died, and was buried with his fathers; it is of that discriminating kind possible to the judge of human conduct,—worked, gathered the fruit of his labours, and was ready to give account; or, by sad contrast, shunned work, but guarded his property, and was ready to hand back again all that he had received. The temptation to neglect effort and allow opportunities to pass unused, our Lord connects with the holder of only one talent, thereby indicating that restricted power is apt to appear smaller by comparison with the possessions of others. Whether properly estimated or not, its comparatively limited influence is contemplated as an excuse for inactivity. Hence often the absence of results which can compare favourably with powers possessed, and painful contrasts. A wise and diligent use of talents, a wilful and persistent neglect of their use,—these are the contrasts in the history of life. Results which the servants can present as an offering to God; nothing to offer at the close of life,—these are the contrasts in respect of outcome. Each servant is well aware how it stands with him; the Lord foresees it in each case, and His coming will declare it to all.

A united service is not contemplated here. It is not suggested that the servants might have placed their money together in one capital sum, to be employed in a joint enterprise. Such union has already been introduced in the parable of *The Husbandmen*. What was there made prominent is now allowed to pass from consideration; and here, when Jesus is dealing with the final award on human conduct, it is indicated that men are not to be judged in groups, but that each one must render account for himself singly. Each individual has received his own distinctive talents, has lived in the midst of his appointed opportunities, and if he has been faithful in service, the work done must be as distinctive as his own individuality.

Verse 19.—"*After a long time the lord of those servants cometh, and reckoneth with them.*"

The time of his absence is described as protracted, the time of his return unexpected, and the reckoning with his servants a thing which had immediate attention, as if it had been the very purpose of his return. What was left undescribed in the parable of The Husbandmen is here introduced as the express object of the parable, thus making it connect with the other to supply what was lacking in that. What is now before us is exactly adapted to the purpose of completing Christ's teaching, describing the return of the master as directly intended by him as the season for passing judgment on the service rendered by those to whom he had intrusted his property.

In interpretation of this verse, it is manifest that our Lord carefully prepared His disciples for expecting a lengthened absence before He should come to judge of the results of their labours. This was, indeed, implied in the unfinished parable of The Husbandmen, and in the representation of a universal sleep found in the parable of The Virgins; but here it is explicitly indicated that His return would not be till "*after a long time.*" When at length He does appear, it will be to judge of the service of His professed disciples. During His public ministry, on which they had attended, He had uniformly said, "I came not to judge the world, but to save the world;" now as this public ministry draws towards a close, He gives warning that when He comes again it will be as the Judge, the separater between the faithful and the unfaithful, and that in accordance with the express testimony given on another occasion, "The Father hath committed all judgment unto the Son." Yet, in the very words in which Jesus gives warning of His coming to judgment, He suggests in a striking and encouraging manner that in relation to His faithful servants His procedure shall not be as that of an avenging judge, nor even as that of one who summons them to judicial investigations. Rather will the procedure of that day be as the friendly reckoning of master and servants, in which both take their part, assured that the reckoning on both sides will harmonise, and the results be satisfactory to master and servant. He will reckon *with them* as in joint calculation. In accordance with this view, each servant is represented as making his own statement, and that is received by the master as strictly reliable. Indeed the whole description has within it the implication that there could neither be error nor deception. Reckoning there shall be, revealing our Lord's expectations from His servants, and their efforts in His service. Christ will commend these efforts, and there will be a common gladness in the results then made known.

Verses 20-23.—"*And so he that had received five*

talents came and brought other five talents, saying, Lord, thou deliveredst unto me five talents: behold, I have gained besides them five talents more. His lord said unto him, Well done, thou good and faithful servant; thou hast been faithful over a few things, I will make thee ruler over many things: enter thou into the joy of thy lord. He also that had received two talents came and said, Lord, thou deliveredst unto me two talents: behold, I have gained two other talents besides them. His lord said unto him, Well done, good and faithful servant; thou hast been faithful over a few things, I will make thee ruler over many things: enter thou into the joy of thy lord."

The day of their master's return was one of interest and excitement, as had been the day of his departure, when distribution of his wealth had been made among his servants. Only now the interest was of a quite different kind. The excitement of expectation moved in the hearts of all the household on that day, as each one busied his imagination with the use to be made of the money unexpectedly placed at his command. Now the excitement was connected with the reckoning and handing over of the results; the public announcement of their work since he left; the impression made on their master and their comrades. Those two who had first received of his substance, and also received most largely, as the most competent and reliable, had a satisfactory account to present. With the five talents were handed over to the owner other five talents; with the two talents, other two. Their lord's favourable judgment of these two servants on the day of distribution is verified on this day of reckoning. The capital is handed back, and in both cases it has been doubled. The talents originally intrusted to them are acknowledged as the source of the gain, but their own work is spoken of by the servants with undisguised self-satisfaction. The delight of their master is complete. He commends them equally, expressing his admiration of the uprightness of their character and the faithfulness of their service. He promises them for the future extended influence in ruling over his possessions, and a closer fellowship with himself, sharing in his own joy.

Such is our Lord's picture of the meeting-time and the reckoning when He shall take account of the service rendered on the earth. The picture is not complete; there is still a companion picture to be hung before us, in a second parable similar in structure; but this is the first representation, most clearly applying to the diversity of circumstances in which His disciples are placed. In this picture the truth lying nearest, full of encouragement while we are in the midst of present work, is, that results proportionate to opportunities will fill each servant with satisfaction on the great and solemn occasion when he renders account of his earthly life. Our responsibilities are fixed for us; what they are is discovered to us by each day of service as it comes; to meet daily obligations by a day of faithful work is to do the part our Master requires of us, and this prepares for ourselves a harvest of joy on the day of His coming. It is not given to us to choose our opportunities, but only our ways of using them. Our obligation is fixed by what we are, what we have, and what opportunities arise in our path. Watchfulness, earnestness, faithfulness are required day by day, to seize our opportunities as they arise. "It is required of a man according to that he hath."

All servants of the Lord shall enter into glory in the day of His glory; He will give them a Saviour's welcome, as those who have trusted in His merit, and are accepted in Him. This consideration is clearly implied. The true servants of Jesus are those devoted to Him in heart, whose life has been consecrated to His service, and who shall equally find a welcome as His ransomed ones. But it is a further truth which here comes into view, absorbing the thought of our Saviour, as He would have it move the heart of His people. Faith secures acceptance, but service receives reward, and the measure of a Christian's service is found in his faithfulness to opportunities offered. Faith unites the soul to the Redeemer from the first moment of its exercise; from the beginning of his trust there is for each believer "salvation ready to be revealed at the last time." But, in addition, we see here the meaning of the Christian's continued life on earth. He is intrusted with service for the Master in the midst of the activities and requirements of daily life: the Master measures the character and extent of this service; and there will be joy in His presence hereafter according to the work which has been done. Faith and faithfulness are companion excellencies in Christian life; dependence on Jesus as the Saviour, and devotion to His service.

The joy of the faithful servant has its counterpart in the joy of his Master. Our Lord's gladness is as His servants', and His servants' is as their Lord's. His joy finds its object in their work, with its abiding results. As He manifests and expresses this joy, it wakens new gladness in their hearts; their joy is thenceforth embraced in His. If we would measure

Christ's joy in His people, its depth is not reached in that rejoicing which is occasioned by their deliverance from sin and condemnation. He has a deeper gladness in the power of a spiritual life awakened in their hearts by faith in Him; in the energy of such life, as it has unfolded in the midst of the toils and trials of the earthly state; in the fruits as these are displayed on the testing-day of His coming, and as they shall continue part of His treasure, adding to the riches of the heavenly kingdom. The grounds of a Saviour's gladness are found in His joy over the varied results of an earthly faith and service, introducing to an eternity of perfect service in a higher sphere.

Our Lord by this parable enables us to enter with some fulness of detail into the sources of His satisfaction; and as these are set in array, it is clear that moral earnestness and worth are the test of excellence. Much additional force belongs to this representation, as we mark that difference in the amount secured makes no difference in the praise bestowed, if only there has been faithfulness to opportunity. Well done! This is the welcome for both. That the one has gained five talents and the other only two, makes no difference in his praise. This difference in amount is even needful in order to make them equally entitled to his approval. In the wealth of the Lord the difference between five and two is a difference among the small things of the kingdom; yet such minor differences are essential for equality before Him who judgeth according to every man's work. Thus the expression of praise from the lips of the master repeats itself, one verse in the parable being an exact reproduction of a verse preceding.

The approval of the Lord concentrates on the same

qualities in both servants: "*Well done, good and faithful servant.*" Character is in each case the key to faithfulness. The basis of moral worth in the servant is that to which the words of the parable point as essential for true service, the beginning and source of it all. Work is commended, and results are justly valued which follow upon work well done; but fidelity in the character is the real test of the work. For a part in the kingdom of righteousness there must be righteousness in the heart. This it must be which manifests itself in faithful service. We know, however, from the whole tenor of Christ's teaching, that He does not point to perfection of character, completed goodness of the whole nature, when He uses the terms "good and faithful" as describing His true servants. A good servant is one genuinely devoted to righteousness. Each one must have his own temptations, and his conflict with evil dispositions. But whatever be the differences in this respect, each one must be determined to contend against evil within as well as without. This conflict is an essential part of God's service, and by success in it the work is done, yielding those results over which the servant and the Lord can rejoice together. To us it may seem as if much more were being accomplished in one case than in another, and according to outward measure or numerical reckoning of talents it is so; but when we compare this difference of result with difference of opportunity, and find equality of faithfulness, we have the key to the equal commendation which our Lord implies in repetition of the same welcome to both servants. A heart devoted to Christ for holiness, a life given to God's service as opportunity offers, and results according to these conditions,—

these are the tests which the Judge will apply. The servant's choice appears in the motive for action; Divine sovereignty in the opportunity; occasion for rejoicing to the servant and to the Lord, in the results of grace and fidelity.

To long-tested faithfulness our Lord appoints enlarged service and greater rewards. Devotedness in this world introduces to enlarged opportunities in the next world. "Thou hast been faithful over a few things, *I will make thee ruler over many things.*" In this description of the future the reference is still to work and reward. In harmony with the analogy the servant is to continue in service, but with greatly wider opportunities. The bounty of the Lord gives enlarged opportunity for energy and usefulness. The "few things" of earth are to be replaced by "many things" which Divine grace provides for the faithful. The close of the earthly life, which seems as the yielding up at once of the capital and the gain procured by it, is followed by introduction into a new and grander order of things, in which larger possessions and wider opportunities are intrusted to each one. The greater power appears as a wider influence and rule under God's government. In the everlasting life procured for us by Jesus, a future is prepared for enlarged work and also for extended reward. In the heavenly kingdom, where righteousness reigns in man and extended favour comes from God, life is progressive in ever increasing ratio.

Verses 24-30.—"*Then he which had received the one talent came and said, Lord, I knew thee that thou art an hard man, reaping where thou hast not sown, and gathering where thou hast not strawed: and I was afraid, and went and hid thy talent in the earth: lo, there thou hast that is thine. His lord answered and said unto him, Thou wicked and slothful servant, thou knewest that I reap where I sowed not, and gather where I have not strawed: thou oughtest therefore to have put my money to the exchangers, and then at my coming I should have received mine own with usury. Take therefore the talent from him, and give it unto him which hath ten talents. For unto every one that hath shall be given, and he shall have abundance: but from him that hath not shall be taken away even that which he hath. And cast ye the unprofitable servant into outer darkness: there shall be weeping and gnashing of teeth."*

The parable closes with a vivid and impressive representation of unfaithfulness on a servant's part, and the consequent displeasure of his master. This servant has made no use of his opportunity, and assumes that he has done his part in returning to his master exactly what he had received. This conduct is treated as unfaithfulness; the property is received back again, and the servant is cast out from the household. This is the parabolic form of our Lord's instruction as to the judgment of condemnation. The sentence is already written in the conduct of the unfaithful one; the result, in separation from God, is what the servant had preferred. Such is our Lord's interpretation of an unfaithful life.

That the man who received *the single talent* is taken to represent unfaithfulness in God's service is a significant fact. Remembering the principle of distribution acted upon by the master, the smallness of the trust committed to the third servant was in accordance with the judgment formed of him. We are thus guided to the state of his character first, and only afterwards to the extent of ability. The result shows that it is character, not restricted ability, which determines the form and direction of life. This truth has already appeared in the equal commendation of both the first servant and the second; and it is now reappearing under the darker colouring of this last scene. Common faithfulness has common approval; unfaithfulness must meet its condemnation. The test is found in the state of the heart, not in the extent of the possessions. We have, therefore, no test of ability in this case, for the servant does not so much as attempt any exercise of his powers, unless we can regard that as some example of effort which is given in burying his master's property. Yet does this act rather indicate his unwillingness to serve, even while he cannot shake off his sense of responsibility. He is not faithful even in the few things, and so will not prove faithful in greater; he cannot, therefore, have more; having voluntarily excluded himself from the position of trust and a share in commendation, he has exposed himself to unqualified condemnation. That he was the holder of only one talent does not account for his state on the day of final award; his character is the single explanation of what he had and did. Small talents do not foreshadow coming condemnation, as they do not imply any loss of approval if only there be faithfulness in the heart. While, therefore, we mark the warning against unfaithfulness, we need to guard against misinterpretation of slender gifts. As we study the picture of this servant burying his single talent, we must remember Christ's words, "Blessed are the poor," and recall that other scene, a poor widow casting in two mites to the treasury of God's house, over which our Lord writes, "She hath cast in more than they all." There is a poverty which is rich in service, and there is a poverty which is itself an index of worse poverty within.

Passing now to the attempted vindication of inactivity and its condemnation, we find the most solemn warnings against neglect of God's service. The excuses behind which inactivity shelters itself our Lord tears away, with the view of delivering victims of self-deception.

Glancing back on the account of *the servant's conduct*, (verse 18), we are reminded that its description was accompanied by no interpretation. "He went and digged in the earth, and hid his lord's money." What was the motive for this we are not told; nor is there any hint as to his expectation of results. This omission is designed as most suitable to the action of men. When men wilfully shun entering upon God's service, they have commonly a very vague notion of their own purpose, and they shun any estimate of the probable issue. It is in keeping with their undefined thought and vagueness of expectation that our Lord does not go beyond the narrative of what is actually done. But the narrative of that is explicit. Men *bury* their talents. They do not merely neglect their use; they actually cover up from view the gifts received from God, shunning the very thought of using them to His glory. They do not proclaim this intention; they do not speak of it as an object accomplished; but they maintain silence regarding it, as if it were a thing they would have no man know. It is not hiding for the sake of preserving the talent, but for the sake of shunning the sense of responsibility, which nevertheless they cannot altogether escape, knowing that the talent is in their keeping, and that a day of reckoning must come.

At length *the necessity for rendering account* of their talents meets the servants. The return of their master made it needful for the one who had received but a single talent to go to the place where he had buried the money, to dig it up, and carry it to the master, to whom he must now make such explanation as he can. When his opportunity had come, he began by reflecting on his master's character, then professed fear of him because of his unjust expectations, and declared his great anxiety to preserve beyond reach of danger what had been intrusted to him.

This is our Lord's description of the incoherence and *self-condemnation* of an attempted defence of neglect to serve God. This mass of inconsistency enables a rational being to cling to some hope for the future. Such a man is ready to reflect on God, fearing Him as a taskmaster, not reverencing His authority. He occupies himself chiefly with thoughts of his own merit. He resents the demands made upon him, thinks of God as a hard taskmaster, and yet is so far from shaping his conduct accordingly, that he deliberately neglects the duty imposed upon him. The main current of his thought is towards self-indulgence. He has the talent and opportunity for God's service, but he does not use them. His life bears witness against him, and when the secrets of the heart are made manifest, attempted vindication will prove condemnatory.

Divine condemnation must follow a life of unfaithfulness. Work neglected, opportunities lost, Self exalted to the first place, God reproached as if He were unjustly requiring service,—all these must be tested before God's tribunal. Feeble admission of wrong-doing must be followed by exposure of all its excuses. Grievous transgressions are not charged against this man. If neglect bring condemnation, how much sorer condemnation must follow upon a life of vice and wilful injustice. But the centre from which all evil comes, whether less or more aggravated, is self-indulgence supplanting the love and service of God. In condemnation of this there is condemnation of all evil. The master's rebuke of his servant anticipates the condemnation of the Judge when He shall appear on the great white throne. "Wicked and slothful servant!" These are the two words which describe the character of the man, and they are the exact contraries of those already used, "Good and faithful servant." This man, instead of being devoted to God, is evil of heart, averse to God and to all that He requires; instead of being faithful to the trust imposed in him, he is slothful, caring nothing that God's purposes are unfulfilled, if only he may take his ease, go out and in according to his own pleasure, be active or inactive, according as he sees opportunity for personal gratification. This description embraces an endless variety of cases. The forms of gratification may be of a coarser or more refined order; they may be degrading or elevating in their influence; yet if they separate men from God and His service, they must be included under a common description. The Judge will make full account of all diversities in degree, and of all intelligent self-direction in shunning darker forms of evil. Nevertheless all faithless life must come under the sweep of a common sentence.

Our Lord makes the parable an impressive unity. He has a single welcome for all faithfulness, whether bringing five talents or two, saying equally, "Well done, good and faithful servant: enter thou into the joy of thy Lord." He has a single condemnation for all who give their chief regard to self, refusing to serve God: "Thou wicked and slothful servant, thou shalt not enter into the joy of thy Lord."

Hard thoughts of God will find their condemnation when brought to the test of Divine requirements. It will then appear that God did not seek to reap where He had not sown; that He did not expect of any one that for which He had not Himself provided both in means and opportunity. He shall ask no more than *that He receive His own with its produce.* Before that demand, hard thoughts shall recoil upon the mind which cherished them; the reasonableness of the demand will be apparent to all, being exactly similar to the expectations of every one who has committed to a fellow-man any trust. God will but say, Now should I have received mine own with what it could produce by its use in the world.

The rules of Divine judgment now become apparent in two distinct forms. *The unemployed talent is transferred to one who will use it well.* There are many Divinely-given talents which so belong to personal existence, that we cannot think of them being transferred to others. In view of this, it will be remarked that our Lord has taken external possessions as affording illustration of the truth proclaimed. The talent of silver intrusted to a servant may fitly represent possessions belonging to a man, as distinct from those essential to the nature of the person.

Possessions which have not been faithfully used will be withdrawn from the holder of them, and will be handed over to another who has given proof of his faithfulness. He that hath not in the form of produce shall have taken from him even that which for a season he has been allowed to hold as a possession committed to his trust.

The unfaithful servant is himself cast out from the presence of the Lord. Possessions which can be taken from him shall be withdrawn; what belongs to his personality may be retained, but he himself must be separated from the presence of the Lord. Where love to God is wanting, there can be no abiding in His presence; where faithfulness has been refused, there can be no continuance in His service; where trust has been betrayed, there must be tokens of His displeasure. The servant formerly described as "wicked and slothful" is now designated "unprofitable." He is a servant only in name, not in reality; he holds his master's possessions, but yields to his master no return. That which in the relationship of earthly life becomes the test of diligence, the gain following from his work, becomes here symbolically representative of the test of faithfulness in God's presence. "Unprofitable" is the sure proof of unfaithfulness, and that is rejected, in harmony with all the conditions of moral life, as with the entire course of Scriptural teaching. So our Lord taught when He likened Himself to a vine and His people to the branches. "Every branch in me that beareth not fruit he taketh away" (John xv. 2). "If a man abide not in me, he is cast forth as a branch, and is withered; and men gather them, and cast them into the fire, and they are burned" (verse 6). Accordingly great fruitfulness is commanded. "Herein is my Father glorified, that ye bear much fruit;" in harmony with which is the desire of an apostle, that believers "may be filled with the fruits of righteousness."

When in the solemnities of the judgment it is shown that the fruits of service become the test of commendation by God, it is not implied that the work of the earthly life affords the meritorious ground of admission into glory. Our Lord has expressly guarded against such a thought by another and quite different use of this same word "unprofitable." In another relation He applies this word to His faithful servants. "Ye, when ye shall have done all those things commanded you, say, We are *unprofitable servants:* we have done that which was our duty to do" (Luke xvii. 10). The whole parable now under consideration is bearing this very lesson. Whether the return brought to the master be greater or less, it is but the natural production from what had been intrusted to each. All that is required of the servants is diligence in the use of what they have received. Accordingly it is their master's property which yields natural return. They are faithful servants who bring such return, and are commended accordingly; but they cannot boast as though they had themselves produced the fruit. They add nothing to the master's possessions, but only bring what is altogether his own. In this respect they are unprofitable,—they have done only what it was their duty to do—only what was the obvious and natural work of their life.

In view of this, the condemnation of the unfaithful servant becomes the more obviously inevitable. He wilfully refuses to serve,—he holds God's possessions, but in such a manner as to prevent their yielding produce. He robs God of that which is His own, and might be condemned as one injurious; but the Saviour finds complete condemnation short of this, in declaring that he is as one who is useless among the servants, and on this account must be separated. Hence the solemn verdict, "Cast ye the unprofitable servant into outer darkness: there shall be weeping and gnashing of teeth." Who they are who are thus commanded to cast him out is not expressly indicated. It may be attendants who are around the Lord, or the servants already commended. We know that the former is the reference in other cases; but our Lord is not concerned with explicit statement on this matter; the doom of the unfaithful man absorbs His thoughts. He who will not live as a faithful servant of the Lord must be an outcast from His presence; and to live apart from the sphere of His favour is to dwell beyond the sunshine of spiritual blessing, in outer darkness. How much this banishment involves no human mind can estimate. But when the inevitable separation becomes a reality in personal experience, there will be found no heart so dulled to sensibility as to escape overwhelming anguish. A wilful refusal of service involves God's rejection of the servant. A fruitless life closes in fruitless remorse, from which there is no escape, outer darkness bearing witness to exclusion from Divine favour and subjection to Divine wrath.

CHAPTER XXVI.

EQUALITY OF GIFTS WITH DIVERSITY OF RESULTS.

THE POUNDS.

LUKE XIX. 12-27.

IN this parable our Lord presents another side of the truth concerning judgment, bringing into view different results attained by servants who are equally favoured in circumstances. There is, however, an immediate end sought by this parable, contrasting with the present purpose to be secured by that just considered. The parable of The Talents carried in it the lesson of *the uncertainty of the time when the Lord might come,* a lesson which had also been conveyed, though less prominently, by the parable of The Ten Virgins; this parable of The Pounds is adapted for impressing men with *the certainty that the time was remote* when the Lord would come to judge of the results achieved by His professed followers. That time is, indeed, far in the distance; but when it comes, it will prove a testing-time for all professed servants of God, and for all who have openly proclaimed themselves His foes. In the one case, distinct results will be computed, and different rewards will be distributed; in the other case, the enmity openly avowed and deliberately cherished will be visited with punishment by Him who is ruler over all.

Verse 12.—"*He said therefore, A certain nobleman went into a far country, to receive for himself a kingdom, and to return.*"

A certain nobleman went into a far country. The indefiniteness of description is still maintained here, as in former parables, though our English version does not make this manifest. The introduction is still "a certain man."[1] This intentional vagueness, which escaped all appearance of identifying a particular individual, served a double object. It avoided a direct reference by our Lord to His personal position in the kingdom of God, a fact which He still felt it needful to keep clouded in a degree of mystery. While thus serving an important temporary purpose belonging to His mission on the earth, and the veiling of His glory until His atoning work had been finished, it directly contributed to His great object as a teacher, by resting the whole order of Divine judgment on principles clearly recognised among men, and applied by them generally in estimating each other's conduct.

While, however, these ends are secured by maintaining an indefinite form of description, there are also explicit references to elevation of rank and sovereign authority, in harmony with the parable of the Marriage of the King's Son. Elevation in human rank, and authority over all orders of the people, here come into view in a manner admirably harmonising with the unique position of the speaker, to whom has been given "a name which is above every name," and who is

---

[1] ἄνθρωπός τις.

"God manifest in the flesh." The leading person introduced is " a certain man *of high birth*,"[1] well born, of noble rank, or, as our version gives it, "a certain nobleman." Thus Christ indirectly alludes to the rank He already holds because of His birth. Beyond this there is the foreshadowing of still greater authority and power than can have any representation in the circumstances in which He was for the time voluntarily placed. He is as one going "into a far country *to receive a kingdom.*" His departure was, indeed, to be through a valley of gloom and suffering, whence in a little while, and for a little space, he should return, not to be seen of the world, but to depart in sight of His chosen people, for the far country, whence also, after a long time, he would return in the majesty of His kingly rank. All this lies wrapt up, concealed from popular view, in this general introduction, to be afterwards recognised by all searchers of the Scriptures who should be privileged to conduct their study in light of the closing events in Christ's earthly history. In the midst of the invisible land, where Jesus shall enter into His glory, He shall *receive* the kingdom from the Father, who shall give to Him all power in heaven and in earth, committing all judgment into the hands of His Son. Such glimpses of glory are granted here, but they are not dwelt upon as though they were the chief objects of our Lord's interest. They present, indeed, the groundwork of His teaching in this passage, but the end to be served is the instruction and stimulating of men in the service of His Father. The life of righteousness, its work on earth, its continuance in glory, its endless reward, these are the things

[1] εὐγενής.

He keeps ever in view,—the things which He would make visible to those dwelling among things seen and temporal.

Having this practical end in view, He emphasises at the outset the certainty of return. This nobleman went "to receive for himself a kingdom, *and to return.*" Practical importance for Christ's hearers concentrates on this return, if only they keep in view that it will be that of their Judge; not the return of a nobleman, nor of a teacher, nor of a mediator, but of a King. He will come to take account of the use made of His teaching, and with sovereign authority to declare all awards, according to the use which His people have made of their opportunities. His return is that which the Christian must ever contemplate,—living under the solemnising, stimulating power of this great expectation, —if he would shun sloth and self-seeking, and be faithful even unto death.

Verse 13.—"*And he called his ten servants, and delivered them ten pounds, and said unto them, Occupy till I come.*"

Distribution is made as the condition of service, and this affords the ground of responsibility, as it also discovers the test of faithfulness. Here, however, we have a wider range of distribution, along with equality of measure, in contrast with what had been depicted in the parable of The Talents. The servants are more numerous, the sums are smaller, the principle of distribution is that of exact equality. These are requisite elements for illustration of diversity of service with diversity of reward. The ten servants place before our view more varied possibilities; the pound to each makes the test of the results, comparative faithfulness in the use of the same opportunities; the smallness of the sum, amounting to little over three pounds sterling, indicates that the judgments concerning our service must apply to our smaller possessions as well as to the grander opportunities placed within our reach. Thus Jesus lays down the principles of righteous judgment, which all must approve, and to the test of which we must daily seek to rise, in order to be assured of our Lord's approval hereafter. The Lord's command is this, "*Occupy till I come*,"—do business with your possessions, trade wisely with them, that they be not left unused, that they be not risked in hazardous enterprise, but continue at your command, yielding return over which the servant himself may rejoice in presence of his King.

Verse 14.—"*But his citizens hated him, and sent a message after him, saying, We will not have this man to reign over us.*"

This reference to a wider circle than that of the professed servants is peculiar to the present parable as illustrating the aspects of Divine judgment. No similar allusion appears in the parable of The Talents, reference there being restricted to the narrower range of distribution belonging to a household, in contrast with what is more appropriate to a wider range of authority. The parable which receives its form by introducing one who is a nobleman, shortly to rise to the rank of a king, makes it natural to adopt a reference much wider than could be appropriately done in alluding to one who is only a householder. In the present case, room is made for an extended field of instruction. Besides his servants, allusion may be made to *his citizens*. The contrast between the two is clearly defined. The one class is devoted to him by voluntary offer of service, in accordance with appropriate covenant. The others are related to him by mere subordination of rank and by dependence, which have awakened resentment and a disposition to resist his claims. This reference here to *citizens*, distinct from the nobleman's family and servants, recalls the allusion in the parable of the Prodigal Son to "citizens" of the far country, and gives striking testimony to the unity of the parables in their teaching concerning the kingdom of God.

"*His citizens hated him, and sent a message after him, saying, We will not have this man to reign over us.*" The state of heart here disclosed is that of intense enmity. Their spirit stands even in contrast with the self-indulgent disposition, which leads to unfaithfulness. Theirs is a cherished animosity, finding expression in strong aversion to everything belonging to God's service. To maintain even an outward semblance of submission appears to them intolerable. United and undisguised expressions of dislike suit well their prevailing disposition, and they are eager to throw off the yoke of their ruler so far as that may prove possible. Yet is the impotence of their rage painfully manifest in the feebleness of the measures to which they resort. They can only protest that they are unwilling to serve; and even that they venture upon only when he has already departed from among them, and started on his way for receiving a still more extended kingdom. Thus does Jesus in most striking parabolic form indicate the intensity and the ineffectiveness of human hatred against God. Only because He seems a God at a distance, withdrawing from active control, and who does not come nigh to judgment, do ungodly men speak boldly of their enmity, deceiving themselves by the loudness of their speaking. But the Lord in going departs to receive a larger dominion, and to return. Then and only then will those who boast of their enmity be brought to the final test of the wisdom of setting themselves in defiance against God. Yet is He a God long-suffering and full of compassion, who desires that all rebels would repent.

Now the second portion of the parable opens before us. The time of the king's return has come. The faithful may bring the fruits of their labours; the faithless must urge some excuse as best they can; the rebellious must try their strength if they are to make good the rebellion which they had loudly proclaimed. The reality will be different from the expectations of all, whether faithful, faithless, or rebellious. The work of judgment will begin, and it will then appear that only a real service can be honoured, and only a real devotion to the king can live in his presence.

Verse 15.—"*And it came to pass, that, when he was returned, having received the kingdom, then he commanded these servants to be called unto him to whom he had given the money, that he might know how much every man had gained by trading.*"

The king has appeared in the place of authority, he issues his mandates, and his servants are called before him that he may know what each one has made by trading. To the nobleman, now saluted as a king, these results are unknown, till the reckoning is submitted and the results presented. But the Lord who comes for judgment needs not to summon His servants for information as to their doings; all things are naked and open to His sight; He but opens the book of remembrance,—no faithful service, however small, has lost a place on that record, and no case of unfaithfulness has passed unnoticed.

Verses 16-18.—"*Then came the first, saying, Lord, thy pound hath gained ten pounds. And he said unto him, Well, thou good servant: because thou hast been faithful in a very little, have thou authority over ten cities. And the second came, saying, Lord, thy pound hath gained five pounds.*"

The reporting to the king and his commendation of faithfulness, are the same here as in the preceding parable. We may, therefore, concentrate on the specialities in this case, as discovering what was lacking in the former, varying degrees of faithfulness and varying degrees of reward. *A life of ceaseless industry in God's service takes the first rank.* There comes a servant who naturally takes the first place. He has been constant in his watchfulness for opportunities, quick to seize them as they have been offered, and untiring in his labours to secure his end. In his hands the possessions of the king have yielded tenfold. The work he has done has stimulated many associated with him, has blessed many more who did not even seek to honour the king, and in all things he has aimed at advancing his master's cause. This is our Saviour's account of Christian life at its best,—acceptance of what God gives; faithful use of it without wearying in well-doing; and a joyful homage in the presence of the Lord at His coming, laying down at His feet all that His gifts have earned. Behind this, but at a considerable distance, comes *a case of genuine devotion but less concentration.* Here also there has been a true sense of responsibility, and delight in the service of God, but there has been more of mixed interest, forgetting and repenting, at times seeking a present indulgence, to the sacrifice of higher ends. Such a servant cannot show the same great results when the time of reckoning comes. Yet is he devoted to the Saviour, joyful in His glory, and ready to lay at His feet all that the labours of a life have produced. Such contrasts as these two there are in Christian life, with many variations between, and not a few examples of life lower still in its results than the second. Of the ten servants, only two are so represented here as to make us certain of results; but besides the unfaithful one whose case reappears in a manner resembling that in the previous parable, there are still seven cases untold, leaving by restriction of the narrative scope for many differences. Differences of result in the service lead on to *diversity of reward*. In the previous parable we have the foundation-truth connected with the application of justice; God will require of a man only according to the ability and opportunity possessed. Restricted opportunity, with limited power, will not hinder any one from receiving the fullest commendation. Here, combining the utterances of the Judge addressed to the two servants specially selected for approval, we have the additional truth, to which our Lord now gives prominence as essential to the administration of justice in the Kingdom of Grace; different degrees of faithfulness will meet equally varying degrees of reward. First, it must be recognised that men far apart in the range of their influence, whose lives wear very different aspects according to actual results accomplished, may equally have the commendation, "Well done, good and faithful servant." This is God's acknowledgment of equal faithfulness. There is, however, besides this, another aspect of Divine justice. The entanglements of earthly circumstances cannot perplex the eye of the Judge, nor can the diversities of individual faithfulness escape His observation and recognition in the awards of His kingdom. Looking on varying degrees of faithfulness, He shall nevertheless have praise for all His servants, because a true devotion of heart and life appears in all. This equality of favour will meet all true servants of the Lord as they appear in His presence; to each one He will say, "Well, thou good servant, thou hast been faithful." But the Lord will also have special praise for each according to the measure of his service on the earth. This is vividly presented to view here by aid of the parabolic form. This nobleman, rising now to the rank of a monarch, and returning to the position where his interests concentrate, and where his influence has been longest and most fully felt, aptly illustrates the truth as to God's judgment, which our Lord would impress on us as His servants while we are in the midst of the bustle of life. This nobleman, having now received the kingdom, returns into the midst of his servants to select from men known and proved those who may be intrusted with wider influence in his newly-acquired dominions. Such is our Lord's representation of the great future lying before His people, when He shall come in His glory to distribute anew of His favour, introducing each one to wider influence. As this earthly ruler said to one servant, "Because thou hast been faithful in a very little, have thou authority over *ten* cities," and to another, "Be thou over *five* cities," so shall it be in the kingdom of heaven. This is one of the certainties under the moral government of God, which the dispensation of favour among His chosen people will make only more conspicuous. Even where all is of grace, still shall distribution be according to justice. All shall, indeed, rejoice together in the glorious sunshine of unmerited favour, but there shall, nevertheless, be differences; and for each one of them the Lord shall have His distinct reason to give in the actual measure of the service rendered on the earth. According as thou hast been faithful, so shalt thou be honoured.

From the principle of distribution, we pass to the representation of *the nature of future reward.* Our Lord does not speak of it as if reward were some external and material gain, some possession to be received by the servant, and thenceforth to be held as property peculiarly and exclusively his own. Reward in the kingdom above consists in *enlarged service.* From proved faithfulness here, the servant is to be raised to extended requirement for its exercise. A wondrous discovery of Divine favour shall break upon His servants in the day of their Lord's coming. The spirit of self-consecration will find extended sphere for its exercise. The contrast in this respect will be great indeed. As the advance from the faithful use of a few pounds of money to the government of five cities in an empire, or even from the same humble responsibility to authority over territory including ten cities, so shall be the immense extension of influence for those who enter into the heavenly kingdom. Continuity of service with widened opportunity for usefulness constitutes the reward of a disciple of Christ. Further source of blessedness will be found in *increased facility* for service within the extended sphere. Increased responsibility in the earthly state carries with it increase of care; the burden grows heavier as influence becomes greater. Even here, however, we can see that there is much in training and experience, which tends to balance things, even though the balance be not quite equal. But what is foreshadowed here is more than the advantage of experience acquired on the earth. The disciple shall be transferred to the new kingdom which his Lord has received, and there, instead of encountering influences adverse to his cherished purpose and to his Master's glory, he shall fulfil his part in a kingdom where all is ordered according to the sovereign authority of Him who hath decreed that "there shall in no wise enter into it any thing that defileth, neither whatsoever worketh abomination, or maketh a lie." Enlarged scope for the service of God shall also be favoured with vastly increased facility in the work. Conflict with evil shall be ended. The discipline and force of character, gained by courageous persistence in the fight, shall be secured for ever, and shall be a spiritual force proving its value continually, yet having the mystery of its development in the darkness and trouble of a state which has for ever passed away. All conditions of life there shall be favourable to joy in fulfilment of responsibility. *Fellowship in service shall be extended, and the bonds of human attachment more closely entwined.* Elevation in honour and influence will not bring separation from those with whom the servants of Christ have been associated in the earthly state. In this world, honour for one often involves severance from those who have previously been companions in labour. Our Lord places before us a prospect the reverse of this. United service on earth shall find its reward in united service hereafter, with contiguity of sphere, and interlacing of the influence of those who have been fellow-workers on earth. As the government of the cities of an empire is a necessary part in its administration, so shall it be with all the service of men in the heavenly kingdom. Widening activity will only more closely entwine the bonds of union. The crowning element in this reward is *closer fellowship with the Lord*. This is the grand prospect, which in the previous parable is made the conspicuous feature, as most surely including all the others here brought into view. There all reward is embraced in this single welcome, "Enter thou into the joy of thy Lord." Here this prospect is again before the view, but in clearer light, bringing out a richer combination of detail. Our Lord "shall see of the travail of his soul and shall be satisfied." He shall find the reward of all His own humiliation and woe in the gathering of a multitude which no man can number, rescued from sin and sorrow. The kingdom of righteousness shall be established; within it, every servant shall find his appointed sphere; entering upon that, he shall *enter* into the joy of his Lord. In experience of this grander joy, all previous experience of fellowship with Jesus will seem as if it had been the attachment of servants rather than of sons. This shall be as the fellowship of those who are permitted to share with the Lord in His rule. Introduction to this shall be experienced as something so entirely new and soul-possessing, that it will be as entrance into the fulness of the Saviour's joy; a first glad and glorious consciousness of what that joy really is in its breadth and depth. This will prove the entrance to an abiding inheritance, the beginning of a perpetual fellowship, eternal as the righteousness of the Most High.

The exceeding brightness of this prospect has here also, as in the former parable, set over against it the darkness and woe of the rejected servant who has refused to serve God, and, besides, Jesus places in stronger contrast the deeper darkness and woe of those who have openly declared themselves rebels against His authority.

Verses 20-27.—"*And another came, saying, Lord, behold, here is thy pound, which I have kept laid up in a napkin: for I feared thee, because thou art an austere man: thou takest up that thou layedst not down, and reapest that thou didst not sow. And he saith unto him, Out of thine own mouth will I judge thee, thou wicked servant. Thou knewest that I was an austere man, taking up that I laid not down, and reaping that I did not sow: wherefore then gavest not thou my money into the bank, that at my coming I might have required mine own with usury? And he said unto them that stood by, Take from him the pound, and give it to him that hath ten pounds. (And they said unto him, Lord, he hath ten pounds.) For I say unto you, That unto every one which hath shall be given; and from him that hath not, even that he hath shall be taken away from him. But those mine enemies, which would not that I should reign over them, bring hither, and slay them before me.*"

The repetition here, in terms nearly identical with those of the previous parable, of the excuse for neglect of God's service on the earth, and of its condemnation, is Christ's strong testimony to the fact that self-indulgence is the peril of professing Christianity, and self-deception its shelter. The same painful callousness, the same self-condemning inconsistency of defence, accusing God in order to excuse self, are here repeated. The completeness of condemnation is also apparent, in the withdrawal of the trust committed to the unfaithful one, and his exclusion from all part in the service, though there is not in this case any description of the outer sphere where the condemned are separated from the glory and joy. Exclusion from Divine favour is the real penalty; God's wrath appears in the condemnation He pronounces; remorse and suffering are the inevitable accompaniments in experience of the condemned.

The special feature on the dark side of this picture is the vengeance which overtakes the openly defiant and rebellious. The sovereign issues his edict that his enemies be slain, and that before his presence. The loving and merciful Saviour thus depicts the certainty and extremity of coming doom. He who has said, "Fear not them that kill the body, and after that have no more that they can do," now selects the extreme sentence of an earthly tribunal to illustrate a more dreadful sentence beyond. That the analogy does not carry in it the hope of some mitigation of penalty, by suggesting extinction of life as the fate of the rebellious, seems clear. A deeper displeasure than that felt against the idle servant is implied, and a more terrible experience as the consequence of the increase of Divine wrath. As the offence against an earthly monarch is small as compared with rebellion against God, the penalty must be greater. To cast away all righteousness is to sacrifice all favour of God; to defy God's authority is to encounter His power. Then shall it be said, "The great day of his wrath is come, and who shall be able to stand?" The Saviour who uses this parabolic form has also said, "I will forewarn you whom ye shall fear: Fear him, which, *after he hath killed,* hath power to cast into hell; yea, I say unto you, Fear him" (Luke xii. 5). Awful beyond conception is the great darkness and dread woe dimly visible in impenetrable gloom. There is nothing in the description here, nothing in the words of Jesus elsewhere on this subject, bearing a rainbow colouring from rays of hope. . There is separation from God's kingdom in the case of all who prove unfaithful; there are special tokens of Divine displeasure for those who openly set at naught all righteousness, in their impotence giving utterance to bitter hate.

Terrible as is this sad record of appointed doom, it is clear that the special design of Jesus is to give encouragement to all who would serve God. The parable speaks of welcome, and reward, and continuity of service in the glorious kingdom above. This is enough to animate each Christian heart, leading to a fuller consecration. To all who are persevering in the service of God through toils and trials, through weariness and pain, Jesus would say, 'Anticipate the day of your release, the day of Christ's coming to receive you to Himself, the day for your entrance upon the joy of your Lord, the day appointed for entrance on a grander career, when the lines of personal influence, the bonds of Christian fellowship, and the tokens of Divine favour shall spread out on every side, and stretch on into the great eternity.' The Lord has made ready in the midst of His kingdom rich reward for all His people. There shall be no ordeal patiently endured, no delays quietly borne, no temptations bravely encountered, no service perseveringly continued, which shall not have its acknowledgment from the Divine Saviour, and its reward above. "Every man shall receive his own reward, according to his own labour."